The *GOLF Magazine*

Complete Guide to Golf

The *GOLF Magazine*
Complete Guide to Golf

By

Gary Wiren, Ph.D., Peter Morrice,

and the Editors of *GOLF Magazine*

Photography in Full Swing, Short
Game, and Putting by Sam Greenwood

THE LYONS PRESS

Guilford, Connecticut

An imprint of The Globe Pequot Press

The Lyons Press is an imprint of The Globe Pequot Press.

10 9 8 7 6 5 4 3 2 1

ISBN 1-58574-510-3

Design and composition by Compset, Inc.

The Library of Congress Cataloging-in-Publication Data is available on file.

Contents

Foreword

At *GOLF Magazine* we use two methods to determine the content of each issue: surveys and guts. In the survey method, questionnaires are sent to thousands of subscribers, asking—among other things—what topics they enjoy most and which kinds of articles they prefer. In the guts method, we editors simply use our intuition as kindred, hopelessly addicted golfers.

But no matter which method we use, the number-one request is always for the same thing: instruction. "Give us more instruction" has been the mandate from our readers ever since the magazine began publishing, forty years ago. The reason is simple: A golfer is happiest when his game is improving.

Recently, however, we've learned a couple of things about how to present our instruction. First, you like it short and sweet. After all, most of the current population were raised on television,

sound bites, and quick delivery of information—
from beepers to e-mail. More than ever, we like
our messages short and to the point.

And the "to the point" part is just as important as
the "short" part. For the last decade or so, the most
popular portion of *GOLF Magazine* has been the buff-
colored section, "Private Lessons," which brings together custom-tailored instruction for five different
kinds of golfers: low handicappers, high handicappers, short but straight hitters, long but crooked hitters, and senior golfers. In this way, we're able to
speak more personally to our readers and help them
more individually with their games.

Why am I telling you all this? Because the same
kind of thinking went into the book that is now
in your hands. When the people at The Lyons Press
came to talk to us about a partnership in golf-book
publishing, we gave them our mantra for success:
instruction, succinct and focused. The result is the
GOLF Magazine Complete Guide to Golf, written con-
cisely, edited mercilessly, and dedicated entirely to
all aspects of playing the game.

The *GOLF Magazine Complete Guide to Golf* assem-
bles a wealth of great advice. We hope you'll use
these pages to raise your game to a whole new level.

George Peper
Editor-in-Chief
GOLF Magazine

The *GOLF Magazine*

Complete Guide to Golf

Book One

Mental Golf

Gary Wiren, Ph.D.

PGA Master Professional
and the Editors of *GOLF Magazine*

Introduction

The human mind has an incredible capacity and repertoire. It can, for example, take you into the past, either recent or distant. In golf terms that means it may literally allow you to remember every shot you hit during the round just completed or leap back to shots made thirty years ago. This ability to recall can be used as a powerful asset in your game, or it can be totally ruinous. Then, within seconds your mind can transport you into an imagined future. This "yet-to-be world," totally of your own creation, also offers the same pass-or-fail double-edged sword in the arena of golf performance. Whether these mental abilities that can skip from past to future end up as your friend or enemy depends entirely upon what pictures you choose to recall.

These are but two examples of the potential of the mind; one of the most challenging elements to master in an already demanding sport. The power of the mind to influence performance should never be taken lightly. Whether you are a new golfer or one who has played for most of your life, I will guarantee you the mind plays a far greater role in your golf success than you realize.

Recognizing the tremendous value in improving one's mental strength for golf, we have produced this succinct practical treatment of the subject, a text you can cover in a short time but use for a lifetime. By working with six powerful mental traits you will be shown their importance, be given great examples of their use, and be provided with a practice tool to achieve greater strength in each area.

As you begin to read this book, let's make an assumption. You would like to play better golf and hope that what you are going to get from this material just might make that happen. Well, banish the thought immediately from your mind that it "just might." For if you honestly apply what you are about to read regarding the development of mental strength for golf, you absolutely will become a better player. In fact, the better player you become, the more important the mental aspect will be in influencing your outcome. Developing mental strength is a guaranteed way to improve your scoring because *every shot starts in the mind, and the body doesn't lie for the brain.*

You'll make your best swings when your mind has pictured a good result.

Golf has been called "the most mental of games." If you have ever encountered any of the following scenarios, you can easily understand why.

1. You had a great warm-up session on the range before you teed off, but once on the course you played eighteen holes and hit only two truly good shots the entire day.

Another bad shot on the course, even after a positive warm-up.

2. During a round you putted well until the last hole. There, with the match on the line, plus a press bet, you faced a straight-in six-foot putt to win and left the ball dead on line for the center of the cup . . . but short.

The greatest scoring mistake: leaving short putts short.

3. After hitting six perfectly straight drives on the easy opening holes, you came to the first one with a narrow fairway and promptly tightened up, slicing your drive into the trees.

Tight fairways can cause tight muscles.

4. It was your best season of playing. You had consistent scores all summer long, until the club championship, when your game fell completely apart and you made an early exit.

5. You were asked two months earlier to play in the big pro-am, but it never occurred to you that when they announced your name on the first tee your knees would be shaky and your hands trembling.

Tournament golf will add tension for the unprepared.

6. Lately when you go to play you can't seem to maintain focus on the course long enough to complete a full round with a decent score.

Some or all of these examples may be quite familiar to you. If they are, how did you react at the time? If they are not, how *would* you react? The golfer with mental strength will handle the previous scenarios

The mentally strong competitor understands there will be tough situations that must be faced.

without having them noticeably affect his or her game. Why? *Because mental strength gives you the ability to maintain composure and control in your performance while facing conditions of stress and distraction.*

Anyone who has played golf seriously will acknowledge the importance of the game's mental aspects. If that is true, then why don't we work more on improving our mental skills, giving them more attention and less lip service? I suspect that we don't because:

- Deep down we don't believe that the mental side of golf is as important as it really is.

- We only have a limited amount of practice time, which seems to be spent hitting the ball.

- We have never been properly taught how to improve the mental game through practice.

The answers to all three of these potential barriers are contained in this book. *I hope to convince you thoroughly of the value of mental strength for improving your play, show you where to find the time, and give you a program that provides sound results.*

One more observation before we start. The golfing world has been struck by "Tigermania," the unprecedented hype surrounding the new man (he's no kid) on the block, Eldridge "Tiger" Woods. Ama-

Golfers participate far more in ball-hitting practice than mental practice.

teurs and professionals alike are amazed not only by his prodigious length but also by his wonderful short game touch. But when I hear someone singing praise for his ball striking or touting his impressive stats I always interject this statement: "Are you aware that he has had a mental coach since he was eight years old!" That's right, since the age of eight. No player before in the history of the game has had thirteen years of psychological coaching prior to launching his/her career as a professional; not Ben Hogan, nor Jack Nicklaus, or Nancy Lopez. "Tiger" Woods is unique in this regard, and it is this quality that made it possible for him to excel at the highest level under tremendous stress and still succeed at such a young age. Believe me, this young man has MENSA-level strength of mind for the game of golf. And believe as well that *he learned to reach that level with mental coaching and by mental practice.*

1

Developing the Strong Golf Mind

So how do we learn to develop a strong mind for golf? And how do we practice? First we'll identify six key qualities that will enhance mental strength. Next, you'll be advised on how to use the Mental Practice Exercises, which are your key to creating new mental habits. There are also some "golden nuggets": observations, truths, and tips that may be just what you need to "turn on the light" and give greater insight into mental strength. Understand that there are a variety of techniques for developing strength of mind. No absolute list of characteristics can define it. But from my forty years as a teacher and player of the game, I feel the following selection will be of great value regardless of your skill level.

Six Qualities of Mental Strength

Relaxation

I often start group golf clinics with a demonstration: I stand in front of the students holding a club lightly between my thumb and forefinger, swinging it freely back and forth in a 180-degree arc. While doing so, I describe the admirable qualities of this pendulum motion—rhythm, acceleration, and consistency, all desirable elements of a good golf swing. Then as the group continues to watch this to-and-fro motion, I say that I'm about to kill the swing—"Watch!"—and it stops dead in a vertical position. My question to them is: "How did I stop it?" The correct answers come in slightly different forms but all point to the same basic cause. "You squeezed it," or "You tightened your fingers," or "By adding grip pressure," all are acceptable descriptions of how to kill a swing. They have just observed and identified the reason why so many golfers find making a consistent golf swing a difficult task. Too much squeezing, tightness, and pressure is a regular occurrence among golfers. This is unfortunate because **the greatest destroyer of a golf swing is excessive**

A pendulum can swing freely until . . .

. . . the grip is squeezed.

muscular tension. That realization is the basis for almost every mental technique on performance enhancement that is described in this book. Muscular tightness, particularly in the shoulders, arms, and hands slows speed, shortens the golf swing's arc length and width, inhibits the squaring of the clubface, and destroys rhythm and timing. Relaxation and muscular tension are mutually exclusive conditions. Knowing that should make it self-evident that *the ability to relax is one of the most valuable tools in the golfer's mental arsenal.* That is why it is the first technique listed among your Mental Practice Exercises.

Relaxation is a very learnable skill that can be accessed in a variety of ways. The form that we offer you is known as differential muscular relaxation, which is induced through imagery. The technique entails progressively working through several key muscle groups in the body and getting them to reach a more relaxed state. One of the advantages to this system is that while it requires some practice to get results, a great deal of practice is not necessary. It is recommended that you use this first technique of the Mental Practice Exercise system in the locker room or parking lot, or wherever you change your shoes prior to going to the practice range or the first tee. A very effective way to practice this relaxation technique is to put the message on a cassette tape and listen to it on a Walkman during your exercise time, or when taking a walk, riding a bike, or other quiet times. When you can induce relaxation by this method and then maintain a similar state during play, your swing performance will improve. *Keep in mind that this is a learned skill that must be practiced, not one to be pulled out only on golf competition days.*

Mental Practice Exercise #1 (for relaxation)

Locate a comfortable chair or seat and sit in your most restful position. Close your eyes, relax, and then say to yourself: "I am in a very restful place—the beach, the woods, a mountain retreat, a lovely meadow, or a cozy room on a snowy night. As I picture my special place I will start to feel more calm; calm and relaxed; relaxed over my whole body. Everything will also begin to feel like *it is slowing down.* **Then I'll focus on my hands and fingers feeling they are warm and relaxed, almost limp. . . . Now my forearms will begin to become free of tension. My biceps and shoulders will relax, feeling warm as my arms and**

To relax before play, find a comfortable space: under a tree, in a golf car, in the locker room.

hands now begin to feel heavy. . . . My neck will relax and my head will feel very heavy . . . very heavy. . . . I will feel my facial muscles relax and my jaw will feel limp. . . . Then the back of my neck and upper back muscles will gradually lose their tension. . . . Next my chest and stomach will begin to relax as my breath-

ing becomes deeper and slower; in and out; deeper and slower. . . . A feeling of warmth will go down into my legs and buttocks. . . . My thighs, then my knees and calves will feel free of tension and very relaxed and heavy; warm and relaxed. . . . I will gradually feel all the tension flow slowly downward and drain out through my toes. . . . I feel very calm; calm and at ease; tranquil and very relaxed."

Let this exercise progress slowly, taking four to five minutes to complete. It will definitely help the rhythm on your first swing.

Additional Insights and Observations on Relaxation

The following are additional insights and observations on relaxation that show how valuable it is to playing better golf.

1. The desired mental brain wave state for performance in golf is alpha. It can be induced through several modalities, one of which is music. While playing in my first U.S.G.A. Senior Open Championship, I used a Walkman with alpha-programmed music to reach that state and relieve tension. It was very effective in helping me to make the cut.

The right music or sounds (preferably alpha rhythm) on a Walkman can keep you calm.

2. Tensing the muscles, holding the tension for a
    few seconds, then completely releasing is
    an effective on-course form of muscle relax-

ation. Give yourself enough time to refocus and create the relaxed but ready state you desire.

3. Controlled deep breathing is an age old technique for trauma reduction. *Slow, deep, but not forced, breathing on the course is an effective tension reducer.*

4. Seeing things in slower than normal motion and matching yourself to that pace can help relieve the temptation to speed up under stressful competitive conditions.

5. There are many techniques that promote relaxation in addition to those mentioned: hypnosis, autogenic training, modeling, positive self-talk, biofeedback, etc. But why not try a very simple one?—*smiling!*

6. I frequently use a technique that I've labeled "creative blindness." It is done by closing the eyes and rehearsing the stroke, particularly a putt, chip, or pitch. When you don't see the ball, a calmness comes over the swinging motion that frees the muscles from restriction. Capture that more relaxed feeling, then very slowly open your eyes, ready to repeat

It is hard to be tense when you are smiling.

the same feeling with the ball in the swing's way.

Additionally, I would highly recommend that the reader investigate acquiring the skill of Transcendental Meditation. It takes considerable practice but produces a deep form of relaxation that is not only good for your golf but also for everyday life.

Closing your eyes on short-shot practice strokes will help you relax.

Confidence

If you really want to become a better golfer, you need to develop a high level of confidence in your abilities; it might be your single greatest mental asset when it comes to an improved game. No performer, be it pianist, actor, stand-up comic, ballerina, high-wire artist, or athlete (golfers in particular), can survive without it. *Confidence is knowing you can do something—not thinking you can— but "knowing."* The exciting news about confidence is that one does not have to be born with it. Not only *can it* be a learned trait, *it most often is*. Those who seem to be "naturally confident" may have a hereditary predisposition in that direction, but a confident attitude is still one that must be acquired. Confidence is a choice, something you can rely on even when things are not going well during a round. You can't always wait for something good to happen to be confident. If you are mentally tough, you stay confident even when the drives are missing the fairway and the putts are missing the cup.

Think of anything that you do well, a skill in which you have a high level of confidence, and ask yourself, "Where did that come from?" The answer will inevitably be the same: practice, experience,

Staying confident when your shots are missing their mark is a part of being mentally tough.

and successful performances. When you practice a skill long enough, hard enough, and correctly, you will develop a level of comfort in performing that skill that exudes confidence.

But what about performing that same skill in the competitive arena? That's where experience plays a role, because an additional psychological aspect is introduced. If the competitive circumstance is unfamiliar, the normal level of comfort may be exceeded and a subsequent deterioration in perfor-

Confidence is boosted by frequent, correct practice.

mance the result. In other words, *practice in itself isn't enough to get you ready for competition. To be successful in the heat of competition you should also include specific "game-like" practice.* The good news is that it can be as simple as simulating situations in your mind as you work on your game. Practicing a putt late on a pleasant summer evening on the green outside the golf shop and imagining that it is for your club's title, or the city publinks senior championship, or to make the cut at Tour Qualifying School, may do the trick when that actual time comes. If you make the experience real enough, when the actual moment arrives you are more comfortable and possibly even confident for having visited this scene before, albeit in your mind.

Confidence promotes trust in what you are doing. The inhibitors of a free-flowing swing, such as indecision, fear, hesitation, tentativeness, doubt, and overconcern with result, disappear with the feeling of trust. That is why you will so often hear teachers of the game saying, "Trust your swing." They know that building trust and confidence will allow you to do all that you are capable of doing.

Learn to memorize *Mental Practice Exercise #2* (page 42) as a form of self-affirmation, of instilling confidence and subsequent trust. Most important is

Be patient: A good shot can wipe out some misplays.

the closing portion of this statement, which is meant to protect you from an insidious habit to which even the best players fall victim—the negative habit of *giving up*. A few bad breaks or bad holes can discourage players enough to make them figuratively throw in the towel. Don't quit. Keep in mind that a series of good breaks can wipe away the sour taste of the previous bad streak.

Mental Practice Exercise #2 (for confidence)

"I am a good player. I am a smart player. Like a professional, I know what I can do. I don't let my fellow competitors, the course, or spectators negatively influence me and keep me from doing what I know I can do. I am tough, I don't quit, and I don't need excuses."

Additional Insights and Observations on Confidence

1. A lack of confidence can lead to these common swing wreckers: *steering,* or attempting to guide the club and consequently the shot to the target; *forcing,* or using excessive muscular involvement in the swing; *left-brain thinking,* or trying to cognitively capture mechanical details while the swing is under way.

Trying to steer or guide the ball just doesn't work.

2. Using selective memory is one mental technique to help maintain confidence. It's easy: Simply remember the good shots and forget the bad. You can't afford to hang on to baggage (bad rounds, bad shots, bad experiences) that steals your energy and undermines your confidence. So put them far on the back shelf of your brain and bring the good ones to the front. My pet term for this is "constructive amnesia."

3. "Choking" in a sport infers that the player has not lived up to his/her potential when tested in competition. It happens when the perceived stress reaches a level beyond which the performer is accustomed. The result is a loss of confidence and poor performance. The answer is to reduce the perception that the outcome is truly threatening and put it in perspective. *Nothing in golf is life threatening. GOLF IS A GAME!*

4. Dyschrony means worrying about the past or future, neither of which will help your golf. *Stay in the present* and simply make the very best shot you can at the time, then go and do it again. That's advice from the late great Bobby Jones, and it is still powerful today.

5. Think of yourself as a biological data-recording system that logs every golf shot you have ever hit. When reporting the result to your brain, put the good shots in **bold type** and the poor ones in agate type. Your shots are creating your golfing biography, and *your biography becomes your biology.*

Put the bad shots in agate type.

6. If you want to handle pressure well and be-
    come a stress seeker (one who plays better in
    competition than practice) rather than a
    stress avoider (one who tends to collapse un-
    der pressure), *use your selective memory* to re-
    call situations in life where you came
    through in "the clutch." Start thinking of
    yourself as "game tough" and tell yourself,
    "I'm good when the heat is on."

Positive Visualization and Imagery

*One of the most commonly used mental tools among
world-class athletes is positive visualization, or mental
imagery.* Springboard divers picture their moves and
mentally rehearse them before stepping onto the
board. Downhill ski racers review in their minds
each turn and twist that must accompany their descent down the slope. Track and field athletes see
themselves clearing the crossbar, sailing over the
hurdles, slinging the javelin without fouling, all in
perfect form prior to their event being called. Top-
class golfers do the same. Do you? If you are like
the vast majority of people who play this game, instead of seeing success, you frequently picture disaster: the ball being topped into the water, slicing or
hooking into the woods, chili dipping into the

bunker. We've all done it. Maybe the better question would be, "What is your most common picture, one of perfect precision or probable peril? If you regularly use imagery, is it negative or positive? Are the divers seeing their foot slip on their hurdle step and their bodies losing control? Do skiers picture themselves falling down, ski tips shooting sky-

Mentally picturing bad shots before you hit makes them come true.

ward, while coming out of the chute? Are high jumpers imagining missing their steps and hitting the crossbar on the way up? Definitely not! That kind of negative imagery interjects worry, adds tension to the muscles, and eventually produces precisely what was pictured; classic self-fulfilling prophecy. *So take a lesson from world class athletes: Create positive mental images if you want positive results.*

Everyone visualizes, albeit to varying degrees. Unfortunately for most golfers, negative pictures dominate positive ones. That certainly is not the case with the "superstar" players. Dr. Bob Rotella, in his fine book *Golf Is Not a Game of Perfect*, relates an encounter with Fred Couples in which he asked Fred about his mental approach to the game. Couples's response was, "I pull up my sleeves and shrug my shoulders to try to get them relaxed, and then I try to remember the best shot I ever hit in my life with whatever club I have in my hand." That, my fellow golfers, is powerful. No mechanical details, only pictures, and pictures of the highest quality.

Use *Mental Practice Exercise #3* (page 50) to stimulate a positive visualization habit. Learn to picture the shot with a particular club just the way you'd like to hit it every time. Start with putting, then imagine playing some chips and pitches while focusing on your technique and how the shot feels.

Picture yourself hitting the putt that is going to go in . . .

On all the shots, see positive results. Change clubs, then move on to full iron shots. Finish with your driver and repeat that swing six times. Let yourself sense how those good swings felt. Take the practice of positive visualization with you to the course and add it to your preparation before each shot. Like Fred Couples, picture the best shot that you have ever hit with that club. If you don't come up with a good picture, step back and start again. The best thing about this procedure is that when you get a negative picture you can always delete it and restart. Call it a "mental Mulligan." If the negative thought is strong, you will have to put yourself into your most powerful mental override mode. You may need several of the mental strength strategies that are recommended throughout this book. Caution: Don't continue your routine while harboring negative thoughts. Stop, then start all over again. Remember, *you and only you control the pictures. Don't miss the shot in your mind before you swing the club, because then it's already too late.*

Mental practice Exercise #3 (for positive visualization)

"I know what my best strokes and best swings look like and I will rehearse by picturing them. Starting on the putting green I will see myself calmly stroking putts in from 3, 6, 9,

and 12 feet, feeling a relaxed flowing motion in each stroke. I'll then visualize making some short chips and pitches, seeing the ball simply getting in the way of my measured swinging motion, which then sends it to the target. Next I will hit a few sand wedge pitches and bunker shots using a bit more body and arm

. . . or the perfect form for chipping.

motion. I will follow with the full iron swing, using a #9, #7, #5, #3, hitting each shot so it lands on the green. Finally, I'll finish with my driver, making six consecutive swings to a balanced finish, seeing the desired ball flight and feeling the power that comes from letting go of tension. I will now picture in my mind a tee-to-green round, seeing only positive results on the course I play next. I'll do this while relaxing, as visualization is enhanced by relaxation."

Additional Insights and Observations on Positive Visualization and Imagery

1. Using images can be tremendously powerful. In fact, *images can be as strong as the actual event*. A United States military officer imprisoned for five years in a Vietnam POW camp visualized in detail playing golf every day. After his release, he returned home and within weeks shot a 75 in a tournament. He had been an 8 handicap player before his tour of duty.

2. Star borrowing, or the *picturing of a great player* and trying to reproduce his/her action, is one form of effective visualization for peo-

ple who have reasonable skills in copying or mimicking. Children are particularly adept, but anyone can do it.

3. Have a videotape made of your swing hitting selected shots with various clubs. Choose your very best swing with each club and have it repeated on the video five to ten times. Watch the tape to fix in your mind a strong image or visual picture of your best swing. This is self-modeling, and can include putting, bunker play, chip and pitch, etc.

Watching yourself on video is a great teaching aid, particularly if it is a loop sequence of your best swing.

If you see straight down the middle every time you step on the tee, you will hit more successful drives.

4. The primary reason players often make spec-
    tacular trouble shots, causing the ball to go
    under, around, and over obstacles, is that
    they work harder on visualizing these shots than
    on those from less demanding positions. This
    fact only serves to further validate the power
    of visualization.

5. Moe Norman, reputed to be golf's all-time
    straightest hitter, says when he is on the tee,
    "all I see is straight down the middle, straight
    down the middle." Wouldn't you consider
    that to be an advantage? Is it available to
    you? Yes, in your mind.

6. One of the greatest putters who played pro-
    fessionally was the late Labron Harris, Sr. His
    mechanics were plain vanilla, nothing fancy.
    So what was his secret? *He made every putt in
    his mind first before he stroked it.* That's positive
    visualization!

Concentration and Focus

If the average round of golf takes four hours, and a
player's normal score is 90, what percentage of that
time would be consumed with actually swinging
the club to hit the ball? Approximately 150 seconds

out of a possible 15,000 . . . or 1 percent. Add to that the preparation time before making the swing and you still have close to 13,000 seconds when you are not playing golf but walking, riding, or waiting to play. *So really, there is only a small amount of time in a round of golf that you need to concentrate.* However, focusing for a few seconds without letting outside thoughts or interference disrupt you is not easy. Try it! Look at an object in the room and let all other thoughts disappear. Do this for only thirty seconds and you will find that it is difficult to keep out flashes of thought, outside interference, or momentary wanderings. Focusing sharply is not as simple as it would seem. Therefore, trying to remain sharply focused, shutting out the outside world for four hours on the golf course, is not really possible. Focusing for a very brief period of time to prepare for and make a shot is much more feasible, but it takes practice.

There are two phases of mental focus on each golf shot. First, is the preparation phase, which Dr. Richard Coop and I called the "analytical phase" in our book *The New Golf Mind*. That's when the left side of your brain is sizing up the problem at hand and taking in information like a computer. After absorbing the available information, the brain begins analyzing it. For example: How far is it to the

It is not easy to focus on a singular object for 30 seconds without being distracted.

flagstick? What is the direction and strength of the wind? What is my ball flight tendency in these conditions? Where is the trouble? How hard is the green? Where do I stand in the competition? *It takes*

Analyze the conditions before club selection.

but a few seconds to gather this information, yet all the data needs to be used in making the decision on the type of shot and club to select.

Now the second phase of mental focus can be entered. That is the "integration," a function of the right side of the brain, which is creative rather than analytical. Details now must disappear and pictures appear. The focus is on sensing, visualizing, rehearsing, centering, settling, targeting, readying, and finally, doing. But it is a totally different mindset than its predecessor the analyzer. The integrator seeks to focus on feel rather than mechanical detail. It lets go of cognitive thought and relies on muscle memory. It seeks flow rather than position. The focus is on allowing rather than causing. *It may be the most difficult task in golf to focus on not trying to overcontrol the result, but rather to let the result just happen.*

All of this can be accomplished with your Mental Practice Exercise #4, which is a well developed preshot routine. *The great value to a preshot routine is that it not only helps you with consistency by adding precision to your preparation but also gets your focus away from result and into process.* In other words, you pay closer attention to the business at hand, the preshot routine and the visualized swing, than to what might happen to the ball once it leaves the clubface. If in selecting a recipe, say for a birthday cake, you choose to deviate from the specific ingredients used on a previous occasion, you will get a result that is not consistent with what you achieved before. It is the same in making preparations for your golf swing. A consistent preshot routine helps overcome one of the game's most difficult challenges: inconsistency. So develop a routine. It will eventually become automatic. You may not need to think about it, yet you must still put your focus on being precise in executing the elements within it. That takes discipline! Consequently, *losing focus on just a few swings per round can ruin what otherwise might have been a good score.*

Mental Practice Exercise #4 (for concentration)

"I have a routine that I follow for each shot, which brings me into focus, allowing me to concentrate on the task at hand."

- **Assess the lie, conditions, distance, and the situation.**

- **Picture the desired shot and where it will finish.**

- **Select the right club to fit the picture.**

- **Begin the preshot routine by seeing the target line and the resulting shot.**

- **Take the grip, aim the clubface, align the body, get the stance, and establish ball position.**

Reading the greens is the assessment part of putting.

- **Waggle for comfort and either visualize your shot or picture your swing again, and capture the feeling to produce the result.**

- **Swing the club while trusting the swing.**

- **Evaluate the result. If it's good, internalize it. If it is not, practice a successful effort and visualize the desired result.**

Additional Insights and Observations on Concentration and Focus

Concentration and focus are important to good performance, providing that the focus is on something that produces the desired result. Too often when the player focuses on "hitting the ball" rather than "swinging the club," the flowing motion is aborted and the finish incomplete. The tightening of muscles in an attempt to strike is so visually evident it appears as though the player were hitting a ball made of steel, or swinging into a solid brick wall. Focus on "slinging," or almost letting go, and that's when you'll feel the flow.

I encounter players who seem to regularly have a couple of bad holes in a round to spoil what otherwise would be good scores. *They consistently look for faulty swing mechanics but should more often investigate loss of focus.*

1. Many athletes in other sports seek solitude just prior to competition, focusing their mind on the upcoming performance. I've often wondered why more golfers haven't seen the need to quietly *focus their mind instead of only focusing on their mechanics during warm-up.* Us-

If you focus on slinging, you will feel the flow.

Other athletes often seek solitude before performing: Why not golfers?

ing either your Mental Practice Exercise card or a prerecorded audiotape in a Walkman can make the experience consistent no matter where you are playing.

2. In studying the greatest putters of all time I found it interesting to note where they placed their attention when putting. Once the reading and aim were completed, *none focused on mechanics; almost all focused on feel and pace.*

3. The deepest form of concentration comes when you are not thinking about trying to concentrate but rather are totally absorbed in the present.

4. The late Harvey Penick often said, "Take dead aim," which is simply another way to tell you to *focus.*

Emotional Control and Attitude

Golf offers its participants the full range of human emotion, from exhilaration after scoring a hole in one, to despair when losing by three-putting the last green from a short distance. *Our emotions have a big influence on our performance, since they possess the ability to chemically alter the body; that same body that swings the club.* Consider the biological effect of anger or fear on the body. Each can produce an elevated heart rate, rise in body temperature, increased muscle tension, a lessened ability to think rationally, and in severe cases nausea and tremors. None of these age-old limbic responses to prepare the body to fight or flee are useful in golf. Yet anger and fear are frequent companions for golfers. How

A bad lie doesn't stop a mentally tough golfer.

well we control these and other negative emotions will largely determine our resulting attitude, and attitude is one of the key components for acquiring mental strength.

We can't control the weather, our opponents, the condition of the course, good and bad breaks, and sometimes not even our shots, but we can control our attitude toward them. *Attitude is nothing more than the emotional response you make to happenings and circumstance.* When Jack Nicklaus hit a perfect drive on the closing hole of the Doral Tournament a few years back needing only a final par to be the winner, rather than being rewarded he found instead he was penalized because his ball ended up precisely in the middle of a large divot hole. What do you think was his reaction? He certainly could have gotten angry or even fearful over the possibility that this could cause him to mishit the shot and lose the tournament. Instead, he took a bit more time to survey the situation, selected his iron, fired the ball cleanly onto the green, and two-putted for the victory. After posting his score and accepting the trophy he was questioned by the press about the obvious bad break on the drive. He said, "Actually, that bad lie may have helped me since I was forced to focus on staying down through the shot." That's putting a definite positive spin on what could have been an emotional "why me" negative response. Nicklaus was in control of his emotions and his attitude.

A hotshot teenage junior golfer from Texas, later to become a PGA Tour player, was used to hitting fifteen to sixteen greens a round in regulation, shooting scores quite often in the low seventies. When he missed more than a few greens, he'd shoot much higher scores and would get visibly upset, displaying fits of anger. His home PGA professional got fed up with the young man's attitude and told him if he wanted to see a real player he should attend the Tour event in town the following week to watch two-time PGA champ Dave Stockton.

The boy did and came back amazed. He said, "That guy Stockton only hit six greens all day. I hit that in nine holes."

"Did he slam his club in the ground when he missed a green?" asked the pro.

"No," said the junior player.

"What did he shoot?" asked the pro.

"Sixty-nine," said the young man, who then added a telling comment: "And he acted like that was the way you were supposed to play!"

"Well now you have seen a real golfer," concluded the pro.

A "real golfer" can do some amazing things. The inspirational para-
plegic trick-shot golfer, Dennis Walters, is a great example.

So what was the lesson? *A strong short game can take you a long way, but a great attitude is a necessary companion.*

When Seve Ballesteros was near the peak of his career he played in our PGA Championship and had two very mediocre opening rounds with a total score that appeared to be higher than the projected cut. He returned to his hotel, made hasty airline reservations for Spain, packed, checked out, loaded the car for the airport, and was ready to leave when a bellman came out and said there was a phone call for him. Tournament headquarters was calling to say that the afternoon scores had been very high and Steve had just made the cut. His tee time was 7:38 the next morning. Think of the situation. He had no realistic chance to win the tournament and was already mentally on the plane home. Yet he dutifully unpacked, checked back in, and played the final two rounds, grinding on every shot and returning scores in the sixties, which produced a respectable finish. At the same time several players of lesser reputation who also had just barely made the cut were simply going through the motions of playing with obvious disinterest, and consequently finished near the bottom of the field, not even making expenses. The difference? *Attitude*.

In all three examples attitude was critical. Nicklaus did not let an obvious bad break anger him or affect his attitude. That's mental strength! Stockton's strong self-image as a player allowed him to maintain a positive attitude despite a day of below-average ball striking. That's mental strength! Ballesteros displayed a remarkable attitude of not quitting, no matter how far back he was in the pack. That's mental strength! All three had a choice. *Attitude is always a matter of choice.* They all chose like champions. In tough circumstances, how do you choose?

Mental Practice Exercise #5 (for emotional control and attitude)

"I know that my emotional state and attitude affect my performance. I also know that I am solely in control of both. Negative emotions like anger and fear produce physiological swing destroyers. So, I will stay cool, confident, and positive. I will have a good attitude, even when things aren't going well, because it will help me play better as well as gain the respect of my peers."

Have some fun in golf: It is better for you than anger.

Additional Insights and Observations on Emotional Control and Attitude

1. Despite any previous performance you should approach each shot with the expectation of success, *desiring it but not requiring it.* That's a good golfing attitude.

2. Many people have *unrealistic* expectations of how well they should play considering how little time they invest in practice. When one

Realize before play that you will hit a few bad shots in the round; then you won't be surprised or get upset. That's realistic.

combines meager preparation with high expectations, the result can create a negative attitude toward the game, the teacher, and oneself. So get real—or at least get realistic! Small efforts produce small rewards.

3. The saying, "As a man thinketh, so shall he be," is a classic concept that has surfaced in other languages and cultures for thousands of years. What you think about life, other people, situations, conditions, and yourself is

what creates your attitude. Knowing that peers can influence our attitude may be why "old pros" suggest that you *hang around good putters because they "thinketh" positively.*

4. What we eat or drink before or during a round can have a biochemical effect on us that influences our emotions. *Caffeine and sweets are examples of poor choices as they can lead to slight tremors and a quick physiological high followed by a sudden low that can negatively affect the emotions.*

5. *Gain a proper perspective* when facing a situation that might cause undesirable emotional arousal. Such an occasion could arise when playing with a famous personality. In such an instance, remember, they are just people. A nurse once told me that she had attended to the rich, the poor, the famous, and the anonymous, and no matter who they were they all needed a bedpan. Not a bad image to keep things in perspective.

6. There is at least one instance I can imagine where *anger can be useful* in golf. That is when you get so angry with your performance that you decide to practice.

If anger motivates you to practice, then it is good.

Motivation

All the good advice, talent, equipment, and opportunity in the world won't make you a better player if you aren't motivated enough to apply yourself. You need some passion for the game—the same passion that you should use to motivate yourself to practice physically, mentally, and biomechanically.

First you must decide what you want, how badly you want it, and what you are willing to do to get it. Is your desire to break 100, own a single-digit handicap, be the best man/woman/junior/senior at your course, become a professional, or to simply beat your know-all-about-it golf neighbor? In order to energize yourself beyond just wishing and into action, you need a goal, an objective, or a dream that becomes concrete. Without such a target, the fires that fuel momentary action will quickly dissipate.

Don't ever discount the power of setting goals! That process is a universally proven tool. The guidelines for goal setting are familiar to most and are quite simple. But many times "simple" does not necessarily mean "easy." The Golden Rule is one example. While the rule of "Do unto others . . . ," is simple and widely known, it is not widely followed. So it is with the motivational technique of goal setting, a valuable tool that is more talked about than practiced.

Check your goals before the practice session.

So, decide what you want from golf. Maybe it has nothing to do with score enhancement, championships, or winning matches with peers. Maybe it's about friendship, exercise, nature, travel, respite from routine, or enjoying the personal challenge. Still you have to know what you want. If not, there is a strong chance that you will get something else. If its solitude you seek then going to the course as a single at 10:00 a.m. on Saturday isn't going to meet your objective. But you must first know what that "deep down" objective is.

Once you decide what it is you want in the golf portion of your life, write down your goal or goals. Putting goals on paper enhances their empowerment. If it's an ambitious goal, say a single handicap when you are now a 23, then it must be broken into smaller minigoals and give yourself an adequate time frame to accomplish them. All goal setting should have some time limit imposed so you stay focused. The time limit can always be adjusted later, but write the completion time down along with the goals and how you plan to achieve them.

Decide what your resources are for meeting your goals. In the case of the 23 handicap player, there could be several: access to golf books and videos at the library; an excellent teaching professional at his/her home course; tournament golf on television providing good models to watch; the Golf Channel for free instruction; a local fitness center where they feature golf exercises; a store or pro shop where they sell learning and practice aids; and a new club-fitting center at the course to get the right equipment. Write those resources down, then make a plan with a weekly or monthly schedule. How much time is available? What are the practice priorities? If you have a teacher, involve him or her.

Proper clubfitting is one of the steps to meeting your goal for better golf.

Practicing with tools and learning aids gives you feedback.

Finally, post the goal or goals, maybe in several places, but at least in one that is in a prominent place that you'll see every day. I put one of my reminders on a Post-it above the door leading out from our master bathroom. It says "WARRIOR?" I know my goal. It's indelibly imprinted in my mind. And the Post-it message is cryptically saying to me, "Are you a warrior or a wimp?" Are you pursuing your goals? It's a strong reminder and a good motivator.

Use your *Mental Practice Exercise #6* (page 72), first to accomplish the goal-setting task, and then to keep yourself focused on that specific target. It's

It is harder to improve without help from a competent teacher.

quite a bit easier to get fired up than it is to stay fired up. As coaches from all sports know, *having the will to win is relatively easy, but having the will to prepare to win distinguishes the champion from the also-ran.* Without motivation, maintaining the desire to succeed is highly unlikely. What would you like to get done in your golf game? If it's better performance through greater mental strength, then use your Mental Practice Exercise program regularly.

You and your teacher should be partners in your quest for better golf.

Mental Practice Exercise #6 (for motivation)

The foundation of good performance is proper preparation. "I will decide what I want, write my goals, make a plan, and follow the plan. There may be interruptions due to sickness, travel, and unforeseen circumstances, but these are only temporary. Progress at times

may be slow or seemingly nonexistent, but I will persevere."*

Additional Insights and Observations on Motivation

1. *Action without a plan is unfocused wasted energy. A plan without action is merely a dream.* You need both a plan and action to stay motivated.

2. It is recommended that self-talk be kind. But self-criticism can sometimes be useful as a motivator, a wake-up call, when your focus has slipped and you have "gone to sleep."

3. Record keeping can be a great motivator. Remember from school days the record boards that trumpeted the accomplishments of earlier track and field stars, swimmers, or a variety of ball players? Those numbers pushed a lot of people to practice harder. Keeping your own stats from rounds of golf can do likewise.

4. Maintaining a ringer score record at your home course is a motivator to *keep trying* dur-

---

*My personal golf plan is located at the end of the book.

Record keeping, like a ringer score, is just another motivational tool.

ing a round even when your game is going poorly. (A ringer score is the best number you have made for the year, or for your life, on each hole of your home course or any one that you play regularly.)

5. *Goal setting during practice sessions* can motivate you to a higher level of performance. For example, "I'm not going to leave until I make three successive putts from six feet."

Setting goals during practice, like making a certain number of putts from a given distance, will help you focus.

Selecting opponents who are more accomplished than you can *motivate you to practice* more and perform better. The choice might be either practice more or get "beat up" a lot on the course.

2

Finding Time Through Built-Ins

You have been given six principles for developing mental strength along with additional insights into their value and how they may be applied. But what about the time factor? Where do you find the time to play, hit balls on the practice range and do this psychological stuff too? The answer is built-ins. If you are creative and attentive you can get all that you need from the material in this book and practice it taking very little additional valuable time. Here is how.

You can get an incredible amount accomplished if you simply attach your new Mental Practice Exercises to daily routines. For example here is one way to complete all or at least some of your Mental Practice Exercises in a normal work day. Your relaxation exercise (#1) takes only three to five minutes. You could complete it around mealtimes, such as part of your lunch hour, a predinner ritual, maybe just before breakfast, or before starting your daily routine. It can always be done at the golf range prior to a practice session, but I would suggest to look instead toward incorporating it into things that you do every day. That's how to develop a good habit. Using Mental Practice Exercises #2 through #6 can all be easily tied into your daily activities. For example, your visualization skill can be done while at the sink in the morning, driving the car, riding the commuter train, doing the washing or dishes, or waiting in line at the store or bank. You can picture your golf swing and never miss a shot. Just use your imagination. Make copies of your Mental Practice Exercise card (page 85) to put anywhere you spend significant time, or carry one with you in your wallet or purse. Soon you won't need the card as you will memorize the key elements and know them by heart. Don't forget the power in the statement, "As a man thinketh, so shall he be." *Use your Mental Practice Exercise card as a constant reminder for mental strength training.*

3

Gary Wiren's Personal Golf Objectives

Earlier in this book we made a case for the value of goal setting in achieving objectives. I believe in its power to sustain motivation and keep you focused on what you are trying to accomplish. With that said, I offer my own personal objectives for golf. In doing so, I give appreciation to former St. Olaf, Minnesota, hockey coach Whitey Aus, who created the model for this list.

1. Set a reasonable schedule of practice and training that you can meet, and then stick to it. There will be emergencies and situations that cause an occasional miss; be as regular as possible.

2. Be positive about yourself, your game, and what you are doing. A negative attitude is one of the most destructive forces in golf.

3. Practice with an objective in mind. Since your time is short, make your practice time of the highest quality. Make each shot (excluding warm-up) as though on the course and counting for score: fewer balls; more perfect shots.

4. When playing, even in a casual round, take enough time to execute properly. As long as you are taking the time to play, even for fun, do it right. Make it a habit.

5. Winners are not always those who have finished first. A winner is someone who gives the most in preparation to reach his/her potential and makes every effort to perform at their highest level. There will be times when that is accomplished and you still aren't victorious; but you are a winner.

6. No opponent is deserving of either lack of respect or an attitude of awe. In any reasonable match of talent, either competitor can win on a given day.

7. You may not have the best talent in a match, but tough competitors often overcome superior talent. Patience and perseverance will pay off in golf.

8. Be consistent in your performance, focusing on the task at hand for the full time you are playing. Don't ease up when ahead or quit when you are behind. You never know what might happen to you or an opponent, so keep your focus. One shot at a time.

9. Self-control is a trait that you should strive to achieve. Loss of self-control is harmful to performance as well as to individual growth as a person. It reveals itself in club throwing, displays of temper, offensive language, verbal abuse of spectators or officials, complaining about the event or facility, etc. **Keep your composure!**

10. Keep your body in good physical shape by observing the following suggestions:

- Eat three balanced meals daily, avoiding as much fried foods, rich desserts, fat and salt as possible. Eat more fruits, vegetables, grains, and cereals, and get your protein. You may have heard this advice many times before, but just don't hear it, do it!

- Limit or abstain from the use of chemicals, including alcohol. Smoking is detrimental to your overall health and is out of the question.

- Get seven to eight hours of sleep a night. Fatigue destroys performance.

- Include a mixture of flexibility, cardiovascular, and strength work in your physical training program.

11. Be committed to your sport, but put competition and outcomes in perspective. There are more important things in your life than golf. Putting it in perspective will help you as a competitor to realize you don't have to win, only to give it your best effort. This attitude promotes relaxation and actually contributes to good performance.

Enjoy what you are doing. If it isn't rewarding or enjoyable, then reevaluate your program and make it so. Golf is a game and is meant to be enjoyed.

4
Conclusion

The reason that people take instruction is to improve. But *improvement requires change*, and change is not easy. Think of any distasteful or annoying habit that is tough to get rid of and you will know what I mean. So it is with bad golfing habits, or lack of good golfing habits, whether they be mechanical or mental. What you have just been given is a formula for greater mental strength, but it is not in itself an answer. You control the final answer which will require patience and effort. Why not go for it? Why not see how much better you could be?

To help you become the best player possible I hope you will make full use of the six keys to developing your mental golf strength that are found on the following page. You might want to remove this page from the book, place numbers 1 through 3 on one side of a 4 × 5 card and 4 through 6 on the other side, and have it laminated so that you can carry it with you for easy recall.

Note: Any references to learning or practice aid devices in this book can be fulfilled by calling Golf Around the World, 1–800–824–4279 or can be viewed at : *www.golfaroundtheworld.com*.

Mental Practice Card

1. I WILL FOLLOW MY PROGRESSIVE RELAXATION EXERCISE BEFORE I PLAY SO THAT I FEEL CALM AND AT EASE.

2. I AM A GOOD PLAYER AND I AM A SMART PLAYER. I KNOW WHAT I CAN DO AND WON'T LET OUTSIDE INTERFERENCE KEEP ME FROM DOING IT. I DON'T QUIT OR MAKE EXCUSES.

3. IN PREPARATION FOR AN IMPORTANT ROUND I WILL FIND A RELAXING SETTING, THEN PICTURE THE COURSE AND THE SHOTS I PLAN TO HIT. DURING THE ROUND I WILL USE MY POSITIVE VISUALIZATION ABILITY TO MENTALLY SEE MY BEST SWING AND MY BEST SHOTS.

4. A DEFINITE PRE-SHOT ROUTINE WILL BE A PART OF MY PLAYING STRATEGY. IT WILL INCLUDE ASSESSING THE CONDITIONS, PICTURING THE SHOT, GRIP, AIM AND SET-UP, TRUSTING THE SWING AND EVALUATING THE RESULT TO EITHER INTERNALIZE OR REPLACE.

5. I KNOW ATTITUDE IS IMPORTANT IN INFLUENCING PERFORMANCE AND THAT NEGATIVE EMOTIONS ARE SWING DESTROYERS. SO, I WILL STAY POSITIVE, EVEN WHEN THINGS AREN'T GOING WELL.

6. SUCCESS IS GREATLY DEPENDENT UPON PREPARATION. SO, I WILL WRITE GOALS, MAKE A PLAN, AND PERSEVERE.

Your Personal Mental Golf Notes

The *GOLF Magazine*

Complete Guide to Golf

Book Two

Golf Fitness

Gary Wiren, Ph.D.

PGA Master Professional
and the Editors of *GOLF Magazine*

Introduction

It's hard to imagine any competitive sport today in which the participants do not physically train for their event; even table tennis and chess players do. *Training is an absolute necessity if participants expect to perform at their highest level.* Yet golfers have been slow to recognize the seemingly obvious benefits of training. Golf professionals from a previous generation were the victims of "old wives' tales" about the negative implications of building muscles for golf. Not so today. That's why you see official PGA fitness trainers on the Tour, college teams that have training regimes, mini-Tour players working out regularly, and national amateur squads with strict physical training programs.

The golfing public started taking more notice of training specifically for golf when the PGA Tour fitness trainers appeared.

The average amateur golfer, however, is still trying to *buy* better performance through exotic clubs, "hot golf balls," and secrets from gurus. Certainly proper equipment and good instruction do help. But you can't win the Indianapolis 500 in a Volkswagen. And you can't make the golf ball respond as you'd like it to if your body can't generate speed or provide control. The "average player" may be limited to "average" by a poorly conditioned body: one that is either too weak, too fat, too inflexible, or all three. So awaken to the reality that *your technique will always be limited by your body's ability to per-*

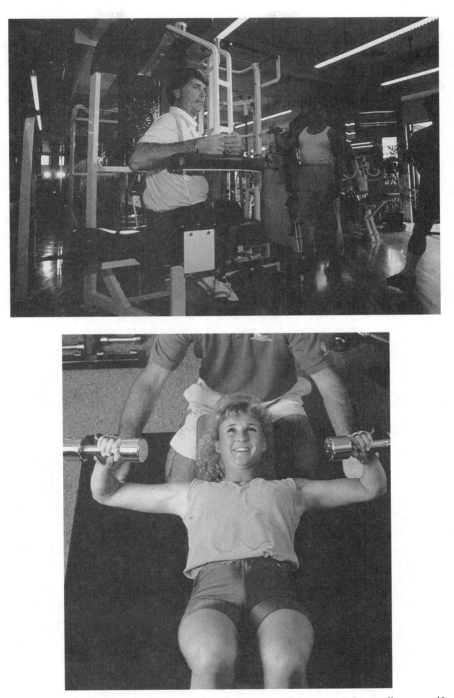

Working out in the training center is a part of every major college golf program as well as for those players competing on the mini-Tour.

form. Let's be honest: Golf is an athletic event. Other factors being equal, the trained athlete beats the untrained one on a regular basis.

Besides performance enhancement, there are at least three other very good reasons to train for golf:

A dynamic full-motion golf swing is a true athletic move.

1. *You will be less likely to sustain injury*, and if you do
    have an injury, you will recuperate much more
    quickly.

2. *You will increase your golfing longevity.* Well-condi-
    tioned golfers can maintain pleasurable golfing
    skills into their seventies, eighties, and even
    nineties, which makes golf "the game of a lifetime."

3. Finally, the greatest benefit to training for golf is
    that you are also training for life. If your desire to
    improve your golf handicap can motivate you to
    adopt a more active, healthier lifestyle, not only
    will your golf get better, but so will the quality of
    your living. *You'll feel better, look better, and play bet-
    ter.* That's quite a combination . . . if you follow
    through with it.

Promise

How can this book help you cash in on the
promises just described? Hopefully, those potential
rewards are sufficient to motivate you to action.
Oh, it will take effort, but the results are truly
worth it. (I say that from a lifetime of personal experience.) So, if somewhere deep inside you there
is an honest desire to be a better golfer, then becoming fit for golf is a goal you definitely need to
pursue. Why? Because it can make a huge difference in performance. This book can give you the
right information to make that difference.

Knowing the demands of a busy lifestyle and realizing that unrealistic expectations often lead to quitting and failure, I have deliberately limited the number of exercises and time for exercising to twenty to forty minutes per workout. To help with the time problem, you are even shown how to build exercise into your life without taking any extra time. Material is offered that ranges from nutrition considerations that are golf specific, to managing your life to protect you from back trauma. So choose from these golf exercise programs what best suits your schedule. Balance them between strength, flexibility, and endurance, and include the whole body. Let's get started—it all starts with warm-up.

1

Warm-Up

The Necessity of Warm-up

When you walk to the first tee without having warmed up, you can expect to be greeted by muscles, tendons, and ligaments that are cold, inflexible, and unforgiving. You are asking (almost begging) for injury or poor performance. Too many times, I have seen the man who leaves the locker room, strolls to the first tee, takes out the driver, makes two swings at a cigarette butt or broken tee on the ground, considers that to be his warm-up, and asks, "How much we playin' for?" Then there is the woman (on ladies' day) whose version of a warm-up prior to the shotgun start consists of a cup of coffee, a danish, and lots of conversation followed by her uninspired

95

practice swings when she arrives at the designated tee location. This is not an adequate warm-up. It encourages injury and discourages good performance.

Compare these examples to other sports. In football the players are on the field forty-five minutes ahead of the kick-off doing calisthenics and run-

This is a great hamstring and back stretch that can be done in the locker room, on the practice range, or on the first tee prior to play.

ning through skill drills to warm up. In basketball (men's or women's) the warm-up starts about thirty minutes prior to the center jump. Then there is baseball (or softball), in which it seems the pregame warm-up lasts almost as long as the game itself. All of these rituals are performed in order to warm up. Why do golfers think they are exempt from the laws of physiology?

Fortunately, the golf warm-up can be done much more quickly than what I've described in these other sports. But just because you aren't tackling someone, jumping for a rebound, or circling the bases *don't think that the golf swing isn't a physically demanding movement that needs its own specific warm-up.* The following pages will give you options to accomplish that physiological need.

Three Warm-Up Options
Home or Locker Room Warm-Up

Taking six minutes to do some stretching before leaving for the course, or in the locker room after you arrive, is a great way to start preparation for your round. The following stretches are suggested for an effective golf warm-up before you get to the practice tee.

Stretch to Ceiling: Interlock your fingers and extend both arms overhead with your palms toward the ceiling. Tilt your head back while looking at your hands. Rise up on your toes as you stretch overhead. Hold the stretch for ten seconds. Repeat three times.

Muscles used: Arms, neck, shoulders, and calves.

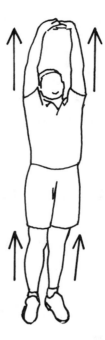

Back Scratch: Stand upright and place one hand in the center of your back. Pull down on the bent elbow with the opposite hand; hold for ten seconds. Repeat three times on each side.

Muscles used: Triceps, forearms, and rotator cuff.

Side Bends: Interlock your fingers and extend both arms overhead. Bend to one side by pulling slowly with one arm toward the ground. Keep your elbows on plane with the body. Hold the stretch for ten seconds. Repeat three times on each side. *Muscles used:* Obliques, upper back, and shoulders.

Wall Touches: While standing with your back about one foot away from a wall, slowly turn your torso until you can place one or both palms flat on the wall. Try to keep your hips facing forward and your knees slightly bent. Hold for ten seconds. Repeat three times on each side. *Muscles used:* Abdominals, obliques, and lower back.

Standing Hamstring Stretch: Stand on one leg. Slowly raise your opposite foot close to thigh height. Rest your heel on a stable object, such as a bench. Interlock your fingers, then slowly stretch forward toward the elevated foot. Hold for ten seconds. Repeat three times on each leg.
Muscles used: Hamstrings, calves, and lower back.

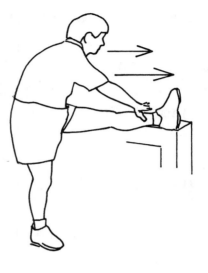

Bench Lunges: Stand two to three feet away from a stable bench and place your hands on your hips. Raise one leg and place your foot flat on the bench. Slowly shift your weight over the forward leg. Don't allow the front knee to extend out over your toes. Repeat five times on each leg.
Muscles used: Hips, quadriceps, and hamstrings.

Golf Car Stretching

The golf car can be a valuable piece of stretching equipment as well as a means of transportation. If you haven't done the home or locker room warm-up exercises, you may wish to do the following stretches, utilizing the golf car, before you tee off. It is a good idea to repeat some of these stretches during the round if you feel yourself becoming tight or fatigued.

Lower Back Stretch: While standing facing a golf car from about one foot away, grab the arm guard with both hands. Fully extend your arms. Slowly bend your knees and sit back away from the car until you feel a stretch in the lower back. Hold for ten seconds. Repeat three times.

Muscles used: Lower back and shoulders.

Rear Shoulder Stretch:
Stand at a 90-degree angle to the golf car. Reach across your body with your outside hand and grab the roof post at shoulder height. Slowly turn away from the car, stretching your rear shoulder and back muscles. Do two repetitions and hold the stretch for ten seconds. Repeat with your other arm while facing the opposite direction.
Muscles used: Rear shoulders, upper back, and torso.

Front Shoulder Stretch:
Stand facing away from the golf car, reach back, and grab the roof post with one hand. Keep your hand at shoulder height with the palm facing out.

Slowly turn away from your hand holding the post. Hold for ten seconds. Repeat twice. Repeat with the opposite arm.

Muscles used: Chest, shoulders, biceps, forearms, and torso.

Middle Back and Hamstring Stretch: Hold on to the roof post with one hand. Slowly lean away, keeping one leg extended out with the toes pointed up. Grab the toes with one hand to stretch your hamstring; sit back to stretch the middle back. Hold for ten seconds. Repeat on the other side.

Muscles used: Hamstrings, calves, shoulders, and middle back.

Gravity Drop: Stand with both feet on the golf car floor, balancing on the forward part of each foot. Hold on to the roof for support and let your heels drop down toward the ground. Slowly lower and raise your heels. Repeat ten times.

Muscles used: Achilles tendon and calves.

Golf Car Lunges: Rest a golf club across your upper back, standing approximately two to three feet away from a golf car. Raise one leg and place your foot flat on the floor. Slowly shift your weight over the forward leg. Don't let your front knee extend out over your toes. Repeat three times on each leg.

Muscles used: Hips, quadriceps, and hamstrings.

Should you find yourself arriving just in time to tee off and no time to do either the golf car stretching or the locker room warm-up, then use the following "No-Ball Warm-Up." You can fit in some of the locker room and golf car stretches while you play the opening holes.

The "No-Ball Warm-Up" on the First Tee

Tour professional golfers arrive at the course allowing one to one and a half hours to prepare before

Hitting balls before play is an advantage that shouldn't be overlooked.

hitting the first tee shot. This provides adequate time to get their equipment organized, do some of the physical warm-up exercises just described, a little ball hitting, short game practice, and putting. Ideally, that's what we all should do. But if you are like most golfers, rarely are you so fortunate. Frequently, you come to the course allowing just enough time to change shoes, check in at the pro shop, and head to the first tee.

Since you seldom have the luxury of arriving an hour before you tee off, and if you didn't do any home or locker room stretches, what can you do when you find yourself on the tee without having done any exercises or hit any shots to warm up? One recommendation is for you to take at least ninety seconds to perform a six-step "No Ball Warm-Up." Here is how you do it:

Step 1 (20 seconds): Take your two heaviest clubs—i.e., sand wedge and pitching wedge— and hold them together in a semi-baseball grip. Feel the heaviness of the two combined and begin making small swings, hands traveling first to hip height, then shoulder height, gradually building up the length to a full swing. The extra weight will not only help you stretch but also will promote a better tempo and true swinging motion. If at any time during these stretches, particularly the next five, you feel a sharp pull of pain, stop and reduce the stress load in the position you are attempting.

Step 2 (20 seconds): Select the club you are going to use from the first tee (probably a driver or #3 wood). Standing vertically, place the club behind your back in the crooks of your elbows and turn a total of 180 degrees, (including back and through swings). Get your abdomen to face the target at the finish and let your weight naturally transfer from your rear foot to your forward foot.

Step 3 (15 seconds): Bend forward from the hips as though addressing the ball. With this forward tilt of the spine maintained, repeat the total of 180-degree turns, allowing your weight to shift from over your rear leg to over your forward leg; again you should be "tummy to the target," looking at your target, not the ground, at the finish.

Step 4 (15 seconds): Standing vertically, place the club across your shoulders and behind your neck, grasping it with the right and left hand spread beyond shoulder's width. Turn 180 degrees; 90 back and 90 through. Use the same lower body finish as before.

Step 5 (15 seconds): Keeping the club in the same position, tilt your spine forward to assume your address position and repeat the exercise. Face the target at the finish.

Step 6 (15 seconds): From the previous position, drop the club behind your back to hip height, keeping your thumbs hooked around the shaft. Raise your arms behind you and make 180-degree turns with your body, always finishing with the weight off the rear foot and on your forward foot. The higher you raise your arms the greater the stretch.

That's eighty seconds of stretching. Allowing ten seconds more to change clubs and positions, and you have a ninety-second no-ball warm-up. Now take a few easy practice swings, gradually increasing your speed until you have reached a comfortable, effective rate; *not your hardest* but your most

After the No-Ball Warm-Up, focus on a good aim and setup.

effective. Tee the ball, go through your preshot routine, and swing with the effort of the last comfortable but aggressive full practice swing. *You'll be starting your round with the knowledge and confidence that you have had an adequate warm-up to hit a respectable drive.*

Then, "make your very best swing," not your hardest hit.

Combinations of any of the three warm-up options just recommended can be used. Obviously, hitting practice shots on the practice range prior to play is desirable to establish your feel and rehearse your routine as well as to stretch and warm your muscles, ligaments, and tendons. The important thing is to warm up in a way that will help you develop the feel for your swing and discourage any chance of injuring yourself.

2

Key Fitness Components

Flexibility

When golfers think of hitting the ball farther, they immediately relate it to physical strength. But strength without the range of motion needed to apply it is of limited value. Power is the result of applying force over a given distance in a specified time. If one has a body with a trunk that can barely turn or knees that hardly flex, arms that refuse to extend, a spine that won't stay tilted, and wrists that resist cocking, the answer to better performance is to *increase flexibility*!

Stretching to increase range of motion and maximize one's power is the hottest, most "in" part of golf exercise among the game's top players. It is an absolute neces-

This hamstring stretch will help reduce potential back problems, thus allowing you to make a strong rotary movement in your swing.

sity for longevity in the game, and one of the surest antidotes for the prevention of injury.

When performing flexibility exercises there are a few important imperatives to follow:

1. Warm up before beginning stretching exercises by performing some total body movement like jumping jacks or jogging in place.

2. Always do stretching slowly. Never bounce to increase range of motion.

3. Don't push your pain level. Distinguish between slight discomfort and sharp pain.

4. Breathe naturally. Exhale as you do your stretch, and continue breathing as you hold the position.

5. To get the most out of a stretching exercise, go to your comfortable limit, relax, then go just a bit farther.

6. Hold your stretch positions from ten to thirty seconds and occasionally longer depending on the exercise. Generally longer is better.

7. Inhale deeply through your nose and exhale through your nose or mouth.

8. Make it a habit of taking stretch breaks during the day, such as stretching when you are just standing waiting for the bus, a plane, in a line at the store, by your desk, in the kitchen or front room; literally wherever you happen to be.

Using the stretches that have been described before you play will provide you with many benefits. It will increase your blood supply to muscles, ligaments, and tendons; elongate muscle tissue; reduce tension; and improve movement around the joints. *These kinds of benefits, which help prevent injury and improve performance, should encourage everyone to do some warm-up related to stretching before play.* For long-term improved golf performance, however, you need a regular program of stretching that is done more frequently than just on days you play. Here is a suggested collection of simple home workout stretching exercises.

Regular Flexibility Home Workout

The following exercises should be done every day to increase flexibility in your trunk and lower extremities. If every day is not possible, then at least every other day is recommended for sustained improvement.

Tuck Roll: While lying flat on your back, pull both knees into your chest with interlocked fingers. Slowly make small rocking motions back and forth between the upper and lower back. Repeat ten times. *Muscles used:* Gluteus, lower back, and shoulders.

Double Toe Tug: While lying flat on your back, elevate both feet into the air. Hood a towel over your toes and slowly pull downward. Push your heels upward to increase the stretch. Repeat five times. *Muscles used:* Hamstrings and calves.

Single Toe Cross-over: While lying flat on your back, bend both knees. Raise one foot in the air, hooking a towel over your toes. Pull the foot toward the opposite shoulder. Hold for ten seconds. Repeat three times on each leg. *Muscles used:* Hips and gluteus.

Hip Extension Stretch: While lying flat on your back, bend both knees. Cross one foot over the opposite knee, then slowly rotate your torso toward the same side as your upper leg. Keep the shoulders flat as you hold the stretch for ten seconds. Repeat three times on each side.

Muscles used: Hip flexors, lower back, and torso.

Trunk Rotation: While lying flat on your back, bend both knees. Cross one foot over the opposite knee. Slowly rotate your torso toward the opposite side of your upper leg. Use your opposite hand to pull. Repeat three times on each side.

Muscles used: Lower back, abdominals, and torso.

Fitness Center Flexibility

Lower Body

The following six-exercise stretching workout is a bit more advanced and may be easier to do at a fitness center. Any of the home exercises could also be incorporated. Hold each of these stretches for ten seconds. Apply consistent pressure during every stretch. Do not bounce. Attempt to exhale your breath out through your mouth as you perform each stretch. This first group of six is for your lower and midbody.

Wall Double-Leg Stretch: Lying flat on your back, place your heels on the wall, keeping the legs fully extended. Slowly pull your toes downward, without bending knees. Alternate feet. Repeat ten times.
Muscles used: Gastrocnemius, hamstrings, and lower back.

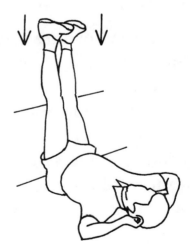

Wall Single Leg/Heel on Toe: Lying flat on your back with your seat close to the wall and legs fully extended, place your heels against the wall. Slowly place one heel on the opposite toe. Apply additional resistance by pressing lightly on your front thigh. Repeat three times. Switch legs.

Muscles used: Hamstrings and achilles tendon.

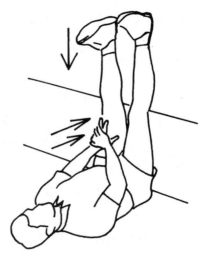

Wall Alternate Instep Pull: Lying flat on your back, place your heels on the wall. Grab the instep of one foot with your same side hand. Press your heel up toward the ceiling. Repeat three times. Switch legs.

Muscles used: Gluteals, calves, and hamstrings.

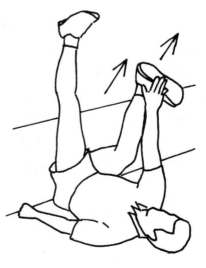

Wall Figure-4 Stretch:
Lying flat on your back, bend both knees until they are in a 90-degree angle. Then, cross one foot over your opposite knee. Pull down on your toes with one hand while pushing on one knee with your opposite hand. You should feel stretching in the back of your leg. Repeat three times. Switch legs.
Muscles used: Gluteals and lower back.

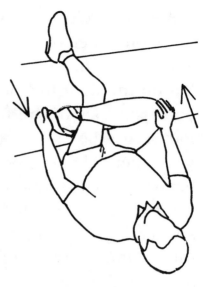

Bench Single-Leg Stretch:
Sit up tall on a bench. Place one leg out in front of you, the other flat on the floor. Interlock your fingers and slowly stretch forward. Repeat three times and hold each stretch at the maximum extension. Switch legs.

Muscles used: Hamstrings, calves, lower back, and shoulders.

Bench Ankle Grab: Place one knee on a bench and put your other foot flat on the floor in front of you. The toes of the front foot must be in front of your bent knee. Slowly bend the knee that's on the bench and reach back and grab your ankle with the same side hand. Slowly pull your ankle forward. Repeat three times. Switch legs.

Muscles used: Quadriceps, hip flexors, and lower back.

Upper Body

For an upper-body flexibility workout at home or at the fitness center, use the following exercises that have already been cited as part of a home or locker room warm-up or golf car stretching routine: **Stretch to ceiling, back scratch, wall touches, side bends, rear shoulder stretch, and front shoulder stretch.** You can utilize these same upper-body exercises and any of the other home stretching or warm-up exercises at the fitness center by inserting them in between the exercises in your strength workout. For example, if you use a back extension machine for strength, you might insert a thirty-second wall touch for flexibility. Matching a stretching exercise to the muscle group you have just worked on for strength keeps you flexible while building additional strength. *The combination of strength and flexibility is the secret for achieving power.*

Strength

The power in the golf swing comes from muscular action, which drives the torso, limbs, and eventually the club to deliver a blow to the ball. It takes an estimated 60 pounds of muscular mass to create a clubhead speed of 100 m.p.h. (240-yard drive). Therefore, *doing exercises to build stronger muscles can definitely increase your potential for distance.* The amount of gain will depend greatly upon where you start. If you are already strong and have good muscle tone, the gains from strength training alone may be small. But if you are in poor muscular condition and have low levels of strength, those gains could be quite large. There is one caveat pertaining to any predictions in performance gain: *You can expect maximum positive results only if you do the prescribed suggested exercises regularly and correctly.*

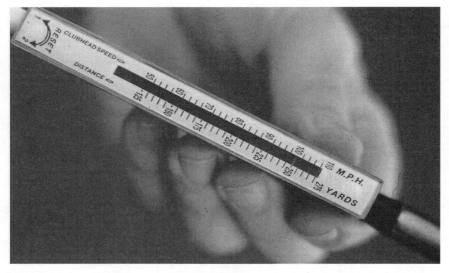

Clubhead speed, as measured by the device shown, is largely a product of a strength and flexibility that is specific to golf, for which you can train.

Here are some important principles you should be aware of before embarking on a strength-building program.

- *It is never too late to get stronger.* Recent research at Tufts University documents strength increases from 10 percent to 226 percent in subjects whose average ages were in their sixties and seventies. Also at Harvard, significant strength gains were demonstrated in a group of both men and women ranging in age from eighty-six to ninety-six.

- *You can't get stronger without stressing your muscular system.* This stress can come from providing a resistance, which could consist of more weight, more repetitions, or more tension, as in an isometric (static) exercise, or by moving the load with more speed.

- *An alternative way to add repetitions is to do a second or third set.* This can be done for any group of muscles on which you wish to focus.

- *Don't go too fast.* Add weight, repetition, or speed gradually and comfortably. The biggest mistake a motivated person can make is to think that two weeks of exercise will undo what has happened to the body over the previous twenty years. Be patient! Go slowly and do it regularly!

- *Rest days in between strength-building days are essential.* Training breaks the muscles fibers down and rest gives them the opportunity to build back up and grow.

- *Don't hold your breath during a lift.* It increases the blood pressure, lowers the heart rate, and can cause blackout. Exhale during the exertion portion and inhale before completion of the repetition.

- *Movements should be steady, not jerky.* Don't choose a load that is so heavy that you lose your good form.

- *Work the large muscles before the small muscles.* Large muscle activity can assist in warming up the smaller ones and they fatigue less rapidly.

At-Home Strength Training

For strength training I recommend using a weight resistance that will allow you to successfully complete at least ten repetitions. When you can complete fifteen repetitions, add weight and reduce the reps to ten again. Dumbbells or hand weights are suggested, but water bottles, cartons of sand, or similar weighted objects can be used. Working out three to four days per week on strength training is recommended. One hard day of strength training per week might maintain your present level, two days would give you some increase, but three to four days of a vigorous (but not intensive) program has been shown to be the most beneficial.

There are also specialized golf strength and flexibility training products that can be used at home.* One of the simplest and most useful for golf is a hand gripper. The hands are the only connection between the power source, your body, and the delivery system, the club. Strong golf starts with strong hands. This is true even more so for control of the club than it is for distance. Home golf training equipment is readily available and quite effective, providing you actually use it.

---

*See the reference at the end of the book.

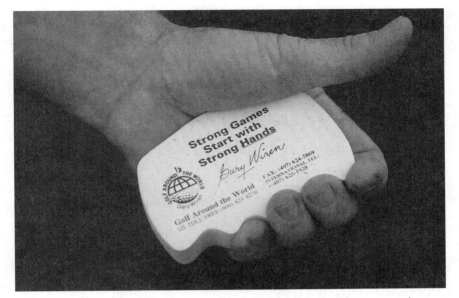

A hand gripper may be one of the least expensive but most beneficial exercise aids you could own.

Rubber tubing has gained popularity among athletes for resistance training in many sports, including golf.

Upper Body

Wall Side Raises: From a standing position, place your back against the wall and spread your feet comfortably apart. Start with your hands at hip height and slowly raise your arms vertically until they are at shoulder height. Lower to the starting position. Repeat ten times.
Muscles used: Shoulders, forearms, and wrists.

Wall Shoulder Shrugs: From a standing position, place your back against the wall and spread your feet comfortably apart. Start with your hands at hip height and slowly raise your shoulders vertically toward your ears. Return to the starting position. Do not rotate your shoulders

or bend your arms at the elbows. Repeat ten times.
Muscles used: Trapezius, upper back, and shoulders.

Wall Vertical Raise/ Horizontal Press: From a standing position, place your back against the wall and spread your feet comfortably apart. Start with your hands in front of your thighs. Slowly raise both hands to your chin, keeping your elbows higher than the hands. Now press your hands straight out in front of you at shoulder level until fully extended. Slowly lower your hands to the starting position. Repeat ten times.
Muscles used: Forearms, triceps, trapezius, and upper back.

Seated Forearm Curls and Reverse Curls: From a seated position, rest the back of your forearm on the top of your thigh with the wrist extended beyond your knee. Slowly raise and lower the weight by flexing and extending the wrist. Repeat ten times, then switch arms.
Muscles used: Forearm flexors and extensors.

One Arm Rows: Bend forward, placing one knee and one hand on a bench, while keeping your back flat. Let your hand with the weight extend toward the ground, then slowly raise your arm until the el-

bow is flexed at a 90-degree angle. Slowly lower the weight to the starting position. Repeat ten times. *Muscles used:* Latissimus dorsi, triceps, and rear deltoids.

Weighted Side Bends: Stand upright with one hand on top of your head and the other hand beside your hip. Place your feet shoulder-width apart. Slowly bend from side to side, keeping your body in a straight plane. *Do not bend forward.* Repeat ten times on each side.

Muscles used: Obliques, lower back, and abdominals.

Lower Body and Abdominals

Calf Raises/Double and Single: (Double) Stand facing a wall with your feet shoulder-width apart. Slowly raise up on your toes until your heels are fully extended off the floor. Repeat for twenty-five repetitions. (Single) Place one foot behind your other heel. Slowly raise up on your toes until your heel is fully extended off the floor. Repeat fifteen times on each leg.
Muscles used: Calves and achilles tendon.

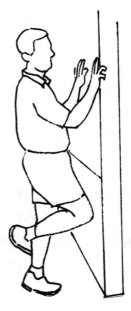

Air Bench: From a standing position, place your back against the wall and spread your feet comfortably apart. Bend your knees and position your feet away from the wall two to three feet. Your

weight should be balanced equally on both heels. Hold your air bench for at least thirty seconds. Repeat five to ten times.
Muscles used: Thighs, hamstrings, and buttocks.

Bent-knee Crunches: Lie on your back and bend your knees to 90 degrees while keeping your feet flat on the floor. Lift your legs in the air, keeping your knees bent at a 90-degree angle. Cross your hands over your chest or support your head with your hands lightly holding your ears. Slowly raise your upper body toward your knees. Keep your elbows pointed at your knees during the exercise. Repeat twenty times.

Muscles used: Abdominal and hip flexors.

Crossover Crunches: Lie on your back with your knees bent so that your heels are flat on the floor. Cross one leg over the other so that one ankle is resting on your opposite knee. Cross your hands over your chest and slowly raise your upper body towards the crossed knee. Avoid putting pressure on your neck by keeping your eyes on the ceiling. Repeat twenty times.

Muscles used: External obliques and abdominals.

Bent-knee Raises: Lie on your back with your knees bent so that your heels are flat on the floor. Keeping your knees bent, slowly raise your knees up toward your chest, then return. Control the move-

ment in both directions, trying not to use momentum. Repeat twenty-five times.

Muscles used: Lower abdominals.

Prone Trunk Raises: Lie on your stomach with your legs together, fully extended and your hands at your sides or crossed over your chest. Slowly raise your upper body toward the ceiling keeping your lower body on the floor. Lift only your upper body. Repeat fifteen times.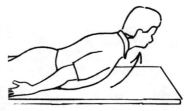

Muscles used: Lower lumbar.

Fitness Center Strength Training

Going to a fitness center gives you the opportunity to work with more sophisticated machines that can isolate specific muscle groups and accurately control weight loads. Utilize the professional staff there to help you assess your current level of fitness and plan a program to meet your goals. Once this is accomplished they will take you through the routine

There are some definite advantages to training with machines at a fitness center.

and show you how to use each machine correctly. There are fundamental principles for exercising (some of which have been mentioned) that when followed can make a great deal of difference in your progress. The staff should review these with you.

The fitness center exercises are recommended specifically for golf, although a local trainer may modify the program after making a personal assessment. In general, it is suggested that you complete at least one set of ten repetitions for each exercise. As you become stronger, add a second and third set of eight to fifteen repetitions. For a more intense workout and greater cardiovascular fitness, you might occasionally do several exercises in a row without resting in between. This will get your heart rate up and put more demand on your lungs. Adding your stretching in between the strength sets will do the same, only to a lesser degree.

Don't hesitate to call upon the staff to help you with technique and some of the details of resistance training with machines, such as seeing that your seat adjustments are correct for your height and that your rhythm on the lift and return are correct.

Upper Body

Chest Press: Using an upright or prone chest press machine, position your body so that your hands and chest muscles are in alignment. Slowly press your hands away from your chest until your arms are about 90 percent extended. Do not lock your elbows. Slowly lower the weight back to your starting position. Repeat ten times. Be sure to exhale when pushing the weight. *Muscles used:* Chest and triceps.

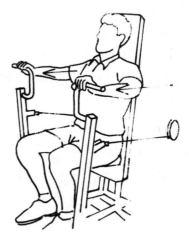

Lateral Raise: Select a lateral raise machine and align yourself in a position so that your forearms rest on the arm pads. Slowly raise the weight up to

shoulder height. Avoid lifting the weight above your shoulders. Slowly lower the weight back to your starting position. Repeat ten times.

Muscles used: Deltoids and trapezius.

Triceps Press: Using a triceps press machine, align yourself in a position that keeps your feet flat on the floor. Select a grip with your palms facing each other. Keep your elbows close to your side and slowly press the weight until your arms are 90 percent extended. Slowly allow the weight to return to your starting position. Repeat ten times.

Muscles used: Triceps and forearms.

Cable-cross Chest Fly:
Stand in the middle of a
cable-cross machine hold-
ing a handle in each hand.
Slowly bring your hands
together in front of you.
Remain stationary, then
slowly return your hands
to their starting position.
Lean your body slightly
forward at the waist. Your
feet should be at least
shoulder-width apart. Re-
peat ten times.
Muscles used: Chest, shoulders, and biceps.

**Isolation Cable-cross
Curls:** Stand up straight in
the middle of a cable-cross
machine holding a han-
dle in each hand. Slowly
bring your hands in to-
ward your ears. Keep your
elbows pointed out as you
squeeze your upper arms.
Slowly return your hands

to the starting position.
Repeat ten times.
Muscles used: Shoulders and
biceps.

Single-arm Cable-cross
Extensions: Stand parallel
to a cable cross machine.
Hold a handle in your
hand that is away from the
machine. Position your
feet shoulder-width apart
and slowly pull your arm
across your body, pulling
your hand down from
your shoulder to the opposite pocket. Keep your arm
straight during the exer-
cise. Slowly return to the
starting position. Repeat
ten times with each arm.
Muscles used: Upper back
and shoulders.

Note: If a cable cross machine is not available at
your fitness center, the following machines are recommended; *chest fly, arm curl, and compound rower.*

Lower Body and Torso

Leg Extension: Sit upright on a leg extension machine. Be sure that your knees are in alignment with the axis of rotation. Select a weight that will allow you to fully extend your lower legs to 90-percent extension. Provide resistance on the downward motion. Repeat ten times.
Muscles used: Quadriceps.

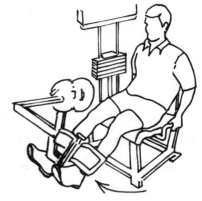

Leg Press: Assume a comfortable position in a leg press machine with feet shoulder-width apart. Slowly lower the weight down toward your body. Do not exceed a leg bend of 90 degrees. Keep the weight balanced equally between both feet. Repeat ten times.
Muscles used: Thighs and hamstrings.

Leg Adduction: Sit comfortably in a leg adduction machine, being sure not to allow your legs to spread too far apart. Slowly bring your legs together by squeezing your inner thigh muscles. Slowly return to the starting position. (Abduction is optional.) Maintain good posture throughout the exercise. Repeat ten times.

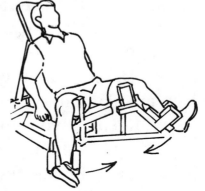

Muscles used: Inner thighs and hip flexors.

Abdominal Crunch: Sit comfortably in an abdominal crunch machine with your feet flat on the floor. Resting the crunch pad on your upper chest, press the pad toward your knees. Your lower body should remain stationary during the motion. Slowly return to the starting position. Repeat ten times.

Muscles used: Abdominals and hip flexors.

Lower-back Extension: Sit comfortably in a lower back extension machine. Be sure that your feet are flat on the platform. Keeping your back straight, press the pad until you are in alignment with your lower body. Do not over extend. Control the weight on the return motion. Repeat ten times.
Muscles used: Lower and middle back.

Rotary Torso: Sit upright on a rotary torso machine, interlocking your lower legs. Slowly rotate the pad, keeping your spine angle vertical. Slowly return the pad to the starting position. Repeat ten times on each side.
Muscles used: Oblique and middle back.

Special Note: Make a sensible choice from the exercises offered on the preceding pages. Do what will fit your time schedule, your fatigue level, and your personal goals. I have offered a number of different exercises so that you can choose the program to fit your situation and also have some variety. Mixing exercises that work the same area of the body has proven to be effective both developmentally and motivationally. Don't become overwhelmed by the number offered. You don't need to do many, but you do need to do some. Selecting a combination of strength, flexibility, and cardiovascular exercises that are mixed on alternate days and that take only twenty to forty-five minutes will make a noticeable difference within sixty days.

Endurance: Cardiovascular and Muscular

The casual pace of golf play does not make heavy endurance demands on the heart and lungs or cardiovascular system; nor does playing golf require intensive repetition (like making five hundred consecutive full swings), which would severely test one's muscular endurance. Nonetheless, golf does make enough demands on the body that endurance *definitely* becomes a factor when it comes to scoring.

Lack of endurance leads to fatigue, and fatigue is detrimental to performance in any skill activity. As one tires, balance is affected, along with speed, club control, even judgment and attention. Doing cardiovascular activities like fast walking, cycling or using a stationary exercise bike, jogging, swimming, stair climbing, even adding repetitions and sets to lighter-weight strength workouts can solve performance problems related to fatigue.

Having a golf car does not mean both people must ride.

The game of golf has built into it a program of cardiovascular fitness; it is called walking. Physicians worldwide extol the value of walking for fitness as a safe, reliable, and effective program. To take it out of the game by riding in a golf car is a health mistake. Golf cars are for people who would be unable to play otherwise due to a physical limitation and for the financial benefit of the facility renting them. Even when the golfer is confronted with the "required riding course" he or she may request that their companion drive or that they share the driving by walking alternate holes. You are not required to sit in the car for eighteen holes, only to rent it and return it. *The health benefits of golf, particularly those involving the cardiovascular and pulmonary systems, are reduced dramatically when the golf car is introduced.*

3

Built-In Fitness Activities

Much of one's success in any endeavor comes from the cultivation of good habits. Being in good physical condition is no exception. But a busy lifestyle unfortunately can turn intention to pretension. Fitness is not a "just pretend" condition. You can't buy it, borrow it, steal it, fake it, nor can you even store it for long. You must attend to it regularly and faithfully. One of the best ways for a busy person to accomplish this is with "built-ins," or fitness activities that you can insert into your daily life without requiring extra time. You do this by connecting them to activities you perform daily. Choose from the following list those you can fit into your lifestyle, or be creative and devise your own. *The secret is to make it convenient, regular, and above all a HABIT.*

Here are six activities around which you could choose to do "built-ins." Doing just one or two from each group should be adequate to produce results, both in your body and in your golf score.

Rise and Shine (Six "Built-Ins")

1. On waking, while in bed, pull your knees to your chest, gently stretching your lower back.

2. When putting on a shirt or blouse, raise one hand over a shoulder and slide it down your back. Push on that elbow with the opposite hand.

3. After putting on a pair of trousers, a skirt, or walking shorts, continue standing and cross one foot over the other and bend at the waist to reach toward the floor, touching it if possible; alternate legs.

4. When standing in front of the mirror, clasp your hands behind your lower back, and while bending forward, raise them as high as possible while the arms are extended. (See illustration.)

5. When putting on your shoes turn your head 90 degrees to the right, then left by gently pushing it with your hand: then hold ten seconds.

6. When finished dressing, get into a half-squat position with your back against the wall. Hold that position thirty to sixty seconds.

Note: What about getting up thirty minutes earlier and taking a brisk walk? That could be the best built-in habit of your life.

In the Bathroom (Six "Built-Ins")

1. Turn on the water. As it gets hot, do side bends, arms overhead and hands clasped.

2. As you lather your face to shave, or put on makeup, tighten your buttocks; hold as long as you can.

3. While shaving or fixing your hair, hold your abdomen in tight and count to fifty.

4. As you brush your teeth, do half squats from fifty to 100 reps; either single- or double-leg.

Half squats are easy to do while you brush your teeth.

5. When applying deodorant, do a single-arm reach toward the ceiling and rise on toes.

6. While putting on aftershave or facial lotion, raise and extend your leg, placing it on the vanity. Then reach forward to touch your toes and stretch your hamstrings. Repeat with the other leg.

Driving the Car (Six "Built-Ins")

1. At stoplights practice deep breathing, filling the lungs completely.

2. At stoplights grip the steering wheel as tightly as possible; release and repeat.

3. At stoplights lace your fingers in front of you, reverse their position, and stretch. Then return

There are plenty of moments during the day when you can build exercises into your life, such as when you are driving the car.

them to the front, palms facing each other, and try to pull your hands apart with an isometric exercise.

4. While driving, do shoulder shrugs.

5. While driving, try abdominal isometrics, holding for thirty seconds.

6. While driving, carry a hand gripper and exercise each hand. (See illustration.)

While Watching Television (Six "Built-Ins")

1. Ride a stationary bike, run on a treadmill, or jump rope.

2. Do bent-knee abdominal curl-ups.

3. Sit on the floor with one leg extended and with the other leg lying flat and bent to 90 degrees so that the foot touches the opposite knee. Reach your

Ride a stationary bike while watching television.

hands toward the ankle of your extended leg and hold that position.

4. Lying on your back with both legs extended on the floor, alternately raise one leg to vertical, then swing it across your body until it touches the floor, so that it rotates and stretches your hips and trunk.

5. Grasp both knees and gently do tuck rolls on the carpet.

6. From a standing but spread-legged position, and while keeping your heels flat on the floor, lean forward until you make a bridge by placing your hands on the floor so you can look back through your extended legs (see picture on p. 20). Hold for thirty seconds.

At Work or Around the House (Six "Built-Ins")

Choose exercises from the previous lists that fit into your average day. You won't do all of these, but you will profit from doing *some* of them. Again, make up your own built-ins if necessary, but put them into your life until they become a habit. *There is so much wasted time in our lives that could be filled with productive fitness activities done on a very casual but regular basis.* Look for those opportunities. One helpful suggestion is to place home fitness products around the house where they are easy to see and convenient to use. A rubber tubing stretch device in a doorway, a hand gripper by the phone, a weighted club in a corner of the family room, or a learning aid such as this Power Swing Fan (see illustration), are all examples of giving yourself a chance to do more built-ins.

4

Other Considerations

Nutrition and Hydration

Even the best-conditioned athlete needs proper fuel, or food, for optimum performance. Seek to maintain your body weight within five pounds of when you felt you were at your top level of fitness. Maybe it was in high school or college and a long time ago, but it is a worthy goal. Eat those foods which over a lifetime of experience produce your best level of energy. The importance of low fat, moderate sugar and salt, and regular intake of water cannot be over emphasized. In fact, never pass a drinking fountain on the course without taking water. It has been demonstrated that a person can live for weeks without food but only days without water. *Water is the elixir of life,* transporting glucose and oxygen to the muscles, eliminating wastes, helping in digestion, cooling the body, and lubricating the joints. Drink eight glasses (64 oz.) in a normal day, more if exercising in hot temperatures. Don't wait until you are thirsty, because that is a sign that you are already liquid deficient, a factor in the deterioration of anyone's play.

Many players unknowingly give themselves the "halfway house blues" by stopping after nine holes for a soda, hot dog, and a candy bar. Stick to fruit, an energy bar, and water or juice. It takes some experimentation to find out which foods seem to work best before and/or during athletic performance, such as a round of golf. Some people can't handle solid foods when nervous and therefore prefer a liquid meal. Personally, I don't like to eat lunch just before playing a one o'clock competition. I focus on liquids and possibly an energy bar. And before an important event I would never introduce some new food to which I am unaccustomed. That is a time to definitely stick with what you know. What we do and don't eat has far greater influence on our state of health than we give credit. *Good nutrition advice abounds everywhere. Have enough willpower to abide by it.*

Finding good nutrition on the course is not always easy, but if a choice is available, water and fruit are better for you and your golf than soda and chips.

Injury and Surgery

Injury is always a possibility when adding more activity to your lifestyle. If you injure your body, don't make the mistake of ignoring the pain. *Listen to your body.* Give your body a chance to recover and don't rush getting back to your previous levels of weights or repetitions. This same counsel applies when you have had to suspend workouts for any reason, including illness, travel, or a busy schedule. Don't push it!

If pain occurs while you are doing a strength or flexibility exercise, stop. We are not talking here about fatigue, the "no pain, no gain" concept. If we want to make the most gain, we sometimes have to push ourselves beyond our comfort level. The pain we refer to here is a sharp pain signaling a potential injury. See your doctor if that kind of pain persists.

By far the most common mistake that golfers make after surgery, particularly seniors, is immediately attempting to match their previous activity level. For example, in hip replacement surgery the nerves in that area are cut more thoroughly than in some other locations like the knee, and the patient cannot feel when he is overstressing the joint. Too much load can lead to reinjury. So while it is important to work hard during rehabilitation, you must also be patient.

Rest

After strenuous physical activity the body needs rest to rejuvenate the cellular structure and muscular tissue and to replace energy reserves. That is why vigorous workout days are scheduled on alternate days with a day's rest in between. Stretching and light cardiovascular workouts can be done daily, but otherwise, include rest days.

Adequate sleep is often overlooked by the enthusiastic individual who has a busy lifestyle. If a commuter stays after work to exercise at the gym, comes home for a late dinner, spends time with the family, and catches up on the mail, news, and phone calls, it can be past midnight before the opportunity for sleep is available. If the morning alarm rings at 5:30 A.M. on a regular basis, he or she is probably not getting enough sleep.

This is one of the most efficient short-term resting positions you can use.

Don't make the mistake of thinking you can make it up by "sleeping in" on the weekend. Your body develops a waking pattern that should be maintained. If you do need to catch up, go to bed earlier but keep your rising time close to normal. There is no correct set amount of sleep needed by every individual, but most adults require seven to eight hours in order to properly give their body and mind adequate rest. Experiment over a one-month period by modifying the amount you receive, monitoring it and determining which amounts of sleep make you feel the best. Getting the proper sleep or rest is vital to a strong mind and body, and hence performance on the golf course. That is the very reason why most touring professionals, even those in top condition, will not play more than three to four weeks in a row without taking a week off to rejuvenate both mind and body.

Protecting Your Back

Back problems can force a complete halt to your game. It's the most common cause of a golfer's physical "downtime." Don't risk injury to your back by reaching over to lift a heavy golf bag from a car trunk or bending over to pick the ball out of the hole while standing with your legs straight. Protect

Danger! Reaching foreword to lift with your legs straight is a back killer. (I strained my back, which is normally strong, while posing for this picture.)

your back by building the strength and flexibility of the trunk region of your body, particularly the abdominal muscles. Combining this with stretching your hamstrings should help prevent back injury.

5

Conclusion

If you have wanted to improve your golf and your lifestyle by increasing your level of fitness but didn't know what to do, well now you do. There is no excuse. So don't wake up one day and say, "Gee, I wish I would have. . . ." JUST DO IT!

Note: If you are about to embark on a program suggested in this booklet, please check with your physician to see that your workout choice is appropriate. Start moderately when using weights or doing new exercises. Select a comfortable level of effort and progress gradually. **The biggest mistake made by those determined to start an exercise program is to push too hard for fast improvement. Be patient!**

Any reference to an exercise or training aid in this text can be fulfilled by calling Golf Around the World at 1-800-824-4279 or can be viewed at www.golfaroundtheworld.com.

The *GOLF* Magazine

Complete Guide to Golf

Book Three

Course Management

Gary Wiren, Ph.D.

PGA Master Professional
and the Editors of *GOLF Magazine*

Introduction

When I am asked, "What does it take to play winning golf?" my reply is always the same. It takes six elements: 1) sound technique, 2) physical conditioning, 3) mental strength, 4) proper equipment, 5) regular practice, and 6) sound course management, all of which are touched upon in this series of books to improve your game. While the first five generally capture more attention in the media, the sixth, course management, is just as important and in some cases even more so. I have worked with players, even at the Tour level, who had mastered the first five yet never reached their potential because they failed the challenge of course management. They knew how to hit the ball, but they were still learning how to play the game. If you are talking "winning golf," number six is one element you can't overlook.

What Is Good Course Management?

Good course management means playing smart golf; not smart as in IQ smart but rather as in commonsense smart. A Ph.D. is really of little value on

Academically smart does not necessarily translate to "golf smart."

the golf course. At its best, good course management means being able to curve the ball and manage trajectory when you need to; knowing your game, such as your club distances and shot tendencies; knowing how to handle various lies and situations on the course; how to cope with poor weather conditions; understanding risk and reward; and finally, controlling your attitude and emotions in competitive situations. All of these will be covered in the following pages. Plus, you will be given a simple six-item guide at the end, "The Stroke-Saver System," which in itself is invaluable for doing just what it says for your game, save strokes.

A Valuable Lesson

It was forty years ago: I was a graduate student in Ann Arbor, Michigan, when I got some of the best advice I have ever heard on playing winning golf. I had just finished eighteen holes at the tough University of Michigan Blue Course, an Alister Mackenzie design, and had again been beaten out of a few bucks by a middle-aged part-time Tour caddie with whom I played on occasion. It was always a shock to me, because he didn't have nearly the distance I did, nor as good a swing, and certainly not the quality of my playing equipment. *But*

The player with a great short game is a match for anyone.

he sure had my number. We sat in the snack bar afterward and over a soft drink he said, "Gary, let me tell you about winnin' golf. First you drive the ball somewhere out there where you can find it; after that you knock it up there on, or around, the green, *and then the game she really starts.*"

Having the ability to get up and down from around the green is one skill all serious players appreciate.

My opponent was absolutely right: He knew the value of keeping the ball in play and having a great short game. But what he failed to share with me at that time was the wisdom, the tricks, and the management of himself and his game that made that philosophy work. This book contains much of what he didn't tell me, the things that I have had to learn since he took my few student dollars. And oh how I wish I had known these stroke-saving course management techniques sooner in my golf life. I didn't, but at least I can share them with you now to give you a short cut on your march to a better game.

Two "Greats" on Management

If someone asked you to name the greatest golfer of all time you could return a variety of answers. Based on the record, however, there can be only one: Jack Nicklaus. His 81 PGA and Senior Tour victories, 28 major wins, and 58 second-place finishes support that choice. The interesting fact is with that impressive record he still never won any of the individual statistical titles (i.e., fewest putts, longest average drive, sand saves, greens in regulation, etc.). So while he wasn't the best at producing specific shots, he was the best at playing the game. *His fellow competitors always conceded Jack the title of smartest player, which translates to "best course manager."*

Another all-time great, Sam Snead, once wrote a book with Al Stump called *The Education of a Golfer.* Sam related many experiences from his career and then, at the end of each chapter, shared stroke-saving thoughts for the average player. Part of the book's premise was that Sam could walk eighteen holes with twenty-plus handicap players and cut five to six strokes off their score by simply coaching them to manage their game and thoughts in a golf-smart way.

Throughout the book Sam discusses situations where a player should use a 3 wood rather than

A lower-viewing perspective reveals the slope more accurately, particularly on the greens.

the driver from the tee; and where a 7 iron chip and run is a higher percentage choice than a sand wedge pitch. He provides other great tips as well, including how a positive frame of mind and seeing good pictures before the swing reduces tension; how to aim away from trouble; and a better procedure for reading putts. The result when these coaching tips were put into practice invariably produced a lower score. *So take it from two of the greatest golfers who have played the game and proven it by their results: Good golf is smart golf . . . and here is how you do it.*

1

A Game of Control

Being in control defines smart golf. That includes *shot-making control, decision-making control, and emotional control.* Smart golf is also adapting to what you can't control, such as the performance of your opponent, the weather, course conditions, or the bounces that the ball takes, good and bad. Anyone who has played competitive golf, at either the club level or Tour level has experienced an opponent (like my Michigan acquaintance) who doesn't have a particularly good swing, can't hit it very far, doesn't impress you with any particular part of his/her game, yet manages to win the match. That opponent seemed composed, rarely made a mistake, and when he did, managed to somehow recover. It was like the opponent possessed an advanced degree in scrambling.

Green speed is a condition you don't control. You have to adapt to it.

But what he really had was a thorough knowledge of how to use his experience, intelligence, and good judgment to produce the most effective shots and make the fewest errors. What they own is course management skill. They are in control.

Ball Flight Laws

If we accept the fact that smart golf is golf that is in control then what is it we have to control? The most important thing is the ball. So good course managers have a clear understanding of the factors that influence ball flight.

What are the elements of ball control over which you have some influence? These elements can be described using the five laws of ball flight from the model **Laws, Principles and Preferences:**[*] 1. Clubhead speed; 2. centeredness of contact; 3. swing path; 4. clubface alignment; and 5. angle of clubhead approach.

Clubhead speed is the most important of the laws of ball flight in producing distance, assuming the other four are reasonably correct. If you don't know your clubhead speed, it can be accurately measured by training aid products that range from simple clip-on devices to sophisticated electronic

---

[*]The model, Laws, Principles and Preferences was created by the author in 1978 and is a part of the *PGA Teaching Manual,* 1990. It presents a three-tiered description of the mechanics of ball flight that the player can influence by his/her application of fundamentals, or **principles,** and technique, or style, labeled as **preferences.**

A club held upside down and swung to create a *whooshing* sound is a good speed indicator. The louder the sound the better.

instruments. You can work on increasing clubhead speed using auditory feedback. In other words, just by listening. When making a practice swing hold the club at the neck end, swing it, and listen for a *whooshing* sound. The greater the speed the louder the sound. You'll discover that lighter grip pressure, particularly in the right hand, will help increase the sound. *Feeling like you are going to "sling" it rather than "hit it" will create lighter grip pressure and increase clubhead speed.*

Centeredness indicates where on the clubface you make contact with the ball: toe, heel, high or low. Any contact made away from the center will reduce distance and can contribute to misdirection as well. An easy way to determine where on the face you are making contact is by applying stick-on face decals. You'll be surprised how often you don't hit the center of the clubface (a good testimonial for perimeter-weighted clubs). *Your best center-face hits will come with correct ball position and arms and hands that stay extended without tension during the swing.*

The **swing path** on which the clubhead is traveling through impact is one of the two most important factors influencing the ball flight direction. The

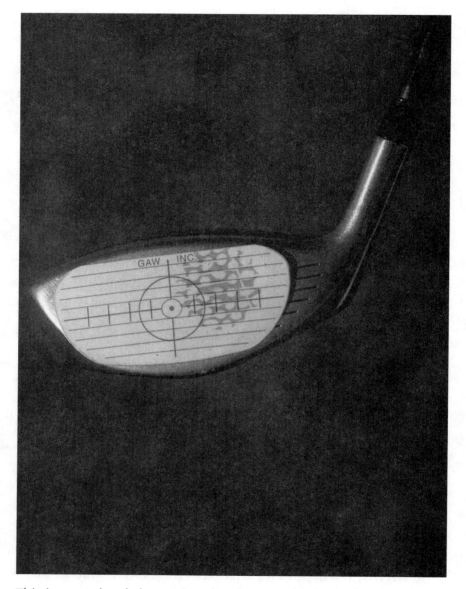

This impact decal shows that the shot was hit in the heel, probably losing about eight to ten yards in distance from a normal 240-yard drive.

path can be influenced by many factors: where you aim your body; the sequence of forward motion through impact; and your intentional arm and hand swing direction to a target. Developing a consistent swing path is one of the most important tasks a golfer can undertake to become a good player. *Much of the success or failure of your swing path will be the result of your body alignment and ball position before the swing ever starts.* There are several commercial alignment devices on the market that could help. But one of the easiest and most convenient methods to improve your body alignment is to put parallel clubs on the ground to identify your target line and foot line. You may have seen or heard that recommendation a thousand times before, but don't take it lightly. It is simple but effective. Once the clubs are in position, aim your hips and shoulders parallel to those lines, and on the forward swing follow that parallel image of your shoulder line.

The next ball flight law, **clubface alignment** (known hereafter simply as "face"), is the single greatest contributor to the shot direction and shape. At impact the face will either be open, closed, or square to your swing path, determined largely by one's grip; or by the left wrist position

The learning aid, Impact Bag, gives accurate feedback on where the club and body should be at the moment of truth, at impact.

(for right-handers) at the top of the swing; or by the amount of forearm and hand rotation, called "release." Timing the face to be square is one of the great challenges of producing accurate shots. *The most effective tool we use in teaching the position is an Impact Bag,* which captures the clubhead in the forward swing and freezes the position of the body.* The soft resistance of the bag gives kinesthetic feedback to the player so he or she can identify the correct body, arm, and hand positions that produce square clubface contact. This correct impact position is repeated until it becomes habit.

The final ball flight law, the **angle of approach,** affects the trajectory of a shot. For example, on a pitch shot or bunker shot if you simply steepen the backswing by cocking the wrists abruptly, you'll produce a sharper angle of swing descent resulting in a higher shot. You get a similar but unwanted result when skying a wood shot (too steep a descent from activating your hands prematurely).

Also, the steeper the descent on a full shot, like a drive, the greater amount of backspin is created to lessen its overall distance. The shallower the club-

---

*See reference at end of book.

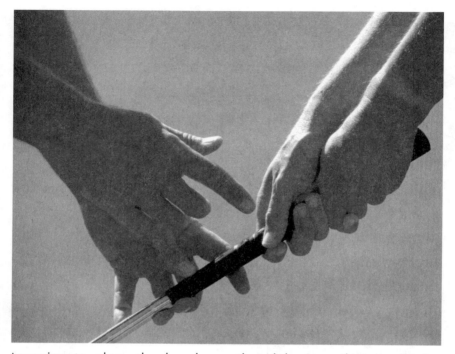

Learning to place the hands on the club correctly is one of a player's most important tasks.

head approach the more the force is directed to the target, resulting in less backspin and greater distance. You can practice this shallower approach by holding your club in the air about two feet above the ball and making baseball-like practice swings as though going after a low pitch. Then tilt forward at the hips until you assume your normal address position and make a similar swing at the ball. *This modified baseball swing practice will help re-*

duce the angle of steepness in the clubhead's approach to the ball.

You have just been introduced to the five ball flight laws and suggestions for improving technique in applying them. Understanding this information provides you with the fundamental physics behind ball flight. This is the foundation for shot control. Now let's look more closely at strategies for making these shots and playing the course.

Shot Control—Understanding Cause and Effect

While golfers cannot completely control their shots, they ought to know the technique necessary to make the ball go high, low, left to right or right to left, longer or shorter when applied correctly. To be most effective in course management a player must be able to exert this kind of control over his or her shots.

Shot Shape

Intentionally curving a golf ball can be accomplished by having some knowledge of simple geom-

When the face and path are at right angles as demonstrated by this learning aid—called the "Shot Maker"—the ball will travel straight.

etry and physics and applying it. Shaping a golf shot is a skill that can certainly come in handy when you need a ball to go around a tree or some other obstacle. Honestly, it is not that hard! *By combining the two elements of clubface alignment and swing path you can create almost any amount of curve that you desire.* Whenever the swing path and clubface line up to make a *right angle* (geometry), no matter in what direction the swing path is going, then the principle resultant *vector force* (physics), the ball's directional flight and velocity, is projected forward along the path the clubhead is taking. If that path is to the right the shot will be a push, to the left a pull.

When the face and path are not at right angles, the ball is struck a glancing blow causing sidespin, which makes the ball curve. If the face is open to the path for right-handed players the ball will curve to the right. If slightly open it will be a fade, or if more open, a slice. When the face is slightly closed to the path, it will produce a draw; when more closed, a hook. *Where the ball starts is generally determined by the path of the swing and where it curves by the face.*

There is, however, the possibility of "clubface override." This can happen when the swing path travels to the right of the target line (from inside to out) yet the

When the clubface is open to the path, as is shown here with the Shot Maker, the ball will slice.

ball starts to the left of the target line. Such an event is the result of a dramatically closed clubface. An example of this would be if the path is 4 degrees to the right but the face is looking 8 degrees to the left. The same holds true with a swing that goes to the left of target (outside to in). With a clubface position grossly open, the ball will not start to the left but rather to the right of the swing path line. In other words, the face position "overrides" the path.

This is a demonstration of "clubface override" in which the starting path of the ball will reflect the position of the club face and not swing path. If the club face is closed, as shown here, the ball will start left.

You can practice shaping the ball and test your path and face combinations by placing a target marker about thirty yards in front of you, where it is easy to trace the starting path and shot shape. Experiment with different swing paths and different face positions to discover how the combinations work. *Path is most easily changed by the alignment of*

An umbrella has been placed in the ground to use as a reference point around which to shape the ball flight.

feet and more important, shoulders. Your club swing path will naturally want to follow your shoulder alignment. The clubface can be preset to an open or closed position, always aiming to where you want to finish. The amount you open or close it will depend upon how much curve you desire. This shaping skill can come in very handy on the course and is not really hard to do (see illustration). In addition, it will help you to understand why your unintentional curves happen.

Trajectory

In the quest for better scoring, it is a great advantage to be able to control the trajectory (height) of your shots; low under obstacles or when playing into the wind and high over barriers or for soft landings on the greens. *There is one principle that controls trajectory other than the loft built into the club; it is the relationship of the grip end to the clubhead end, or the angle of shaft tilt.* The more the grip end is tilted forward, ahead of the clubhead, the lower the trajectory. The farther back the grip end is leaned the higher the shot will travel.

Moving the ball back in the stance at address will naturally tilt the shaft toward the target. This is the way most players create lower trajectory shots. The

Foreword tilt of the clubshaft at impact translates to lower flight.

The more vertical the shaft becomes the higher the ball flight.

Try using trees and mounds when practicing trajectory control.

reverse holds true when you move the ball forward and tilt the shaft to more vertical, giving the ball a higher trajectory. Adjusting the ball position at address is not a guarantee of trajectory since you could play the ball back in an attempt to hit it low and make an early release of the hands. This scooping-style swing negates the original forward leaning shaft angle, possibly even causing it to have a backward lean, which sends the ball high rather than low. So while ball position helps to bring about the desired result, in fact it is the lean of the shaft at impact that really counts.

To practice trajectory control go to the side of the practice area where there may be some trees and experiment with different ball positions and impact shaft angles in trying to play shots under and over branches. This is one of the easier principles to learn and apply.

Decision-Making Control— Knowing Your Game and the Course

One of the mistakes that causes a player to make poor decisions is allowing the ego to entice him/her into trying to match the shot making of a superior ball-striking partner or opponent. Golf matches and tournaments aren't always won by the best ball striker. On the contrary, in matches of reasonably equal talent, winning golf is more often the product of knowing and staying within one's circle of competence; in other words, doing what you know you can do and not attempting the heroic. Playing "your game" is achieved by knowing what you can do and making good decisions after the important factors have been considered. Unlike some of the other vagaries of golf, the decision-making process is one over which the player does have complete control. The question then becomes, "How well do you know your own game?"

Getting the Distance

Golf is a game of both distance and direction, with control of distance being an important part of the equation. *If you don't know the distances you hit your clubs—and most golfers honestly don't (they tend to overestimate)—then you are giving away a lot of shots on the course.* How far do you hit your 5 iron, driver, or pitching wedge? Is the yardage figure you come up with all carry or does it include roll? Does your answer represent "your best ever" distance or your average distance?

For example, if there is a bunker at the corner of a dogleg 237 yards away, can you carry it in the air? Or let's say you are trying to play safe and not roll into the long grass fronting the green on a par five hole. The distance to the grass is 218 yards: Do you know what to hit? How about a shot to the green that is over water that extends right to the front of the putting surface; the carry is 174 yards with the flagstick eight steps back; do you know the right club? Having an accurate knowledge of how far your iron shots to the green carry and tend to roll also makes a world of difference in how long your putts will be. Face up to the fact that the length of your first putt on the green correlates directly with how many putts you are going to take. The statistics from touring professional players indicates that from 6 feet they make roughly 65 percent, from 12 feet 32 percent, and from 30 feet only 12 percent. And for amateurs, the percentage is surely much poorer. *Isn't that in itself enough reason to learn your club distances?*

So how do you learn your distances? When teeing off with a driver, make note of where you are playing from in relation to the permanent tee marker and the length of the hole. Let's say it is a 385 yard par four. When you arrive at your ball, seek out the nearest fairway sprinkler head or other distance markers to see how far you have remaining to the center of the green and subtract it from the total distance of the hole to determine your driving distance. This won't tell you the carry for the drive unless the fairways are unusually soft and your ball has made a plug mark, in which case you can also determine the carry from the mark.

A more techno-centered means of finding your length with each club is to use an electronic distance-measuring device. You may find these at such places as indoor playing and club fitting centers; golf learning-aids catalogs or in specialty golf stores; and handheld electronic range finders that can be taken on the course. Indoor golf centers tend to have their machines "jacked up" to make the clients feel good, so a realistic outdoor measurement may be more accurate. One tool that is right on the money for distance that you can acquire and take with you when you play is the Bushnell 600 Range Finder, an optical monocular high-quality instrument, accurate within a yard up to 600 yards.[*]

Electronic tools aside, the more traditional way to get your distances for irons and sometimes even

---

[*]See reference at end of book.

The Bushnell 600 is excellent for getting your yardage on the course and on the practice range.

fairway woods has been to monitor shots on the par-three holes. A permanent marker in the ground or a post should indicate the distance to the center of the green from that spot. Step off the distance from the marker to the location of the tee blocks to be accurate. Add or subtract yardage as needed. Hit your shot, then check your result in relation to the center of the green, not to where the flagstick is located. Also on iron shots to the green, pay close attention to the fairway sprinkler heads and the permanent 100-, 150-, and 200-yard markers. Take your steps from them to your ball, add or subtract yardage, and then note what clubs you need to get to the green. Find where your pitch mark is on the green to determine carry and roll.

Half Shots

Knowing correct distances also applies to less than full shots. In fact, these shots are often more difficult because they require judgment for the swing length and effort. That's why you may hear good players talk about "laying up" on a par-five to play from a distance where they can take a full swing rather than getting closer and be faced with a half shot where more touch is required. How much shorter does your ball go when you choke down on the grip by one inch, two inches? In my own case, it is ten yards for every one and a half inches. How far do you take the club back to hit a thirty- to forty- or fifty- to sixty-yard wedge shot? This question can be answered in a couple of good practice sessions by doing the following: Go to a practice area and measure off distances in ten-yard increments from thirty to sixty yards, placing a marker at each location. Take your sand wedge, or whatever club you use for that length, and hit balls to

Practicing distance control with a sand wedge.

each successive target, noting the length of back-swing it takes to produce the correct distance. When former Open champion Tom Kite has a full pitch shot and asks his caddie how far they are from the flag, he doesn't accept a comment like, "About forty-five yards." He wants to know, "Is it forty-six or forty-four?" That precision comes from having measured the distances in practice and frequently rehearsing the swing length to have the feel of how to make it happen.

The Target

Once you know how far the ball goes with each club (full swing, half swing) then it's important to know for sure how far the target is from your ball. We have mentioned permanent markers and sprinkler heads in the fairways as well as the permanent marker on the tee ground. It is important to understand that on a par-three hole the scorecard distance and the actual playing distance are very seldom the same. How far away are the tee markers from the hole's permanent marker as printed on the scorecard? How many yards or steps are the tees in front or behind the permanent marker? What is the flagstick location today in relation to the center of the green? Are you going to have to either add or subtract yardage? Is the green uphill or downhill from the tee area? This could make a difference from a half club to maybe even two clubs; it will require more club for uphill and less for downhill. Is there a wind that will help or hurt? Will you need to increase or decrease one, two or even three clubs to compensate for it? A crosswind also will affect the distance of your shot, depending upon which side it is coming from and whether you draw the ball or fade your shots. If you *consider all these factors you can then come up with the actual "play-*

ing distance" for the hole, not the scorecard distance. Finally, where is the most severe trouble on the hole? Is it over the green, in the front, or on the side? If you judge incorrectly, would it be better to be too long or too short to miss on the right or the left? On

This is the kind of shot where distance control is critical.

the par-three 15th at PGA National in Palm Beach Gardens, Florida, which is fronted by water, you don't want to be short. In different years, both Don January and Ray Floyd left it short and it cost them respective PGA Seniors' Championships; one making five, the other a seven. For safety's sake it is wise to use more club than normally necessary if the penalty for being short is severe. The reverse (use less club) is true if there is a penalty for being long. It all goes into the equation known as "club selection," an important part of good golf course management.

Percentages

Given five shots with a driver to a fairway that is less than thirty yards wide with trouble on both sides, how often do you feel you can place your ball into that space? There are times in a golf round when such a shot is required. If your answer is one out of five with a driver, but three out of five with a fairway wood, then you'd better play the percentages and hit the fairway wood. If on a par-five, the carry over the water on your second or third shot is 215 yards and you can hit your 3 wood a maximum of 220, then what are the odds that you will hit it perfectly? If on another hole the flag is tucked behind a bunker, it's a firm green, you are downwind and playing a hard two-piece ball, do you go for the pin or to the open part of the green where you can land short and bounce the shot on? *A golf round gives you lots of opportunities to make decisions like these, and these decisions should take percentages into consideration.*

The reason that Las Vegas can build multimillion-dollar casinos is because people who go there are willing to take a gamble, even when the odds in the long run are never in their favor. Therefore, they lose more often than they win. When you are on the golf course, leave the gambling to Vegas unless the odds are in your favor or the risk-to-reward ratio is worth it. Consistency is golf's toughest challenge and reckless gamblers on the course are seldom consistent. When you are going to attempt a high-risk shot ask yourself, "Am I comfortable or nervous making this attempt?" and "Do I believe I could pull it off three out of four times if given the chance?" If your answers tell you to go, then go, providing the risk is worth it. Keep in mind, however, that more often than not, it isn't worth the risk.

Tendencies

Another factor to consider is your tendency under a given circumstance. Let's assume that you are

Do you risk it? Make your decision based upon the odds, the circumstance, and your personal history.

playing a 165-yard par-three with a green surrounded by water except on the left where there is a bail-out area. The flagstick is on the right-hand side of the green near the water and the wind is blowing strongly left to right. The odds for hitting a good shot may be reasonable; you may even feel good about your chances of getting close. But if your historical tendency in that situation is to push-fade the ball because you tighten up, then you'd better take that into consideration. Aim left where there is enough margin for error that a push-fade would still hit the green and where a straight shot may miss the green but give you an easy chip. The point is, you have taken the water out of play by acknowledging your tendencies.

Self Control

Another factor to consider is your behavior in certain playing situations. For example: Do you press for more distance when playing with long hitters, only to find you lose control and shoot higher scores? Have you recognized that when playing with better players, particularly pros, you rush your shots to get out of the way? Does being held up on the course because of slow play irritate you to the point where you get upset and it affects your game? Does playing with people about whom you don't particularly care change your normal approach to the game and cause you to lose focus? These are cases in which you need to control yourself more than control the ball. *If you have a tendency to let these kinds of circumstances negatively affect your performance, then you must either avoid them when possible, or acknowledge them and adopt a strategy to overcome them.*

Handling Course Conditions

Equally important to knowing your game is knowing *the* game, which means knowing how to handle course conditions.

A golf course presents a monumental test of one's ability to handle varied conditions. Think for a moment of the possibilities: wind, rain, cold, heat;

Being able to "read" bunker sand (having a feeling for how the ball will come out) is part of the course management learning process.

up-, down-, and sidehill terrain; deep grass, short grass, and no grass; fast, slow, grainy, undulating, flat, and wet greens; tight, narrow, and sloping fairways; elevated, downhill, and around-the-corner targets; fine and coarse bunker sand with various depths; trees and bushes, lakes, rivers and oceans, they all add up to challenging your adaptability, creativity and courage— qualities of a good course manager.

Wind

Wind is the most common weather element we face on a golf course. The fact that it comes from different directions and at different velocities during a round, or even during one hole, makes for some interesting adjustments.

When playing into the wind off the tee many players try to hit harder. But attempting extra distance will likely cause you to lose control. This mistake is made even worse because ball flight errors are really magnified in heavy winds. A typical shot that would curve ten yards off line under calm conditions will deviate only five yards when hit downwind but twenty-five yards when stuck into a strong headwind. Trajectory is critical, since you want to keep the ball lower, to get under the wind. Most players when playing

into the wind attempt to keep the ball down by teeing the ball lower on wood shots. However, this can
be counterproductive, as it tends to steepen your
angle of approach to the lower teed ball, thereby
adding backspin. This type of swing produces what
is known as a "riser," or ball that starts low and
climbs abruptly but then drops with little forward
roll. It is not a strong shot into the wind. A shallower or more level angle of approach using any tee
height will produce a greater vector force traveling
toward the target and a ball with less backspin. That
is why you will sometimes see a player competing
in a long-drive competition teeing the ball high,
even into the wind, seeking a more level swing.

When playing iron shots to the green you can
keep the ball lower and under a heavy wind by
simply taking a club with less loft and either shortening your hand position on the grip or limiting
your backswing. Either of these adjustments will
affect distance control. Taking a stronger club than
you would normally think to use when hitting into
the wind is almost always a good idea, since the
tendency, even for professionals, is to not use
enough club. Remember that a drawing or hooking
ball will fight the wind better because the trajectory
will generally be lower. More important, it will
have less backspin.

This shot into the wind is being played with a restricted backswing to help keep the trajectory down.

When hitting a tee shot with the wind behind you (a following wind), the lift and drag are reduced and so is the trajectory. In order to achieve the optimum trajectory you may need to tee the ball higher. To get optimum distance from a side wind, shape the shot to ride the wind rather than playing one that fights it. This is because riding the wind reduces drag.

Rain

The Boy Scouts' motto, "Be Prepared," is a good place to start when considering the challenges to scoring that weather presents. Rain is one of the most common and most difficult conditions. Being prepared for

A large golf umbrella is a necessity for the frequent player.

rain means having a sixty-two-inch golf umbrella; two large towels that you keep dry by carrying them under your umbrella struts or in the golf car; at least three extra golf gloves; a rain suit that is truly waterproof; a rain hat (one with a broad brim if you wear glasses); waterproof shoes; a nonslip grip product that can be used on your grips if they get slippery in wet weather or a special glove that grips better when wet; and a hood for your golf bag to keep rain from going inside. If you are in a golf car without a cover attached to the back, restrap your bag so it doesn't stand vertically but rather hangs out to the side where the water won't as easily run down into it and get your grips wet. Do this maneuver by pulling the cart strap through the bag handle and angling your clubs off to the side. If you choose to do this, be more careful driving the car, since your clubs are "sticking out." The best situation is to have a cover that goes over the entire car, including your clubs.

That keeps everything and everybody protected from the elements. The number one rule is, *whatever it takes, keep your hands and the grips on your clubs dry.*

Shot making needs to be adjusted for rain as well. You will not get your normal distance for several reasons, such as: wet ground that cuts down

Hanging your clubs to the side, then using a towel over them, will help keep rainwater from getting on the grips.

roll; wearing extra clothing that may hamper your swing; and the rain itself creating "heavier air." Don't try to press for extra distance from the tee or in the fairway, as the wet conditions make it easier to produce errors during your swing. Trying to hit harder will only exacerbate the situation. And certainly don't expect your normal distance when playing from wet, heavy rough. Just get the ball out and back to the fairway.

There is one instance during wet conditions where the loss of distance is reversed. When water gets between your clubface and the ball, reducing the amount of backspin, the result is known as a "flier," a shot that travels farther than normal. This commonly happens when your ball is resting in light rough and the wet blades of grass "grease" the clubface to make the ball shoot forward on a lower, "hotter" trajectory, with less backspin to stop it once it hits the ground. However, "fliers" can happen in any wet condition, not just from the rough. If you anticipate the "flier" possibility you can use one less club (a 6 iron rather than a 5) or you can swing with less effort than normal.

Combating Cold

Two other common weather hazards are extreme cold or heat. *For cold weather preparation, focus on the warmth of your hands, feet, and head.* Carry gloves for keeping your hands warm in between shots, a handwarmer in your pocket, a cold weather hat or cap, and either an extra pair of regular socks or thermal socks. Wear loose-fitting clothes that don't hamper your swing, preferably those that are tested for their thermal effectiveness. Carry two extra golf balls in your warmest pocket and rotate them with the one in play on every other hole. Cold golf balls do not go as far as warm golf balls because the material from which the ball is made does not respond as efficiently as it gets colder. A shot that travels 200 yards at 70 degrees F will only go 185 yards at freezing. Superficial heating does little good if the ball has been exposed to the cold over several hours. Heat three of four balls by setting them at the base of your kitchen freezer (where the warm air comes out) the night before you play. Then keep them in your hand warmer pocket and alternate them every hole. (When I travel by air and have to

A stocking cap, loose upper clothing, and rain pants kept this golfer warm.

play shortly after getting off the plane, I carry a sleeve of balls in my briefcase since those in the luggage compartment are exposed to extreme cold.) Just as effective in cold weather as in rain is the golf car cover that surrounds the whole car with four transparent walls. It will both shut out the wind and keep in the heat. Drinking warm liquids like soup, hot chocolate, tea, or coffee can help you retain body heat; but watch the caffeine as it tends to make one jittery.

Playing in the Heat

Very hot days can negatively affect your game just as well as cold if you are not prepared. The essentials that you will need to combat the heat are a broad brimmed hat (at the very least a cap or visor, although neither protects your ears or neck from the sun as well as a hat); U-V–rated sunglasses; sun screen with a minimum 15 protection rating; at least one towel; three extra gloves to replace those soaked with perspiration; and a water bottle. *I try to never pass an opportunity to drink water on the course, even on temperate days.*

Protection from the sun has even more to do with avoiding skin cancer than performance. Since golf is a game often played under intense sun, it is a problem to be taken very seriously. Still, don't underestimate the possibility of heat exhaustion, sun stroke, dehydration, or just plain fatigue in affecting your game. To avoid such problems you should be taking in liquids, preferably water or an isotonic drink rather than a carbonated sugary beverage. *Fi-*

Water is still best to drink on the golf course.

Isotonic drinks replenish liquid loss and have some nutritional benefits but are usually high in sugar.

nally, rule number one for your equipment in hot weather as in wet weather, is keep your grips dry.

Uneven Terrain

My experience tells me that fewer than 50 percent of amateur golfers understand the influence that uneven terrain has on ball flight.

Do this simple exercise to better visualize what happens once you discover that you are not living in a flat world. Hold your dominant open hand out in front of you so that the palm is flat and is facing an imaginary target to your left, like a golf green. Raise your hand six inches and the palm of your hand will still face the imaginary target; lower it and the result will be the same. Now go to the starting position again but tilt your hand backward, creating loft. Make the tilt resemble the loft in a pitching wedge. Raise your hand six inches again and see where the palm is now facing; markedly left of your imaginary green. Lower your hand and notice that it faces well to the right. This is precisely what happens to your clubface when you are on a slope where the ball is resting either above or below your feet. Although the leading edge of your club is still at a right angle to your target, the clubface is definitely not. This is true whether you are playing a full shot or a pitch. The ball will rebound off the clubface in the direction the face is looking. The more the loft, the more it will aim off line.

To adjust for this aim discrepancy I have developed a simple system. If you are on the course facing an iron shot to the green where the ball is above your feet, set your hand in front of you in a

Model your hand position to match the loft in the clubhead.

position that compares with the loft in the face of the club you are about to hit. Then raise your hand to match the tilt of the ground. Look in the direction your palm is pointing. Then rotate your body and hand until your hand, which is still tilted, is

Raise your hand to match the slope of the ground and see where the club points.

aimed in the direction of the flagstick. Your body alignment will definitely be to the right. You may want to allow for a slight draw as shots hit where the ball is above one's feet are more apt to produce that shape.

When the ball is above your feet, adjust for starting aim but also know that this lie will encourage a draw.

Playing Safely Out of Trouble

There are two shots that I learned relatively late in my career that have been very useful. My regret is that I didn't come across them sooner.

The first is the chip out. That may not sound too exciting but think of the many times you were in trouble, simply trying to play out to the fairway and then fluffed what seems a simple shot. Usually the conditions are similar to one of these. Your ball is in the woods resting 1. on loose pine needles; 2. sitting on ground with a sandy base; 3. nestled deeply in heavy rough. The cardinal mistake that is most often made in these three conditions is hitting behind the ball. Do it and the ball travels only a few feet, necessitating a repeat attempt to chip out and causing one more stroke to be added to your score. A very effective solution is to play the ball back farther in your stance than any shot you have ever hit, i.e., *slightly back of your rear foot.* Lean a little left, make no attempt in the swing to lift the ball up, and you will make solid contact with the ball (rather than hitting behind it), using whatever club you have chosen to escape your predicament. Use something like a 4 or 5 iron if you have to keep it low under branches, and a pitching or sand wedge

The secret to chipping out from a difficult lie is to hit the ball first, an action that can be encouraged by positioning the ball far back in your stance.

to come out of the tall grass if producing a higher trajectory isn't a problem.

Recovering with a Special Shot

Occasionally, you'll have the chance to produce a spectacular recovery. Such a time could be when you are in the woods and could chip out to the fairway, but instead you see a path through the trees to the green. The problem is that you are only 125 yards from the flagstick and would have to use a 3 iron to stay under the branches. How do you know how hard to hit a 3 iron and make it go only 125 yards? Let me explain how I do it, and then you can adapt the technique to match your own distances.

Normally I hit a full 3 iron 195 yards. When I lower my hands on the grip (choke down) by one and a half inches the distance, with a full swing, is reduced to 185 yards, gripping three inches down becomes 175 yards. Now I am at the lowest point on the grip, just above the steel. If I next shorten the length of my backswing (I estimate it to be about five inches) the ball will travel approximately 165 yards, five inches more 155, gradually bringing my arms down in those five-inch increments to 145, 135, and finally 125 yards! So I end up swinging with normal pace a 3 iron that is gripped down to

Knowing how to hit a long club short distances comes in handy when you are in trouble, and it will save you strokes.

the steel, using a backswing that has been shortened by 25 inches and I will get it very close to the green, sometimes on and sometimes even close to the flagstick. Course conditions will make a difference and may require you to make some adjustments. If the grass is wet and slow, add on some distance; if dry and fast, subtract. If it is slightly uphill add more backswing; downhill, subtract. Those things will be handled by your imagination. But try this technique and you will be amazed at how effectively it works.

Emotional Control . . . Using "the Next One"

At the beginning of this book we said that being in control was instrumental to good course management. That meant controlling the ball, controlling your decisions, but also controlling your emotions. In this series, the book *Mental Golf* provides a detailed system for developing greater mental strength, including ways to keep your emotions in check. But let me add a thought here that can truly help you with the emotional control aspect of course management.

Anger produces physiological responses that are frequently self-destructive when playing golf. We

Anger carried to the next shot is a tension-producing response, a negative for good golf.

all have witnessed and some have experienced the feeling of human rage that emerges when a person has hit a bad shot. I've seen players who have graduated from Princeton and gone on to Harvard Business School, yet out of anger over a mishit golf shot, announce to the world that they are "stupid idiots," as if their 135 I.Q. had just dropped by 50 points. Anger produces tension, and tension is the great destroyer of the freewheeling swing. So this is not a good course management response.

PGA Senior Tour professional Rick Acton uses an interesting approach to maintaining composure in such a situation. He says, "It is not the shot you just hit; that's over. It is *the next one* on which you should focus." Example: Your iron shot to the green fades far to the right, leaving you an almost impossible pitch. You play a lofted sand wedge to the fringe and the ball continues rolling across the green and amazingly drops in the cup. You see, it wasn't the weak approach to get concerned about but "the next one." Losing your emotional control over the first shot may have put you into a state that would not allow you to successfully produce "the next one." Ask Larry Mize if you don't believe its true. (Do you recall his fabulous winning pitch shot from the right of the green on #11 at the 1987

Davis Love won the 1997 PGA trophy after a near win in the U.S. Open the year before.

Masters to beat Greg Norman? It happened to be "the next one" after missing the green.) Acton recommends controlling those potentially destructive feelings during play by dismissing "this one" after it has been played, and focusing on "the next one." And why does this make such good sense? Because there is nothing that you can do about the last shot after you have hit it. The only thing you can do is to make a fresh start by focusing on the prospects of the next one being good.

Conversely, imagine that you have just hit a lovely shot to the green and are looking at a chance for a birdie. You may already be celebrating on your way to the putt. But then it takes you three putts and you bogey. You see, it wasn't the shot you just hit but "the next one." that should have captured your focus. Ask Davis Love, who suffered through this very scenario. He knocked it on the final green of the 1996 U.S. Open with a chance at a birdie putt to win, only to three-putt and lose. (The good news was that he came back to subsequently win the 1997 PGA Championship. In a sense, that was "the next one.")

Experienced players realize that golf is not a game of perfection. They are going to hit a certain number of bad shots a round. But the best performers do not lose composure when those shots surface: They just focus on "the next one." In this way they are in control.

2

Conclusion

As you have seen, there is a great deal to learn about being adept at managing your round on a golf course. It takes time and experience to learn the many nuances of conquering the challenges that golf offers. Even the most experienced players make errors in course management. Gary Player, for example, once mentioned to me that he made about five or six course management errors per round. How many then do you think you make? Certainly reducing the number would produce better scores. I leave you with a simple proven guide to put you on the right track. I call it the "Stroke-Saver System—Six Rules for Managing Your Game on the Course.

The Stroke-Saver System

1. **I will use enough club on my approach shot to comfortably get to the flagstick.**

Don't consistently come up short on your approach to the green; use enough club.

2. **I will have a routine for every shot focusing on grip, aim, and setup.**

Have a routine for all of your shots, including putts.

3. **I will hit my shots with positive thoughts and pictures in mind and back off to restart if they are negative.**

Having positive thoughts and seeing good mental pictures will allow you to make a more relaxed full motion swing.

4.　**I will not swing with more effort than that which is needed to produce my effective swing speed (ESS). I will stay in complete control.**

Finishing in perfect balance is an excellent sign that you have maintained your effective swing speed.

5. **I will, when playing a full shot into the wind or to an elevated green or when chipping or pitching uphill, use a less lofted club; downwind, downhill, or to a lower level green, a more lofted club.**

Downhill chips should be made with more loft, since the tendency is to be too long.

6. I will not leave makable putts short.

When in makable putt range, I always want to give the ball a chance to go in by at least getting it to the hole.

You will be surprised at how many shots you can save by simply applying the previous six rules as often as possible. It will take discipline and practice, but combined with the other information you have read, your scores on the course will definitely improve.

You will have become a good course manager.

All references to learning aids or practice devices can be answered at Golf Around the World, 1-800-824-4279, or at www.golfaroundtheworld.com.

The *GOLF Magazine*

Complete Guide to Golf

Book Four

Full Swing

Peter Morrice

and the Editors of *GOLF Magazine*

Photography by Sam Greenwood

Introduction

It's hitting that career drive or nipping a long iron off the fairway. It's watching an approach shot climb with a slight draw, float over the pin, and pull up next to the hole. The object of golf may be to make the lowest score, but these are the things that make golfers tick. You may respect the guy who sprays it all over but manages decent scores, but the player who bombs it off the tee and attacks the pins . . . he's the golfer you want to be.

Not to knock the short game. It's well established that some 60 percent of the average player's score comes within 100 yards of the hole. That said, if you want to see your scores come down, grab your wedges and your putter and go to work on the short stuff. But that's like being told to eat your vegetables: You know it's good advice but you just can't get yourself to do it.

Simply put, the long game is too tantalizing to pass up. Watching a well-struck ball soar through the air has an intoxicating effect on golfers. That's why they spend their practice hours at the driving range instead of the putting green. Hitting balls is entertainment; practicing putting for any length of time feels like solitary confinement. And while a better short game may be the quickest way to lower your scores, this book presumes that golf is more to you than just posting a number.

In the pages that follow, we'll pull apart the golf swing and tell you what has to happen and why, but first we'll take a detailed look at the setup. To put it bluntly, you simply cannot be an effective golfer without solid, consistent address positions. Truth is, much of your performance is predetermined before you even take the club back by the angles and positions you create at address. Physics tells us that.

Once we get the setup down, we'll start on the swing itself, from the takeaway to the finish, in simple, understandable terms. No bizarre ideas or unproven theories here, just the time-tested, mainstream teachings that the world's best teachers and players have relied on for years. With an understanding of the basic parts of the swing, you can learn how to blend them together into a cohesive, effective swing motion.

Our next step will be to define common problems, such as slicing, hitting fat, and topping, and discuss what causes them. As random as they may seem, all bad shots have a logical explanation. We'll take a brief look at how the most common come to be, and then we'll finish up with a section on how to get the most out of your practice time.

Throughout the book, you'll also find a recurring feature called "Best Tip," a sampling of the greatest tips ever published in *GOLF Magazine*. Most of this instruction comes from *GOLF Magazine*'s Top 100 Teachers, the industry's definitive collection of swing doctors. We dispense their ideas in every issue of the magazine, and here you'll enjoy some of their best full-swing tips and drills in a single volume.

Whether you're a newcomer to golf, a frustrated middle handicapper, or a hotshot looking to take your game to the next level, this book will provide you with a brief yet comprehensive look at the fundamentals of the swing. With a little dedication and a well-formed improvement plan, you can become the player you dream of being. Let's get started.

1

Preswing

Next time you go to the driving range, take a look at the folks around you. Chances are, you'll be standing in the midst of middle-handicap America. Ask around and you'll find they're trying to fix their slice, get more distance, hit the ball higher, and so on. All noble intentions, but most golfers think they'll naturally groove a better swing simply by hitting ball after ball until their hands throb. In the end, all they get is tired.

Now compare this scene of panting, ball-beating middle handicappers to the practice area at a professional tour event. If you've never been to one, trust me when I tell you the pros hit balls about half as fast as amateurs do. And what are most of them focusing on? Preswing fundamentals. Things

Tour pros work long hours on perfecting their setup.

like alignment and ball position and posture. They know that how they set up either promotes or prevents the right positions during the swing. They also know it's a lot easier to monitor and change static positions than swing positions.

You may find it amazing that the world's best players work on simple things that many amateurs think they had figured out years ago, but it's true. Every day the pros go back to the basics, knowing these are the building blocks of the golf swing. Let that be a revelation to you.

Jack Nicklaus, in his instruction manual *Golf My Way* wrote, "I think it [the setup] is the single most important maneuver in golf. . . . If you set up correctly, there's a good chance you'll hit a reasonable shot, even if you make a mediocre swing. If you set up incorrectly, you'll hit a lousy shot even if you make the greatest swing in the world." Actually, you *need* to make a faulty swing if it starts from a faulty setup. In effect, by making errors at address you require in-swing errors to compensate for them.

So, put aside that feeling that you already know how to set up to a golf ball. If you'd like to play better, do what the pros do and perfect your address positions. It's the only logical place to start.

The Grip

If you're like most golfers, the last thing you want to hear is that you have to change your grip. Golf is a humbling game in which you're constantly trying to assert control yet often feel like you have none. Your grip is your one connection to the golf club, and whether it's good or bad, it's yours. You rely on it for a sense of control, and no golfer wants to give that up.

But before you dismiss the idea of changing your grip, answer this: Would you like to get rid of that slice of yours? How about hitting the ball another 20 yards? Ahhh, now I've got your attention. Fact is, how you grip the club at address in large part determines the position of the clubface at impact, which plays a major role in the direction of your shots. The grip also figures prominently in how much power you can produce during the swing. In short, if you care about how far and how straight you hit the ball, you need to care about your grip.

Hitting It Straight

The way you grip the club influences how the clubface rotates during the swing—from open to square to closed like a swinging door. And the position of the clubface at impact dictates how the ball will curve in the air. For example, if the clubface is angled to the right, or "open," when it contacts the ball, the ball will pick up left-to-right sidespin and curve to the right. If the clubface is angled to the left, or "closed," the ball will take on right-to-left sidespin and curve left. It's that simple: The squareness of the clubface when it meets the ball is the only factor that affects the curvature of the shot.

But how does the way you grip the club affect clubface position at impact? Consider this: Your hands are pulled into certain positions on the downswing by the centrifugal force of the swing, like they would be in a game of tug-of-war. Let's call these "natural positions." If the hands don't match these natural positions at address, the clubface will either open or close when the hands assume these positions on the downswing.

The natural position for your left hand is however it hangs at your side; this is how it will return to the ball at impact. The position of your right hand is a different story, as the right hand makes a striking, or spanking, action at impact. To promote this, your right palm should point to the target at address. If your hands start in these positions and your clubface is square to the target, your clubface will return square at impact without manipulation.

Power Is in Your Hands

How does the correct grip promote more power in your swing? Think about what happens to your wrists as you swing back and through: They hinge the club up going back, unhinge coming down, and

Position your left hand on the grip however it naturally
hangs at your side.

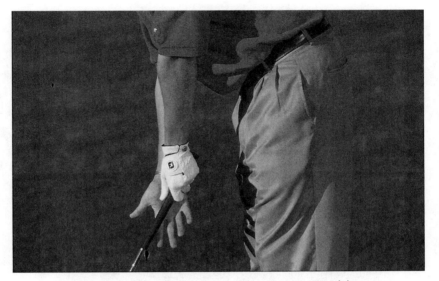

Your right palm should face the target at address.

then rehinge on the follow-through. Get a club and try it. This may seem like a natural and inconsequential action, but it is a major power generator in the golf swing.

As the wrists hinge going back, they create an angle between the left arm and the club, thereby introducing a second lever to the swing. (The first lever, a straight line from the left shoulder to the clubhead, is established at address.) As wrist hinge produces this second lever, the clubhead can travel through a much longer arc than it could in a single-lever motion. And a longer arc means more room

Proper wrist hinge promotes a full swing arc.

for the clubhead to accelerate on the downswing. Furthermore, as centrifugal
force on the downswing
unhinges the wrists, pulling
the left arm and the club
back into a straight line, the
clubhead is flung into the
ball with great force. That's
the whipping action you
see in good players.

Believe it or not, the grip
is at the root of this wrist action. To understand this, get
a club and place the grip di-
agonally across your left
palm, running from your

> **Handle With Care**
>
> Grip thickness is one equip-
> ment variable that receives
> little attention. While stan-
> dard, off-the-rack grips are
> fine for many golfers, make
> sure your grips are right for
> you. The critical check is in
> the left hand. Take your
> normal left-hand grip and
> check that the tips of your
> middle two fingers are
> lightly touching your palm.
> If the fingertips are either
> not reaching the palm or
> digging into it, your grips
> are the wrong size, which
> can have a profound effect
> on how you move the club.

forefinger to your heel pad, and close your fingers
around it. Now, with your hand at your side, try to
cock the clubhead up in front of you simply by hinging your left wrist. Not easy, right? Now grip the club
again, this time holding the handle across the base of
your fingers, and try that same exercise. You'll find
you can cock the clubhead up farther and with
greater ease with the handle in your fingers.

This is precisely how the left wrist should hinge
during the golf swing and the reason the handle

The popular Vardon, or overlapping grip.

must be held in the fingers of the left hand. Like-wise with the right hand, as the right wrist also must hinge. With the handle placed correctly and the hands in their natural positions on the club, the hands and arms can contribute significant power and also square the clubface at impact.

How to Find Your Best Grip

Let your left hand hang at your side. Your palm probably doesn't directly face your left leg; with most people, it's rotated slightly inward. To demonstrate this, lay a pencil loosely in your fingers and again let your hand hang. Is the pencil sticking straight out? It's likely pointing slightly to the right. This is the natural position of your left hand, a position it will seek out unless forced otherwise, so place your hand like this on the grip.

Generally speaking, the handle should run from the middle of your left forefinger to just under the heel pad of the hand. When you close your fingers around the grip, feel as if you're holding the handle against your palm with your fingers, the butt of the club sitting firmly under the heel pad. Then add the right hand, also setting the handle in the fingers. The visual here is that the right palm should face the target at address, matching the clubface, as it will make a palm-to-target striking action at impact.

As for how to join the hands, most instructors recommend the Vardon, or overlapping, grip, where the little finger of the right hand hooks around the left forefinger. For most golfers, this arrangement offers the best combination of control in the fingers and range of motion in the wrists.

BEST TIP: *The Impact Test*

Centrifugal force causes the joints of the left wrist, elbow, and shoulder to line up in a certain way at impact. An effective grip delivers a square clubface as this lining up occurs.

You can simulate this pulling force as follows: Grip a 5-iron in your left hand as you normally do and hold the club out in front of you with the toe straight up. Have a friend hook his fingers around the clubhead. Then slowly lean back, letting your body weight straighten out your left arm (see photo at right). This is how your joints will line up at impact. If your grip is good, your clubface will remain square, or toe-up, as you lean back. If the clubhead twists left or right, adjust your left-hand grip accordingly.

—Robert Baker, *GOLF Magazine*
Master Teaching Professional

BEST TIP: Follow the exercise at left to see if your left-hand grip promotes a square clubface at impact.

Tension Control

There are all sorts of images out there for monitoring grip pressure. Sam Snead used to say to pretend you're holding a baby bird, while another image equates grip pressure to squeezing a tube of toothpaste. While these thoughts may be helpful, you alone have to determine how much pressure is right for your swing.

You should feel as though you're gripping as lightly as you can without losing control of the club during the swing. Due to the swing's high velocity, you need a secure hold with your fingers, but you don't want to create undue tension in your wrists and forearms. Setting the handle in your fingers, not your palms, will help keep the wrists and arms relaxed, as flexing the hand muscles sends tension up the arms.

Experiment on the practice tee with different levels of grip pressure. When you find one that seems right for you, rate it on a scale of 1 to 10 (1 being the lightest; 10 the tightest). If your ideal grip is a 5, for instance, make that one of your preswing checkpoints. You'll be amazed how much faster you can swing the club with a lighter grip.

> ## BEST TIP: *The Pincher Drill*
>
> Excessive pressure in the last three fingers of each hand causes the forearms to become rigid. To relieve this tension, make some pitch swings using a "pincher grip," with just the thumb and forefinger of each hand gripping the club and the other six fingers flared out. Notice how well you can control the club with such little grip pressure. Try to incorporate more "pinch pressure" into your normal grip.
>
> —Kip Puterbaugh, *GOLF Magazine*
> Top 100 Teacher

Aim and Alignment

Golf is a game of precision disguised as a walk in the park. Think about it: You stand on most tees and gaze out over a 40-yard-wide target, any part of which you'd be happy to play your next shot from. Then you hit into greens bigger than most backyards—and again, you'll take any shot that ends up on the putting surface. In fact, it seems the only time you have a specific target is when you're putting. And they call this a target sport?

They do, and it most certainly is. However, many golfers get lulled into complacency, even sheer sloppiness, by the apparent size of their targets. They set up to shots as if direction is of little concern, and then can't believe it when their ball sails into trouble. It's crazy: Golfers try so hard to get their swing right so they can hit the ball well, and when they do, it goes in the wrong direction because of careless aim and alignment.

Granted, there are legions of faults that cause shots to fly off-line, but poor aim and alignment are among the biggest culprits. And since they occur before the swing begins, they are the easiest to rectify. Unfortunately, some golfers find the aiming process mundane and therefore disregard it; others fail to appreciate the consequences. Whatever the reason, the golfer who neglects these preshot essentials is leaving his performance up to chance: A perfect swing is wasted if it isn't preceded by good aim and alignment.

A Game of Direction

First, let's get our definitions down. "Aim" refers to the position of the clubface relative to the target, while "alignment" refers to the position of the body relative to the target line—an imaginary line drawn from the ball to the target. It's useful to think of

"Aim" is the angle of the clubface relative to the target.

aiming and aligning as two different actions, because they affect shot direction in different ways.

Aiming sets the clubface at address, which often determines its position at impact and therefore the way the ball curves in the air. But ball flight is a function not only of curvature, but also of the shot's starting direction; this is where alignment enters the picture.

On full shots, the path of the swing primarily determines the ball's starting direction; the momentum of the clubhead propels the ball in whatever direction it's tracking on. This swing direction tends to

Swing path mainly determines a shot's starting direction.

follow the alignment of the body lines—imaginary lines across the feet, knees, hips, and shoulders. Although the body lines tend to line up with one another, the shoulders are the key, since the arms hang directly from the shoulder sockets. So, instead of checking the squareness of your stance to assess alignment, as most golfers do, have a friend hold a club across your shoulders to see where they're pointed; they have the biggest impact on swing path.

I have already touched upon clubface aim and how the grip plays a leading role in the rotation of the clubface during the swing. But the positioning of the clubface at address drives the entire aiming process. If you watch the pros, you'll see they aim the clubface first, then step into their stance and align their body. This order is critical: At address you have a better view of the clubface then you do your various body lines and can therefore aim the face with greater accuracy. Then, a square clubface can serve as a valuable reference point when you align your body.

How to Aim and Align

Should all golfers employ the same aim and alignment? In a perfect world, they would. If the clubface is perfectly square at impact and the clubhead is moving directly along the target line, the result is a shot that flies straight to the target. And straight shots should be preceded by square aim and alignment. However, golfers know such shots are few and far between.

More likely, you get into the habit of aiming and aligning a certain way as a reaction to your typical ball flight. For example, if you slice, you may start aligning to the left to make room for your left-to-right curve. The opposite goes for the golfer who tends to hook. But these are individual variations we cannot cover here, so let's establish a method for setting a square clubface and square alignment. You can vary from the model as necessary.

Starting from behind the ball, pick an intermediate target—an old divot hole, a patch of discolored grass—a few feet in front of the ball and directly on your target line. Walk to the side of the ball and set the clubhead behind it, positioning the leading edge (bottom) of the clubface perpendicular to your target line. This is where that intermediate target becomes helpful. It's much easier to square your clubface to a spot a few feet away than to a target a couple of hundred yards away.

Using the square clubface as a guide, position your feet, setting your stance line perpendicular to

First, square your clubface to your intermediate target.

Then, align your body parallel to the target line.

the clubface, which is also parallel to the target line. Check to see that imaginary lines across your knees, hips, and shoulders are all parallel to your stance. If they are, you have a square clubface and square alignment to match.

BEST TIP: Use an Aiming Station

Proper aim and alignment come from good habits. You have to learn to establish your target line and use it to aim your club and align your body.

To d o this, set up an aiming station the next time you go to the practice range. Lay down a 12- to 15-foot piece of rope to represent the line you want the shot to start on, then place a club on the ground in front of your toes and parallel to the rope. Lining up your feet with this club will effectively square your stance.

Hit some balls from this setup, first setting the leading edge of the clubface perpendicular to the rope, then setting your body lines parallel to the club on the ground. Getting into the habit of squaring the clubface and then matching your body will serve you well on the course.

—Jim Flick, *GOLF Magazine*
Master Teaching Professional

Ball Position and Stance

Of all the preswing elements, stance and ball position are probably the most instinctual. Ball position relies heavily on innate eye–hand coordination. Plus, you get direct feedback: If you're hitting behind the ball, it's too far forward; if you're hitting the top of it, it's too far back. Even rank beginners figure that out. And your stance is simply a way of arranging your feet to maintain balance during the swing, which you do naturally to support any motion.

The downside to these elements becoming second nature so quickly is that golfers tend to forget about them. As they gain more knowledge of the mechanics of the swing, they have "bigger fish to fry" than these elementary setup positions. Such thinking is a grave error, for although ball position and stance may not be exciting, they have a tremendous impact on performance. And they, too, can slip off track.

Take ball position. It's one of the first things Tour pros check when their ball-striking starts to slide. If this surprises you, consider why it's important in the first place. In order to fully benefit from the power and precision you work to create in your golf swing, you must hit the ball flush. To do this, you have to make contact with the ball at precisely the right point during the swing—or else your effort is wasted.

So where is this right point? With the driver, it's just after the clubhead has passed the low point in its arc and started to ascend. For all other shots, contact should come just before the clubhead reaches the low point. Remember, nothing ensures solid contact better than proper ball position.

Where to Play the Ball

Although many great players, including Jack Nick-laus, have been successful playing the ball in the same position for all shots, it's generally accepted

Play the driver off the left heel for a square hit.

Center the ball for the wedge for a descending blow.

today that the ball should move progressively farther back in the stance as the clubs get shorter.

First, understand that the swing will tend to bottom out directly below the swing center, or the sternum. The key to solid ball-striking is having the ball positioned so that you create the right sternum-to-ball relationship at impact—sternum behind the ball for the driver, about over the ball for a 5-iron, and slightly in front of the ball for a wedge.

If the driver is played off the left heel, as most teachers recommend, the 5-iron should be two to three inches behind that, and the wedge in about the middle of the stance. Why such big changes? With the longer clubs, the golfer moves aggressively toward the target on the downswing, which moves the swing arc forward and requires a forward ball position. With the shorter clubs, there's little lateral body thrust toward the target and therefore the ball should be played below the sternum to create the proper impact.

Customize Your Ball Position

You can easily determine your optimum ball position with each club based on your own individual swing. Grab your driver, 5-iron, and pitching wedge and find any flat grassy area. Starting with the wedge, make some normal practice swings, noting where the clubhead cuts through the grass. Do the same with your 5-iron, then your driver, marking their respective touchdown points with tees.

The location of the tees will tell you where you should position the ball for each club. Keep in mind, the exact ball position should be slightly behind the touchdown points for the irons, as you want to make ball-first contact. For the driver, position the ball slightly in front of the touchdown spot to promote a slight upswing hit. With a little experimentation, you'll identify the optimum ball position for the various clubs; then it's just a matter of keeping tabs on it from shot to shot and round to round.

BEST TIP: Distance from the Ball

Golfers often ask me how far they should stand from the ball. To answer them, I refer to a composite computer model that Dr. Ralph Mann and I generated from a biomechanical study using 54 PGA Tour pros. With the driver, the pros we tested addressed the ball with their left toe approximately 32 inches from the ball. Shorter golfers may want to increase that to 33 inches, taller players to 31. For a 5-iron, the pros stood 23 to 25 inches away; with a 9-iron, 19 to 21 inches. So, the next time you go to practice, slip a yardstick in your bag and see how you measure up.

—Fred Griffin, *GOLF Magazine* Top 100 Teacher

Good Standing

We've touched on the stance already, but let's take a more in-depth look at the basic rules. There are really two areas to consider when you position your feet: how wide apart to set them and how to angle them in relation to the target line.

Your stance should never be wider than it has to be for stability, as a wide stance restricts the natural motion of the hips and legs. In general, as the clubs become shorter, your stance should become narrower, your narrowest stance coming with the wedges. This is because the shorter clubs produce a steeper swinging motion and limited weight transfer and therefore don't require a wide stance for balance. The faster, more powerful swings made with the longer clubs produce weight transfer and rely on a wider stance for stability.

So how wide is right? Picture vertical lines drawn down from your shoulders. With a wedge, the outer edges of your feet should line up with these vertical lines; with a 5-iron, the middle of your feet should be on the lines; and with the driver, your insteps should correspond with the lines. Flexible players can spread their feet a bit more, but keep in mind, the more you widen your stance, the more you restrict body coil.

With a wedge, set the outsides of your feet at shoulder width.

Angling the feet at address also has a major influence on how the body works during the swing. Assuming the stance is square to the target, flaring either foot outward affects the body's turning capacity. If you flare out the right foot, the hips and therefore the shoulders turn more easily away from the target. Turn out the left foot and you facilitate

With a driver, set your insteps at shoulder width.

body turn toward the target on the downswing. Try these variations; you'll feel the difference.

Many teachers recommend a square right foot, set at a right angle to the target line, and a slightly flared left foot, opened roughly 20 degrees toward the target. Squaring the right foot limits the hip turn going back, providing resistance as the torso

A square right foot creates a tight backswing coil.

turns and letting the body coil like a spring. Flaring the left foot presets a quick uncoiling of the lower body on the downswing, a powerful move all golfers should strive for.

BEST TIP: A Guide for Wide

Your stance should never be wider than your normal walking stride. Most golfers err on the wide side, as they feel more powerful. Ironically, a wide stance actually reduces power by restricting body turn.

> Here's how to establish your ideal stance width: Take a normal step forward with your left foot and stop. Spin 90 degrees to your right, keeping your toes in place. That's how wide you should stand with the driver. For each successive club, narrow your stance a half inch, which puts your feet five to six inches closer together for the short irons.
>
> —John Redman, *GOLF Magazine*
> Top 100 Teacher

Posture

Good posture, whether it be at the dinner table or walking down the street, makes a person look alert and confident. Poor posture, on the other hand, suggests sloppiness and fatigue and makes a person seem careless and decidedly less athletic.

In life, such generalizations may be unfair, but when it comes to golf, they do hold some truth. Fact is, the better your posture at address, the better your chance of making a powerful, consistent golf swing. This is not to suggest that your back has to be ramrod-straight, with your chin jutting high in the air; rather you should find a balance between textbook-perfect posture and posture that is comfortable for you.

Physics and kinesiology tell us there are ideal angles at which the body moves fastest and most efficiently. But when a golfer cannot easily create these angles at address or sustain them during the swing, he must make adjustments to his setup or else risk in-swing compensations. For example, a person with rounded shoulders should naturally slump over more than a person who has perfect posture. Point is, strained positions create tension, and tension is the number-one killer of golf swings.

It's a Balancing Act

One of the irksome things about this game is that the golf ball lies on the ground and the golfer stands almost upright. Immediately you're faced with a dilemma: how to get the clubhead down to the ball. There are two primary ways to lower yourself toward the ball: Tilt the torso forward (upper body) and flex the knees (lower body). Sounds easy enough, until you learn that effective posture is a delicate balance of the two.

For starters, the upper body should pitch forward from the hip sockets while the knees assume a

To set your posture, first tilt forward from the hips.

slight or "athletic" flex, like those of a tennis player awaiting a serve. The order in which you introduce these angles is critical: You must tilt the upper body first, which sets your weight forward, then you flex your knees just enough to redistribute the weight toward the middle of the feet. If you start with the knees, you'll tend to bend them too much and then

After you've pitched forward, add a slight flex to the knees.

set the upper body too upright, the most common posture fault among amateurs.

Once you assume your posture, you should feel balanced and stable, as if you could react in any direction without losing your footing. Golf is unlike many other sports in that you're not physically reacting to an opponent's moves; but in the case of address posture, try nevertheless to create a "ready" or "anticipatory" position, as if some action were coming your way.

BEST TIP: Get Vertically Aligned

The body posture to strive for at address is called "vertical alignment." This is a fancy way of saying you want your upper body balanced over your lower body. More specifically, you achieve this position if a straight line extending downward from the back of your shoulders (viewed from the side) would pass through your kneecaps and into the balls of your feet. Have a friend hang a club from the back of either shoulder to see how you line up at address.

—Rick McCord, *GOLF Magazine*
Top 100 Teacher

A Second Tilt

Besides tilting toward the ball, your upper body should also tilt a few degrees away from the target at address. This slight lean to the right presets the coiling action of the upper body and weight trans-

Good Advice Gone Bad

Beginning golfers are constantly being told to keep their head down, because they tend to look up prematurely to see the shot. As a result of these constant reminders, many golfers become "ball bound," meaning they fixate on the ball at address. When this happens, the head invariably droops down, burying the chin in the chest. Then, when the shoulders try to turn on the backswing, the chin gets in the way and thereby cuts off the coiling action and shortens the swing. To prevent this, remind yourself at address to keep your head up and look at the ball through the bottoms of your eyes.

fer to the right leg on the backswing. The good news is, this tilt occurs naturally—if you let it.

Here's what happens: When a right-handed golfer grips a club, he places his right hand below his left on the handle, by about four inches. This position drops the right shoulder lower than the left and, since the shoulders are connected to the spine, tilts the spine slightly to the right. From there, the body will "load" onto the right side as the backswing is completed, setting up a powerful return to the ball.

There's more. When your spine tilts to the right, your head has little choice but to go with it. And that's a beneficial position as well, as your head needs to be behind the ball through impact to maximize the power and leverage of the swing.

Placing your right hand below your left on the grip tilts your spine away from the target.

Preshot Routine

Now that we've discussed the preswing compo-nents, we need to consider a system for putting them into place before every swing. This may

Is Your "K" Okay?

One of the most enduring images in golf instruction is the reverse "K" address position. It's created by the slight tilting of the spine away from the target. To see it, take your address facing a full-length mirror.

Draw an imaginary line from your left foot to your left shoulder; it should be fairly straight and tilt slightly away from the target. Then envision a similar line along your right side. It should run from your right shoulder to your waist, then kink and go down your right leg. Together these two lines should resemble the letter "K" turned backward. Check this position often, as it promotes many correct moves in the golf swing.

sound like a lot to keep track of, but the good news is human beings are creatures of habit: We thrive on the familiarity that habit brings. The trick is to make sure you form the right habits, which then serve as a barrier to keep the wrong ones out.

What you need is a sensible method for organizing the various elements of the setup. The best way to do this is to establish a preshot routine, a series of simple preparation tasks designed to get you physically and mentally ready to execute the shot at hand. As you think about making a preshot routine part of your game, remember that the better your setup, the better your odds of consistently making an effective golf swing. Address positions are literally the foundation of the swing. Get them right and you have something reliable on which to build.

Why All the Fuss?

The purpose of the preshot routine is twofold. First, it provides a logical framework for organizing the setup components; and second, it creates a consistent approach from one shot to the next. A good preshot routine ensures that you give due diligence to the setup and then sends you into the swing feeling confident and relaxed, knowing you've done everything possible to prepare yourself. This way you can ask your body to execute a golf swing and reasonably expect it to respond.

For starters, understand that in the moments preceding every shot, your mind and body will be engaged in some form of activity. If you use that time well, meaning you establish your setup and promote relaxation, you're putting yourself in position to perform well. If you use that time unwisely, thinking about too many things or just fidgeting over the ball, your performance is a crapshoot. The first step to consistent performance is consistent preparation.

Next time you watch the pros on television, notice how they all perform their own preshot routine. Some look simple; others seem elaborate and tedious. But the common denominator is they repeat their routine before every shot they play. They know that golf is a complicated game, and the more you can standardize it from shot to shot, the more you simplify it. So stop reinventing the wheel every time you step up to your ball. Start with an effective preshot routine and your performance and confidence level will soar.

A Few Preshot Guidelines

It's true that every preshot routine has its own personality, but that's not to say they don't have common components. Every routine should start with an assessment of the target area and should end with a relaxation check just before the start of the swing. In between, the various setup elements should be established, and extraneous thoughts and actions should be kept to an absolute minimum.

The best starting place for any shot is directly behind the ball, where you can clearly view the target area and envision the ball flight in your mind. This signals the start of your preshot routine, indicating it's time to clear your mind of any negative thoughts and to focus on creating a perfect setup. The theme from start to finish should be simplicity and structure. In the end, your routine should not be mentally taxing and should be easy to repeat time and time again.

Get a Good View

Standing a few paces behind the ball, first establish your ultimate target. This may not be the middle of the fairway or the flag, due to the proximity of hazards or the ideal angle for your next shot. For instance, if you're a short hitter playing a hole that doglegs to the left 250 yards out, you may want to play to the right side off the tee to set up a clear approach. Whatever the case, pick a target that's realistic for you, always considering your next play.

Keep in mind, your target line probably isn't the line you want to start your shot on. If you tend to curve the ball either left or right, you need to borrow some room to allow for that curve—perhaps 10 to 20 yards. Once you establish a starting line for the shot, pick an intermediate target, as described earlier, directly on that line and a few feet in front of your ball. You'll use this intermediate spot at address to establish precise aim and alignment.

Some players like to take their grip while standing behind the ball, which is fine. Since we've already discussed how to arrange your hands, just note that you must make sure the clubface is square once your grip is complete. To do this, raise the clubhead up to waist level after you've taken your grip: The clubface is square if the leading edge,

From behind the ball, pick an intermediate target directly on your starting line.

or bottom, of the face is perpendicular to the ground. Now you're ready to step into the shot.

Step to the Side

If you wish to take a practice swing, do so as soon as you walk to the side of the ball. Practice swings can be useful in relieving tension or rehearsing a particular swing, but eliminate them if you feel they interrupt the flow of the preshot routine or offer little preparation value. Players who lack patience or find themselves rushing through the preshot process should consider skipping the practice swing and focusing on the essential preshot elements, such as aim and alignment. It may be reassuring to rehearse your swing, but to do so in lieu of a proper setup is only hurting your chances.

Once you're ready to step up to the ball, your first objective should be to square the clubface to your starting line. Locate your intermediate target, then tilt your upper body forward to lower the clubhead to the ball. Set the leading edge of the clubface behind the ball and perpendicular to your starting line. If you haven't already completed your grip, now's the time to do it—left hand first, then

Square your clubface before taking your stance.

right. Make sure the clubface is square to your starting line when your grip is complete.

Using the clubface as a guide, set your feet parallel to your intended starting line. To do this, it might help to picture your setup as a T square, with your clubface flush to the ruler's edge and the tips of your shoes up against either end of the "T." Although your other body lines tend to follow the alignment of your feet, it's a good idea to run your eyes from your toes to your shoulders, making sure these lines are parallel to one another.

At this point, your body weight should be favoring your toes, as you've tilted your upper body forward to sole the clubhead. To counter this, flex your knees slightly to redistribute the weight toward the middle of each foot. Remember, keep your knee bend to a minimum. Your lower body should feel ready to support the momentum of the swing but not be in a strained or aggressive pose.

One last thing before you start your swing: Check your relaxation level. Tension at address leads to a fast takeaway and limited range of motion. The two most popular ways to curb tension are waggling the clubhead and taking deep breaths. The waggle keeps your hands and arms supple so they can create a smooth start to the swing, while deep breathing can relieve muscle tension throughout your body. Although it's a good idea to monitor your breathing throughout the preshot process, the most important time is just before you start the club back. Feel the breathing down in your diaphragm, not just in your upper chest. The relaxation you create will really pay off.

It's a Golfer's Best Friend

Golf at times seems a cruel and lonely game. But with an effective preshot routine on your side, you can create a sense of familiarity and reassurance be-

> ### A Sample Preshot Routine
>
> Behind the ball:
> 1. Pick your target and starting line for the shot.
> 2. Select an intermediate target in front of the ball.
> 3. Complete your grip.
>
> Beside the ball:
> 4. Make a practice swing to rehearse the feel.
> 5. Using the intermediate target, square the clubface.
> 6. Using the square clubface, align your body.
> 7. Complete your posture.
> 8. Relaxation check: waggle or deep breath.

fore every swing you make. It's a lot easier to be relaxed over the ball knowing you've achieved the correct setup positions and done all you can to ready your mind and body.

Furthermore, a reliable preshot routine will do wonders for your performance under pressure. When a stressful situation arises, such as teeing off in front of a crowd or playing sudden death in a match, most golfers either speed up or try to carefully control every step of the process. The speedsters wind up swinging before they've adequately prepared their mind or body, while the deliberate types only add to the gravity of the moment. The key in pressure situations is using the same routine you've grooved when the pressure wasn't on; that's the best way to counter the anxiety you feel.

BEST TIP: *Perform at Peak Concentration*

The amount of time it takes to perform the preshot routine is critical yet often overlooked. Each golfer has his own capacity to concentrate, and for every shot he faces, there's one moment in time when his concentration is at its peak. Your objective should be to reach that peak and act then.

Over the years, I've timed about 50 PGA Tour players to see how long they take to hit a shot. Three-quarters of them took between 18 and 22 seconds from the moment they clicked "on" their concentration to contact with the ball. Each had his own preshot routine, which never varied from shot to shot, and each took a consistent amount of time to hit the ball.

Experiment with preshot routines of varying lengths on the practice range and have a friend time each one with a stopwatch. Over time, your performance and patience level will tell you if you need a concise or detailed approach. Once you know, create a preshot routine to fit your concentration capacity and then use it before every swing you make.

—Dr. Richard Coop, *GOLF Magazine*
Mental Game Consultant

2

The Swing

Think of the golf swing like a game of dominoes: Set it up, get it started, and the rest takes care of itself. Okay, it's not quite that simple, but the swing *is* a natural chain of events—and doesn't have to be as complicated as many amateurs make it. With all the mental and physical factors you can try to control, it's no wonder the average player often seems frustrated and confused. He is, much of the time, simply overwhelmed.

But it doesn't have to be that way. First of all, understand that the outcome of your shots is largely determined by decisions you make before you step up to the ball, such as club selection, shot selection, and target orientation. If any of these factors are off, your outcome will suffer despite how well you execute your swing. It's during the preswing period that the golfer has to be a thinker.

After these preliminary decisions, your focus becomes the setup, which we've established as a major factor in performance. How major? Look at it this way: You take your setup—a structured, step-by-step procedure—and all that's left is making the swing itself, which should be an instinctive, flowing action. This is where athleticism must take over.

Remember, almost all of the thinking you do on a given shot should be completed before you take the club back. The angles and positions we are about to discuss should be grooved on the practice tee, not on the golf course. Mechanical thoughts cause tension, and tension is your swing's biggest enemy. So, consider yourself forewarned: Think while you practice and before you execute. Once you start your swing, rely as much as possible on your athletic instincts.

Starting Back

Put simply, the takeaway sets the shape and pace of the golf swing. A swing that starts off smoothly, the arms and body moving in sync, has a good chance of producing favorable results. One that starts quickly or out of sequence demands in-swing compensations, which are unreliable at best.

There are several keys to a good takeaway. First of all, it should not start from a still position, one good reason to waggle the club at address, as described earlier. Another effective preswing motion is the forward press, whereby the golfer pushes his hands slightly toward the target immediately before starting the club back. In this case, the takeaway is essentially a rebound of the forward press.

Starting back, the hands, arms, and shoulders should move the club away together. This is called a "one-piece takeaway." Such connection at the start is critical to creating the right path and shape for the swing. You should feel like the left shoulder is pushing the club back, without any conscious twisting or hinging of the hands or wrists.

When the clubhead reaches hip high, there are three important positions to check. First, the shaft should be parallel to the target line, the butt end of the grip pointing just left of the target. Second, there should only be a slight hinge in the

Tailor Your Waggle

Aside from kick-starting the swing, the waggle can also serve as a rehearsal of your takeaway. Consider this: Most golfers either lift the club abruptly on the takeaway or else drag it back with tense arms and stiff wrists. If you have either problem, design a waggle to prevent it. Use a wide, one-piece waggle to head off an abrupt start, or a loose, wristy waggle to avoid a rigid, mechanical takeaway. Take advantage of your rehearsal.

At hip high, the shaft should be parallel to the target line.

During the takeaway, the wrists should hinge only slightly.

left wrist, as this initial move is a wide, sweeping motion. And third, the toe of the clubhead should be turned upward, as the forearms naturally start to rotate. With the clubhead hip high, the leading edge of the clubface should match the forward tilt of your spine. Get these positions right and you've created a wide extension and the proper path for your golf swing.

The only other factor to consider on the takeaway is tempo. This needs to be the slowest part of your swing. If the takeaway is fast or abrupt, the swing will follow suit; likewise, if you start with a smooth, wide extension, you're likely to maintain good rhythm and width throughout your swing. So remember, think slow at the start: The swing is plenty long enough to produce acceleration without any quick bursts of speed in the early going.

BEST TIP: Get a Head Start

To groove a wide, smooth extension away from the ball, hit some practice shots starting from a fully extended postimpact position. (Set up as usual, then move the clubhead out a few feet toward the target, fully extending your arms as you do after impact.) From there, just take your normal backswing. Starting from a full extension (see photo at right) promotes a wide, smooth move going back.

—Dick Tiddy, *GOLF Magazine* Top 100 Teacher

To the Top

Once the clubhead reaches hip high, the majority of the body weight should already be on the right instep. This weight transfer occurs as a natural result of the arms and shoulders extending the clubhead away from the ball. If your weight is still centered at this point, chances are you've made an

BEST TIP: Try the exercise described on the previous page to groove a good takeaway.

abrupt takeaway by lifting the club with your hands and cocking your wrists.

From the hip-high position, the wrists will start to hinge the club upward, as long as they are free of excess tension. In fact, by the time the hands are opposite the right ear, the wrists should have cocked the club into a 90-degree angle with the left arm, creating a distinct second lever in the swing. This second lever not only allows the clubhead to swing through a much longer arc in the backswing, but also sets up a powerful release of energy on the downswing. Wrist cock is one of the hallmarks of a powerful swing.

Just Plane Talk

Swing plane is a daunting topic to many golfers, so let's simplify it. The plane of the golf swing is established by the angle of the shaft to the ground at address (looking down the target line). As a general rule, a swing is called "on plane" if the club stays parallel to this address angle throughout the swing. Longer clubs create a flatter plane, as the golfer stands farther from the ball to accommodate the longer shafts, while shorter clubs put the golfer closer to the ball and therefore produce a more upright swing plane. But while the shaft angle at ad-

Going back, the wrists should hinge the club into a 90-degree angle with the left arm.

dress varies from club to club, the shaft should stay roughly parallel to this starting angle throughout the swing—and that goes for every club in the bag.

To further understand the concept of swinging on plane, picture your target line extending infinitely both toward and away from the target. At address, the shaft points directly at this line. As the club starts back, it sweeps inside and starts to elevate, but the shaft still points directly at the extended target line. As the swing progresses and the wrists hinge, the club turns upside down. Now the butt end of the club points to the extended target line. In fact, either the clubhead end or the butt end, whichever is closer to the ground, should point to this extended line throughout the entire swing.

Although the plane of the swing actually should get slightly flatter coming down than it was going back—as the forward thrust of the lower body on the downswing pulls the club into a flatter position—for simplicity's sake, stick to the extended target line image to check your swing plane.

Load Before You Fire

The purpose of the backswing is to position the club and coil the body in such a way that the downswing

At halfway back, the grip end should point to the ball.

is a simple reversal of events. As I've said, the farther along you get, the harder it is to assert control over the swing; by the time the downswing begins, if not sooner, you have to be on automatic pilot.

After the wrists have fully hinged, the hips and shoulders continue to turn to complete the backswing. It's important to remember that once the shoulders stop turning, the arms should stop swinging back. If they don't, the body will likely start down before the arms are ready, throwing the swing out of sync. Ideally, the shoulders turn 90 degrees and the hips 45 degrees from their starting positions to the top of the backswing. This relationship between the upper body and lower body coils the torso like a spring, setting up a powerful uncoiling on the downswing.

Now let's discuss the role of the lower body in the backswing. Most teachers view the lower body as the support base for the actions of the upper body. As such, the legs do not initiate any backswing action. In fact, the lower body should resist the turning of the upper body to create the springlike effect that will power the downswing. In short, the legs should simply maintain their flex and react to the coiling of the torso, the right leg serving as the axis over which the upper body rotates.

If the lower body stays passive, the torso coils like a spring.

> ### BEST TIP: Light Up Your Line
>
> Here's a good visual for checking your swing plane. Line up two clubs on the ground, one on either side of the ball, to represent your target line. Then tape two flashlights together end to end, so the beams shine in opposite directions. Grip the flashlights like a club and take your setup, shining one beam on the ball. Take some slow-motion half-swings: If your swing is perfectly on-plane, the beam from one flashlight, then the other should shine on the clubs going back. Coming down, again one beam, then the other should track along the clubs.
>
> —Rick Grayson, *GOLF Magazine*
> Top 100 Teacher

Checkpoints at the Top

The top of the backswing offers one last chance to check yourself before "letting it go." Not that you should have swing thoughts at this point; your thinking should be geared toward the setup and maybe the very early part of the swing. But, when practicing, it is useful to swing to the top and assess what your swing looks and feels like. The downswing happens too fast to include reliable compensations for bad positions at the top.

At the top, the upper body should feel fully coiled, with the left shoulder turned under the chin. The left arm should be fairly straight, although not stiff, and the back of the left hand should be in a straight line with the left forearm, neither cupped nor bowed. Ideally, the club should be parallel to your target line and in a fully horizontal position. A square clubface at the top, assuming you've swung it all the way back, puts the leading edge at the same angle as your left forearm—roughly 45 degrees to the ground.

The lower body should feel stable and ready to start moving toward the target. Most of the body weight should be distributed between the right instep and heel, never to the outside of the right foot, and the left knee should be kicked in slightly.

Most golfers keep their left heel planted throughout the backswing, although inflexible players may consider letting the momentum of the backswing pull it an inch or two off the ground to allow for a fuller swing. Nevertheless, even if the heel is lifted, the left toe should still be gripping the ground, as the body must be in position to shift left and drive toward the target.

For a full coil, feel your left shoulder turn under your chin.

Stay in Those Angles

An effective backswing winds the body up and sets the club in a position at the top from which it is easy to simply reverse directions and deliver the club forcefully to the ball. The key word here is "simply," as many golfers make moves on the backswing that have to be undone on the downswing if the clubhead is to accurately return to the ball.

The most important area when it comes to keeping your swing simple is posture. In short, you have to maintain the same body posture from address through impact in order to achieve any degree of ball-striking consistency. If your posture changes going back, meaning you raise up or shrink down, you have to make the exact reversal of that move on the downswing to strike the ball solidly.

As noted earlier, posture is a combination of forward tilt from the hips and flex in the knees. Although these critical body angles vary from player to player, based on individual physique, once they're established at address, they must remain fixed through contact with the ball. This can be a challenging endeavor, especially for less flexible players, since the address position can feel awkward even before the body starts coiling.

To add to the difficulty, the coiling action of the backswing jeopardizes these angles in two ways. First, it's easier to turn your shoulders from a more upright position, which encourages you to raise up as the shoulders near their rotational limit. Second, as weight transfers to your back foot, it's easy to let it drift to the outside of the foot, which often causes

---

BEST TIP: *Feel a Good Coil*

Coil is created when you wind the upper body against the resistance of the lower body. To feel this, sit on a bench or chair and lean forward 30 degrees. Grip a club and start to swing back, turning your left shoulder toward your chin. Since you can't turn your hips at all while sitting, you'll feel the large muscles of your back start to stretch almost immediately. Try to reproduce this coiled feeling in your golf swing.

—Carl Lohren, *GOLF Magazine* Top 100 Teacher

---

the back knee to straighten. These tendencies make it all the more important to be aware of maintaining your posture through impact.

One good way to make sure you're staying in posture is to swing in front of a full-length mirror with a mark or piece of tape indicating your head level at address. Swing back and through several times, looking up to check that your head doesn't move above or below its starting position until it turns up on the follow-through.

The Transition

We've said that the takeaway sets the overall shape and pace of the swing, but the transition from backswing to downswing has the most direct effect on the shape and pace of the down-swing. In other words, the way the golfer changes direction at the top in large part determines his position at impact, which is the only position that dictates where the ball goes.

The keys to a good transition are proper sequence of motion and smooth tempo. Most teachers hold that the downswing should occur from the ground up, starting with a weight transfer or lateral "bump" back to the front foot. From there, the body should start un-winding, lower body leading and pulling the upper body, until the club is pulled through by the momentum of this uncoiling action. There need be no conscious flipping of the hands through the hitting area: If the body is allowed to unwind in sequence, centrifugal force will properly position the hands and arms at impact.

If the downswing is simply a reversal of the back-swing, it must begin with a return of the weight to the front foot. In fact, the lower body actually should

---

Don't Pause

Players who tend to rush the club back down to the ball are often told to pause at the top. This is dangerous advice for two reasons. First, the swing should always be thought of as one flowing motion: Any conscious starting or stopping disrupts its natural rhythm. Second, a pause at the top reduces the resistance between the upper and lower body, promoting a downswing in which the entire body unwinds together. The result is a lack of leverage on the downswing and a dramatic loss of power.

The downswing starts with a lateral "bump" back to the front foot.

start toward the target a split second before the upper body finishes turning back. This stretches the muscles involved in the coil even more and gives the appearance that the clubhead lags behind in the downswing sequence. The immortal Bobby Jones described this action in his book *Golf Is My Game* as follows, "The all-important feel which I experience as the swing changes direction is one of leaving the clubhead at the top of the swing."

> ### *BEST TIP: Uncoil from the Ground Up*
>
> Grip a three-foot-long piece of rope as if it were a golf club and swing it back, letting it flip over your right shoulder. From there, swing the rope down and through, letting the lower body lead the uncoiling action, pulling the rope taut and making the tip trail through the hitting area. This drill proves that the downswing is a pulling motion, as the lower body must lead the upper body for the tip of the rope to whip through last.
>
> —Martin Hall, *GOLF Magazine*
> Master Teaching Professional

Watch Your Speed

Just like the first move away from the ball, the transition from backswing to downswing should be smooth and unhurried. In fact, a graceful transition is one of the most aesthetically pleasing parts of the golf swing.

Think of the great players you like to watch. I'll bet they include such smooth swingers as Fred Couples, Ernie Els, and Steve Elkington. These players seem to have effortless power—no sudden bursts of speed, yet an aggressive whip into the ball. Much of this graceful power comes from a smooth transition, which allows them to gradually accelerate the club through impact. The simple truth is that the more you rush the swing from the top, the less speed you'll have at impact. Your swing can only have one fast point—save it for when it counts.

If you think smooth tempo is an intangible quality and either you have it or you don't, you're half right. The world's top golfers are gifted athletes with a natural sense of rhythm and timing, but that doesn't mean you can't improve your own speed control. If you can calm the instinct to "hit from the top" and trust that gradual acceleration will yield maximum swing speed, you'll groove a more powerful, more consistent golf swing.

How to Find "The Slot"

If, as we've said, an effective downswing should simply undo the positions achieved on the backswing, this means the arms, which travel in and up going back, must reverse that motion so that they move down and out—in that order. Unfortunately, most golfers don't let the club drop down before they swing it out to the ball. As we'll see later, the "over-the-top" downswing that results is one of the most prevalent faults in the game.

The fall of the arms at the start of the downswing is one of the marks of an accomplished player. The good news is, it's a move that happens naturally if you follow the correct sequence of motion from the top. In other words, you don't have to consciously pull your arms down; a proper transition will drop them into position.

Let me explain. From a fully wound position at the top, your first move down—a lateral shift back to your front foot—will cause your arms to drop downward toward your right side. As the uncoiling of the body begins, the left shoulder pulls away from the chin, which also pulls the arms downward. Again, this dropping action is merely a response to the body's move toward the target, not a conscious action.

If the arms remain passive at the start of the downswing, they will fall into a position called "the slot," with the right elbow tucked close to the right side, the wrists still fully hinged, and the butt of the club pointing to the ball. This position sets the stage for a powerful delivery from inside the target line. Virtually all good ball-strikers, despite any idiosyncrasies on the backswing,

Don't Get Down

The idea that you have to hit down on the ball is one of the biggest misconceptions in the game. Truth is, the club should move at about a 90-degree angle to the spine on the downswing. The up-and-down appearance of the swing is created by the forward tilt of the spine at address. The golf swing is very much like a baseball swing; it just starts from a more bent-over position.

If the arms stay passive at the start of the downswing, the club drops into "the slot."

drop the club into the slot. Stay relaxed and let your swing unwind and you can, too.

Through Impact

Once you get into the downswing, you've reached the point of no return. You simply cannot manipulate the swing from this point forward with any degree of consistency. You've had your chances to affect the fate of the shot at hand, from club selection to setup positions to even a simple thought at the change of direction. Now the swing is on its own. The flight of the ball will tell you how well you've done.

This is not to suggest that you shouldn't be sensing anything through impact, only that trying to time specific positions when the club should be freewheeling into the ball is unwise and unreliable. You can, and should, feel certain sensations as the body uncoils, but they are "flowing" sensations that occur throughout the downswing. Among them are the transition of weight to the front foot and the pulling of the torso and arms by the lower body. Let's try to isolate these feelings and thereby create a sensory framework for the downswing. You may not be able to "save the swing" at this point, but you can sense how it's going.

Shift, Then Turn

While the lower body plays only a supporting role on the backswing, it takes center stage at the change of direction. After the initial forward shift of the lower body, the hips should start to rotate aggressively toward the target. This rotation, or "clearing," of the hips gives the downswing its rotary shape

After the weight shifts forward, the hips start rotating to the target.

and also preserves the resistance between the upper and lower halves created on the backswing.
Maintaining this resistance well into the downswing allows you to unleash the power of the coil
at impact.

By now the majority of the weight should be on
the front foot. It's worth noting again that sequence

BEST TIP: Attack from the Inside

To groove an inside path into impact, practice hitting balls with your right foot pulled back 12 inches from its normal position and set on its toe. Make a normal swing from this stance and your right arm and shoulder will naturally drop to the inside as the swing changes direction, setting up a powerful in-to-out path through impact. Hit several balls from this stance and then try to incorporate the feeling into your normal swing.

—Jane Frost, *GOLF Magazine* Top 100 Teacher

of motion is crucial: Your lower body must lead the way, first with a lateral weight shift to the front foot, then with a rapid rotation of the hips. Since the hips turn fairly level, the unwinding force they create drops the club onto a flatter, more rotary plane, which brings the clubhead downward. This flattening of the swing plane sets up a powerful approach from the inside.

With the weight shifting forward, the left leg will serve as the axis around which the upper body turns through the ball, just as the right leg functioned on the backswing. This aggressive shifting and turning of the lower body clears a path for the hands and arms to deliver the club from the slot position—the key to strong, accurate ball-striking.

Narrowing of the Arc

A powerful swing features a distinct narrowing of the clubhead arc on the downswing. To understand this, consider a simple image. If the clubhead left a trail in the air like a skywriting plane, the downswing part of the trail, viewed from a face-to-face position with the golfer, would be much narrower, or closer to the body, than the backswing portion. It would look as if the golfer has yanked the grip in closer to his body on the downswing. This narrowing of the arc proves that the proper sequence of motion has occurred and also indicates stored power.

When the lower body leads the downswing, the right shoulder and arm are pulled downward, dropping the right elbow to the right side. Compare this position to its backswing counterpart and you'll notice there were several inches between the right elbow and the body going back, giving the backswing its wide, sweeping shape. By contrast, the right elbow virtually rides on the body coming down. Furthermore, the wrists are still fully cocked when the hands reach hip high in the downswing, which is exactly where the wrists *started* to cock on the backswing. This sharp wrist angle dramatically shortens the return path of the clubhead.

There is another reason the clubhead arc appears so much narrower on the downswing: the lateral shift of the hips. On aggressive full swings, the hips move about six inches toward the target at the start of the downswing—the "bump" I referred to earlier. This lateral move shifts the clubhead arc six inches forward. So, while the clubhead actually does stay closer to the body on the downswing, the repositioning of the lower body serves to exaggerate this narrowing effect.

BEST TIP: *Check Your Width*

To make sure you have the right sequence of motion on your downswing, compare your clubhead arc halfway down to its position halfway back. Set up next to a bush or small tree so that your clubhead just reaches the leaves halfway back. Then take some practice swings, stopping to check the clubhead position halfway down. Your lateral move toward the target to start the downswing and the subsequent body rotation should pull the clubhead at least a foot inside the leaves on the downswing.

—Craig Shankland, *GOLF Magazine* Top 100 Teacher

Your Power Source

It's easy to say that brute force has no place in the golf swing. It's decidedly more difficult to sell this idea to a golfer who has just seen Tiger Woods or John Daly hit a tee shot. The explosion of power that these great players produce at impact makes it seem that they are attacking the ball with every ounce of energy they have.

Although they may be doing just that, it is important to remember that they are employing swinging force, not hitting force. That's the difference: The pros let the clubhead swing through the ball, while average golfers throw the club at the ball. Impact is not a position to the pros; it is simply an action that occurs between the backswing and the follow-through. To borrow an age-old saying, "The ball just gets in the way."

That's not to say that strength is not a power factor in golf. But upper-body strength typically associated with muscular people—the upper arms, chest, and shoulders—actually does little for the golf swing. The strength and flexibility of the trunk and the core muscles (abdomen and lower back) have a much greater impact

> ### Clubhead Follows Grip
> Wherever the grip end of the club points on the downswing is where the clubhead will swing through the hitting area. When the club drops into the slot, the butt end should point at the ball. As the swing continues, the butt should turn upward and point to the right of the target, indicating an on-plane swing and an approach from the inside. If the butt of the club points left of the target, the clubhead will swing out to in through impact, and the ball will tend to start to the left. If you slice, you probably suffer from this over-the-top move.

on your power potential than a muscular upper body. We've all seen our share of muscle-bound strongmen who can't hit the ball 200 yards off the tee. You wouldn't tell them they lack power—if you're smart—yet they are not powerful golfers.

So where does the power come from? Most of it is generated by the tension created as the upper body coils around the lower body. The more you can wind the torso against the resistance of the hips and legs, the more power you will store going back and then unleash coming down. This pivoting action of the body relies more on flexibility than strength: You'd much rather have elastic muscles that can produce the winding and unwinding motion than hulking muscles that limit your range of motion.

Other factors in creating power include weight transfer and your body's lever system. Driving your weight to the target on the downswing is critical because it initiates the uncoiling process and establishes the left side as the point of resistance for the full release of the right side through impact. As with so many aspects of the swing, weight transfer on the downswing is set up by the proper loading on the backswing. In other words, there's no weight to transfer if the backswing didn't do its job—yet another reason to focus on the early part of the swing.

BEST TIP: *Towel Drill*

Train yourself not to rush the club down from the top by making practice swings with a towel wrapped around the head of your driver. The air resistance of the towel trains you to build speed gradually on the downswing. With the uncoiling of your torso leading the way, the arms do not waste energy with an early hitting action and the clubhead achieves maximum speed through the bottom of the swing.

—Jeff Warne, *GOLF Magazine* Top 100 Teacher

As for your lever system, the biggest power producer is the wrist cock. When the wrists hinge on the backswing and create that 90-degree angle between the club and the left forearm, they store a tremendous amount of potential energy for the downswing. This is where so many golfers cheat themselves of power: They fully cock their wrists going back and then, in an attempt to create power, release this angle too early in the downswing with a hitting or swatting action. To take advantage of the power you've stored, you have to let centrifugal force unhinge the wrists, pull the left arm and the club into a straight line, and sling the clubhead into the ball. You have to simply let that happen.

Centrifugal force pulls the club in line with the left arm at impact.

The Moment of Truth

While it's true that the golf swing is an intricate chain of events, impact between clubhead and ball is the only position that really matters—the only position that the golf ball reacts to. Impact is when you either cash in on a well-timed, well-ordered move or you pay the piper for shortcuts or compensations taken along the way.

This being the case, you may be wondering why we've spent so much time discussing everything that precedes impact. Why not keep it simple and just describe where you need to be at impact? The answer is easy: because you have no conscious control over what the clubhead is doing when it collides with the

---

BEST TIP: Extend for Power

Power hitters maximize swing speed by making a full release of the club and a wide follow-through arc, the left wrist remaining flat and the left arm straight well past impact. To sense this extension, make some practice swings with your driver, letting your right hand slip off the grip as the clubhead approaches the hitting area. Without your right hand, your left arm will fully extend to the target and your left wrist will stay flat, as long as your body keeps rotating.

—T. J. Tomasi, *GOLF Magazine* Top 100 Teacher

ball. The swing is happening too quickly to manipulate the club in any reliable fashion. For this reason, the way you perform your downswing, your backswing, even your setup, is how you affect the position and speed of the clubhead as it reaches the ball.

There are, however, a few sensations you should be aware of through the impact area. First, make sure the clubhead is approaching from slightly inside the target line on a semicircle arc. In fact, on practice swings, you should be able to pick up the blurred path of the clubhead, even though it may be moving at speeds upwards of 100 mph at the bottom of the swing arc. Many good things have to happen in the downswing for the clubhead to approach on this path.

Next, you should feel like your right hand and arm are extending to the target. The old image for this is that you're skipping a stone across the surface of a pond with a sidearm motion, elbow leading the hand until the stone is released. To achieve this sensation, your left side must

Don't Return to Address

Forget the old instruction adage that says get into the same position at impact as you were at address. Although the clubhead must return to the ball, your knees and hips should be several inches closer to the target at impact, and your entire torso should be rotated well left. Think of impact as a driving, dynamic move to the target—a brief instant that sometimes eludes even the fastest cameras.

straighten up slightly to provide a point of resistance for the throwing action. Many teachers say you should feel like the right hand and arm make a slapping or spanking motion through the ball.

The important point to remember is that the entire right side should make an aggressive release through impact, aided by centrifugal force and the momen-

Through most of the downswing, the right elbow leads the right hand.

tum of the swing. The long-standing idea that the right side should be passive in the golf swing, so as not to overpower the left, does not apply in the hitting area. In short, no right-handed golfer should suppress the hitting power of his dominant side. Perhaps the legendary Ben Hogan put it best in *Five Lessons: The Modern Fundamentals of Golf* when he said, "As far as applying power goes, I wish that I had three right hands."

To the Finish

With the ball on its way, many golfers think the shot is over and their work is done. Well, you could argue that point, as you can't affect the fate of the ball after it leaves the clubface—despite any midair pleas or threats. You can, however, learn a lot from how you feel after impact and the positions you reach at the finish. Fact is, every motion in the golf swing flows into the follow-through, giving clues as to the correctness of the actions that got you there. Working backward from the finish is one of the most effective learning tools at your disposal.

Let's focus our analysis of the follow-through on three areas: weight transfer, body rotation, and arm swing. First, as you continue to push off the right side and onto the left, your head should remain in its starting position. In fact, it may even move slightly away from the target by impact to counter the driving force of the lower body through the strike. At the finish, all of your weight should be on the outside of your left foot, with your right foot on its toe and serving only to maintain balance.

The body rotation, as it has throughout the downswing, follows the transfer of weight toward the target. The lower body continues to clear the way for the upper body, with the right side now powering the motion and pushing the body into the follow-through. At the finish, the right shoulder should be closer to the target than any other part of the body, and your belt buckle should point slightly left of the target, your chest even farther left. This fully rotated body position proves that the body pulls the arms and the club through impact—the key to maximum leverage and power.

As the body pulls the arms, the right side joins the party and applies some hitting force of its own. The

---

Heads Up

It's a good idea to let your head swivel in response to the shoulder turn, both on the backswing and downswing. After impact, track your eyes down the target line after the streaking ball, instead of pulling up out of your posture. This will help you maintain your forward tilt through the shot to ensure solid contact. In fact, two of today's top stars, David Duval and Annika Sorenstam, actually rotate their eyes down the line before impact, their heads swiveling, not lifting up.

Relaxed arms naturally rotate and extend through impact.

At the finish, the right shoulder is closest to the target.

right hand and arm fire through the strike, rotating the shaft as the right forearm rolls over the left. This is not a conscious action: If the hands and arms are free of excessive tension through the hitting area, they will naturally release the club. After impact, you should feel like the clubhead is chasing the ball to the target.

The momentum of the swing fully extends the arms toward the target, as the left elbow begins to fold, allowing the club to wrap around the body and run out of steam. One more good flowing sensation: The left elbow should point at the ground throughout the downswing and into the finish. If you can do this, the hands will float up to a position above the left shoulder, as you watch your ball soar to its target.

BEST TIP: *Throw on a Scarf*

To fully release your right hand and arm on the follow-through, imagine you're wrapping a scarf around your neck, throwing it with your right hand. Make some practice swings focusing on this image. It should promote the correct rotation of your right arm and also help keep it relaxed; a stiff right arm restricts your follow-through.

—Mitchell Spearman, *GOLF Magazine*
Top 100 Teacher

3
Faults

When it comes to swing technique, it's fair to say the end justifies the means. In other words, if you break all the rules of swing mechanics but consistently get the club into a good position at impact, more power to you. No one can argue with good results. As renowned British golf instructor John Jacobs wrote in *The Golf Swing Simplified,* "The golf swing has only one purpose: to deliver the head of the club to the ball correctly. How that is done is immaterial, so long as the method used permits correct impact to be achieved over and over and over again."

That said, you must understand that there are certain parameters when it comes to individual style in the golf swing. Clearly, you can't stray too far from the ideal setup and swing positions discussed in the previous sections and still expect good results on a consistent basis. For example, if you cut across the target line slightly through impact, you may be able to get away with it; but if you slash the club dramatically across the line, impact will be weak and your shots will dart off line. It's all a matter of degree.

But how do you know which faults are acceptable? Your ball flight is your guide. The distance and direction of your shots tells you what happened at impact, which tells you what happened during the swing. It's all very logical. Then you have to decide if you can live with the *good* shots you're hitting. If you can, your focus should be on hitting those good shots more consistently, not overhauling the mechanics of your golf swing. You want to be able to hit serviceable golf shots. Forget about creating textbook swing mechanics. That's something even the best can't emulate.

Look at the great players: They have their own individual swing styles, which often vary greatly. Colin Montgomerie has a long, flowing golf swing, with the hands high on the backswing and again at the finish; David Duval is more around the body, making a powerful trunk rotation back and through. Is one way better than the other? It is for each of these guys. And as good as they are, if one tried to swing like the other, we'd probably never hear from him again.

Point is, there is no perfect golf swing for everyone. It all boils down to how you position the clubface at impact; that's the acid test of the swing. The difference between mechanical faults and unorthodox moves is only the results they produce. An unconventional swing that consistently delivers good shots is absolutely flawless. The end truly does justify the means.

Why Shots Go Where They Go

Before we look at specific faults, it is important to have a basic understanding of what makes the ball go where it goes. Simply stated, as the clubhead swings through impact, the clubface acts on the ball in several ways. This exchange lasts only half a millisecond (.0005 of a second) before the ball is on its way, executing the flight plan by traveling a certain distance in a certain direction.

This interaction between clubface and ball largely determines the identity of the shot, along with certain equipment specifications and environmental conditions. The ball doesn't care if your takeaway is laughably fast or you lift your head up six inches on the backswing; it only reacts to the position and speed of the clubface at impact. This is not to say that quirky moves cannot have a dramatic effect on the shot—they do, but only if they influence the clubface at impact. That's why such unorthodox swingers as Lee Trevino, Raymond Floyd, and Jim Furyk have excelled: Their idiosyncrasies allow them—even help them—to deliver the clubface correctly at impact, and that's the only position that really counts.

In all, the clubface "reports to the ball" in five areas. Together, these five impact factors, in large part, produce the outcome of every shot you play. They are in no particular order:

1. Swing path: the path the clubhead takes through the hitting area.

2. Clubface angle: the squareness of the club-face in relation to its path.

3. Clubhead speed: the velocity of the clubhead when it meets the ball.

4. Point of contact: where on the clubface the ball makes contact.

5. Angle of approach: the steepness of the club-head's approach to the ball.

The combined effect of these five impact factors dictates the distance and direction of the ensuing shot. The first two—swing path and clubface angle—largely determine direction, a combination of the

The ball starts in the direction the clubhead takes through the hitting area.

shot's starting direction and any curvature. On full swings, the ball basically starts out in the direction the clubhead takes through the hitting area, as the ball is propelled by forward momentum. If the ball then curves in the air, it means the clubface was not square to this path at the moment of impact.

Distance is a function of the three remaining impact factors. Clubhead speed is the most obvious: The faster the clubhead is moving at impact, the harder the strike and the longer the shot. But club-

The angle of the clubface at impact dictates the way a shot curves.

All else being equal, higher clubhead speed means longer shots.

head speed is wasted if contact is not made on the sweet spot of the clubface; in fact, center-face contact is one of the least discussed yet most important factors in maximizing distance. Off-center hits can also influence shot direction, as they cause a twisting of the clubface through impact, but not as much as swing path or face angle.

Face Facts

On full shots, the path of the clubhead through the hitting area primarily determines the shot's starting direction. In some cases, this is not true, due to a circumstance called "clubface override." In short, this means that if the clubface is dramatically open or closed at impact, it can have more of an influence on starting direction than the path. In effect, the clubface angle overrides the path.

Finally, we have the angle of approach, or how level to the ground the clubhead is traveling when it meets the ball. This incoming angle determines not only the initial launch angle of the shot but also the amount of backspin the clubface imparts on the ball by way of a descending hit. Since backspin creates height and height reduces distance, the approach angle has a major impact on how far the ball goes.

So that's distance and direction in a nutshell. Now let's see how these impact factors produce golf's most common mishits. Better still, you will find out how to wipe these bad shots from your full-swing repertoire.

Slicing

You may think there are dozens of reasons why the ball slices. Not true. There is actually only one root cause of the slice: an open clubface at impact. By this I mean the clubface points to the right of the path of the clubhead. For example, if the clubhead tracks straight down the target line through impact and the clubface points right of the target, the ball will pick up left-to-right sidespin from contact with the angled clubface. And sidespin is what makes the ball curve in the air.

But what causes the clubface to be open at impact? This is where the analysis can get a bit thick, so let's focus on two areas that plague most of the slicing population. The first culprit is a "weak" grip, where the hands are turned too far to the left on the handle at address. With this grip, when the hands are pulled into their natural positions by centrifugal force on the downswing, as discussed in "The Grip," the clubface flares open, resulting in a shot that spins off to the right.

The simple truth is that many slicers could straighten out their ball flight with a slight adjustment to their grip. They simply need to rotate their hands farther to the right on the handle, seeing about three knuckles on the left hand at address, and to make sure they hold the grip in their fingers, not their palms. With a better grip, the clubface will square up through impact and shot shape will improve dramatically.

The other major contributor to the slice is a failure to rotate the club through impact. Consider this: In a relaxed, rhythmic swing, the arms naturally release the club, the right forearm rotating over the left through the hitting area and therefore

Why Your Driver Slices Most

Left-to-right sidespin causes the ball to slice; backspin causes it to rise. In most shots, these opposing forces battle it out in the air. As a rule, the lower the loft on the club being used, the less backspin is imparted on the ball, which lets sidespin win the battle. This is why your driver slices worse than any other club in your bag: It has the least loft and imparts the most true sidespin on the ball.

closing the clubface. Unfortunately, many slicers have excessive hand and arm tension, which retards this rotation and leaves the clubface wide open at impact.

To promote a proper release, slicers need to soften their hands and arms, starting with a lighter grip, and let the swinging force of the clubhead turn the right forearm over the left. There's no need to strangle the club to prepare for impact; your body will naturally increase grip pressure to absorb the hit. Remember, a well-timed release will happen automatically—if you stay relaxed and simply let it.

Tense arms fail to rotate through impact, leaving the clubface open.

Without tension, the arms rotate and close the face.

BEST TIP: Turn Your Back on a Slice

Here's a drill to help you feel a full release. Take your address with a mid-iron, then shift your feet 90 degrees to your right, putting your back to the target and the ball off your left side. Hit some balls from this awkward position, half-swings at first. Since the swing can't extend much down the line, your arms are forced to release—right forearm rotating over left—promoting a closed clubface and right-to-left ball flight. After several swings, go back to your normal stance and try to feel the release.

—Rick McCord, *GOLF Magazine* Top 100 Teacher

Hooking

Since the slice and the hook send the ball in opposite directions, it makes sense that they stem from opposite faults. In fact, take everything just said about the slice and turn it the other way and there you have the hook, starting with a closed clubface at impact, which causes the ball to spin from right to left off the clubface and curve to the left.

Again, there are many ways to arrive at impact with a closed clubface, but we'll concentrate on two: a "strong" grip, with the hands turned too far to the right on the handle; and an early release, the hands and arms rotating prematurely on the downswing. If the hands start out in a strong position on the club, the force of the downswing will roll the clubface closed by impact, as the hands seek out their natural positions.

To correct a strong grip, simply turn the hands farther to the left on the handle at address, with the back of the left hand pointing more toward the target and the thumbs more on top of the handle. This will delay the closing rotation of the clubface on the downswing until after impact and thereby produce a straighter ball flight.

Clearly, a strong grip goes hand in hand with an early release, or excessive hand and arm rotation

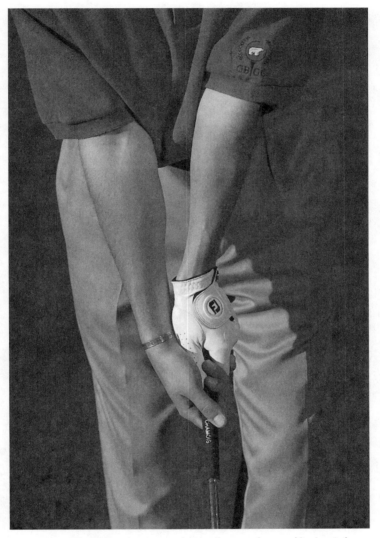

Strong grip: hands turned too far to the golfer's right.

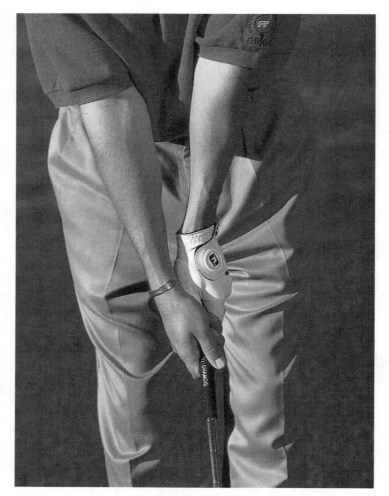

A neutral grip helps keep the clubface square.

before impact. Players who hook tend to create too much rotation with a quick, overactive right hand at the start of the downswing. Focus on letting the lower body start the downswing, keeping the right hand and arm relaxed and passive. Don't forget,

> ### BEST TIP: Swing an Inverted Club
>
> To tame an overactive right hand and arm, turn your driver upside down, grip it around the hosel, and make some practice swings. Try to position the "swoosh" of the swing immediately after the spot where impact would be made. This trains you to save the fast point in your swing for the moment of impact.
>
> —Mike Lopuszynski, *GOLF Magazine*
> Top 100 Teacher

the release should happen by itself; allow the momentum of the clubhead to create the rotation.

Pulling

Like the hook, a pulled shot flies wide left of the target. The difference is the hook curves left, while the pull starts left and flies straight on that line. This type of ball flight tells us two things about impact: First, the swing path cut across the target line from out to in, producing a shot that starts left; and second, the clubface was square to the path, as the ball did not curve in the air.

We should note here that although path and clubface angle combine to determine the direction of every shot, one usually has more influence than the other, based on the loft of the club being used.

Since loft creates backspin and backspin counters the effect of sidespin, the more lofted the club, the less sidespin will affect the shape of the shot. As a result, direction in the more lofted clubs comes more from swing path than clubface angle. Conversely, the less lofted clubs impart relatively little backspin and therefore are more affected by the sidespin imparted by an open or closed clubface. This is why you can pull a 9-iron and slice a driver with the same swing and impact positions.

> ## When Face Matters More
>
> On full swings, swing path *primarily* determines a shot's starting direction, but it's actually a combination of path and clubface angle at impact. The slower the swing, the bigger the influence from clubface angle, as there's less forward propulsion. In fact, on the shortest shots—chips and putts—the starting direction is almost entirely determined by face angle at impact. With these shots, the ball simply deflects off the clubface in whatever direction it's facing.

Perhaps the two most common reasons for the pull are playing the ball too far forward in the stance and swinging "over the top" on the downswing. With the ball way up in the stance, the arms are forced to reach forward at address, which shifts the shoulders left, or "open" to the target. Since the arms tend to swing the club in the same direction that the shoulders are aligned, the swing path will tend to be out to in and the ball will start left.

Swinging over the top often leads to a pulled shot.

Let the lower body lead the downswing to keep the club inside.

First, check to make sure the ball is positioned correctly, and never farther forward than the left heel. It's also a good idea to confirm that your shoulders are not simply open to the target, as that alone could result in a yanked shot to the left. Check shoulder alignment by holding a club across your shoulders and seeing where it points.

Swinging over the top refers to the path of the clubhead on the downswing being over the top of, or steeper than, the path taken on the backswing. This often is caused by starting the downswing with the arms and shoulders, instead of the lower body, and therefore throwing the clubhead out of its natural inside path.

BEST TIP: *For the Heel of It*

Setting up with the ball off the heel of the club-face encourages an in-to-out swing path through impact, as you feel like you have to reroute the club closer to your body to find the center of the clubface. This is a great visual cue for correcting the out-to-in swing path that produces pulls and slices. In fact, look carefully and you'll notice many Tour players address the ball off the heel. Try it and see if your shots straighten out.

—Jim Flick, *GOLF Magazine*
Master Teaching Professional

Fixing an over-the-top downswing requires special attention to sequence of motion at the change of direction. Focus on letting the downswing occur from the ground up, keeping your back turned to the target and your torso coiled until the lower body pulls them into action. This will drop the club onto the desirable inside path to the ball.

Pushing

Often confused with its more popular cousin, the slice, the push is a shot that starts and flies straight right of the target. There is no midair curvature, which is what distinguishes it from the slice. Similar to the pulled shot, the push results from a swing path that cuts across the target line, in this case from in to out.

Two leading causes of the push are playing the ball too far back in the stance and sliding the hips too aggressively toward the target on the downswing. With the ball well back, the shoulders are pulled into a "closed" position, aligned at or right of the target, and the swing will tend to be in to out. Also, a back ball position doesn't give the clubhead enough time to start tracking down the target line by impact; in effect, contact is made too early in the swing. As a result, the ball is sent out to the right.

When the hips slide out in front, the typical result is a push.

To get rid of this problem, simply keep tabs on your ball position, making sure it never creeps into the back half of your stance or even near the middle with your longer clubs.

As for the hip slide toward the target on the downswing, this is the result of a good thing taken too far. The hips *should* move toward the target as you swing down, but when they slide too far, the upper body must hang back to maintain balance, which drops the clubhead back behind the right hip. From there, the swing path cannot get back on

Think "shift, then turn" to calm overactive hips.

the target line by impact and the ball is pushed directly to the right.

To contain this lateral move, simply reorder your aggressiveness. Instead of sliding hard toward the target, try to make a slight lateral bump with the hips and then make an aggressive turn to the left. This will keep your upper body more stacked over your lower body and prevent the clubhead from getting stuck behind you.

BEST TIP: Slide Check

One good way to check how much your lower body is sliding on the downswing is to hit balls with the backs of your legs up against the back of a chair. Set up a folding chair facing directly away from you so that the top-back portion of the chair touches the backs of your thighs at address. Hit mid-iron shots with the chair in place. You'll be able to evaluate lateral movement in the lower body because you will feel your legs sliding along the back of the chair.

—Bill Moretti, *GOLF Magazine* Top 100 Teacher

Hitting Fat

While this blunder needs little introduction, the fat shot occurs when the club contacts the ground before the ball; in fact, the clubface often doesn't touch the ball at all, as a cushion of turf gets trapped between the two. The result, aside from a dead feeling in the hands at impact, is a dramatic reduction in clubhead speed and a miserably short ball flight.

Two of the more common causes of the fat shot are hunching over too much at address and dipping into the ball on the downswing. Let's start with address: If the upper body is slumped over and the

Being too hunched over at address often leads to heavy contact.

Get in a posture that will let your arms fully extend into the ball.

BEST TIP: *The Light Touch*

To ensure solid contact, your body posture must stay constant from setup through impact. To check this, take your normal address with a 5-iron, then stand the club vertically on its toe and hold it with just the index finger of your left hand. Practice swinging your right arm back and down, concentrating on keeping the club vertical and the pressure from your finger consistent (see photo at right). If you can do that, you're maintaining your address posture.

—Bruce Hamilton, *GOLF Magazine*
Top 100 Teacher

---

legs straight in the setup, the arms tend to "get lazy" and bend at the elbows. Then, when centrifugal force straightens the arms on the downswing, the true radius of the swing is realized and the swing lever becomes longer than it was at address. As a result, the clubhead bottoms out into the ground before reaching the ball.

To combat this posture problem, make sure you set up with a lively flex in your knees and that your left arm is fairly straight, although not rigid. You want to feel like you're swinging the club more around your body than up and down, giving centrifugal force a chance to fully extend your

arms and fire the clubhead into the back of the ball.

The other major cause, dipping down into impact, often occurs as a desperate recovery for a lifting action made on the backswing. Problem is, if you dip down a hair more than you lifted up, which is often the case, the clubhead will dive into the ground behind the ball. Again, a good setup goes a long way toward fixing this fault, as good posture is easier to maintain than poor posture.

Get into a relaxed, athletic position at address, then focus on winding your body over your right leg and then letting it unwind over your left leg, staying at the same height throughout. Maintaining the flex in your knees and the forward tilt of your spine through impact is the key to consistently returning the clubhead to the ball. If these critical angles are compromised, contact becomes a game of chance.

Popping Up

Pop-ups occur mostly on teed shots, especially driver shots, as they are caused by the clubhead glancing the ball on a steep descent and making contact on the very top portion of the clubface. Most pop-ups result from the player lunging toward the target with his upper body on the downswing and therefore having to drop the club steeply to get it back to the ball.

The ball flight of a pop-up is not only high but also very short, making it not exactly the most playable card in the deck. The height comes from the steep angle of approach, with the clubhead

Lunging the upper body forward causes pop-ups off the tee.

Keep your head behind the ball for a shallow approach.

grazing the ball on its way to the ground, thereby imparting a tremendous amount of backspin. This glancing contact transfers little energy from the clubhead to the ball, producing a shot without much forward momentum.

The steep swings that produce pop-ups are characterized by an up-and-down chopping motion with the arms. The best way to flatten out a steep swing is to add body turn. Since the shoulders move on a more horizontal plane than the arms, focusing on turning the shoulders leads to a shallower approach into the ball. But in order to trust that you'll make solid contact with a shallow approach, you must keep your head and upper body behind the ball through impact. That will correct the body lunge.

BEST TIP: Swing Uphill for Solid Contact

To learn to deliver the clubhead solidly at impact, practice hitting mid-iron shots from an uphill lie. The slope forces you to swing under and through the ball, which you can accomplish only by lowering your right shoulder. Hitting from an upslope also provides instant feedback: If the right shoulder stays high, a common mistake, the club will chop down into the hill. Think about swinging the clubhead up the slope rather than into it.

—Dana Rader, *GOLF Magazine* Top 100 Teacher

Hitting Thin

Flush shots occur when the clubface contacts the bottom half of the ball, except with the driver, when impact is more toward the middle. However, on most shots when the face meets the ball at or near its equator, you experience thin contact and a hollow feel that reverberates up the shaft and into your hands. The result is a line-drive trajectory and minimal backspin. However, the thin shot does approximate the distance of a well-struck shot, as the clubhead still meets the ball at full speed.

As with the fat shot, thin contact can be traced back to the setup. The player who overflexes his knees tends to set his spine too upright and is therefore asking for thin shots. Such posture promotes a very shallow, rounded swing plane, with the clubhead skimming the ground through impact. While this can be a beneficial swing shape for tee shots, it does not lead to pure strikes with the rest of the clubs.

Is It Fat or Thin?

It's commonly called a "drop-kick" when the clubhead hits the ground and ricochets into the ball. I suppose it qualifies as a fat shot, because the clubhead bottoms out into the ground, but it certainly feels thin, as contact occurs high on the ball. For advice on how to avoid this ugly mishit, see the discussion on reverse weight shift under "Hitting Thin," as most drop-kicks can be traced back to that fault.

If the weight moves left going back, it will fall right coming down.

To promote good posture, make sure you tilt your upper body first when taking your address, then flex your knees slightly to balance your weight on your insteps. Flexing the knees first leads to excessive flex and therefore a more upright spine, as posture is a balance of the two.

Another common cause of thin shots is the reverse weight shift, where the body weight moves to the left foot on the backswing and the right foot on

Loading onto your right side sets up a shift back to the target.

the downswing. When the weight shifts away from the target at impact, the left shoulder tilts upward, which starts the clubhead swinging upward to soon, leading to contact high on the ball. The thinner the contact, meaning higher on the ball, the lower and shorter the ball flight.

The key to combating a reverse weight shift is loading your body weight onto your right foot going back, led by a wide extension of the arms away

> ### BEST TIP: Practice in a Fairway Bunker
>
> Because of the lack of solid footing, hitting balls from a fairway bunker is a great way to promote proper weight movement. If you make a reverse weight shift in a bunker, you're likely to lose your balance. Hitting from sand teaches you to keep the lower body quiet, letting your weight transfer naturally to your rear foot going back and to your front foot coming down. It will also help improve the tempo of your swing.
>
> —Todd Sones, GOLF Magazine Top 100 Teacher

from the ball. If you can load up going back, your weight will naturally transfer to your left foot coming down. With your weight driving forward, you set up the descending angle of approach necessary to pinch the ball off the ground.

Topping

Hitting thin shots is bad enough, but topping the ball may be the golfer's most embarrassing miss. A topped shot is essentially a shot hit so thinly that the leading edge of the clubface contacts the ball above its equator, causing the ball to compress into the ground and dribble only a short distance.

The topped shot can have a devastating effect on the golfer's psyche. For one, topping is associated with beginners, who lift their heads anxiously in an effort to see where the ball is going. The problem is that lifting your head means lifting the arc of your swing as well, which pulls the clubhead well off the ground at impact.

Experienced golfers sometimes still make the mistake of peeking too soon, but more likely their topped shots come from the same faults that cause thin shots, only exaggerated. They make such a severe reverse weight shift and put so much weight on their rear leg at impact that the rising arc of the clubhead nearly misses the ball completely.

When the weight transfer problem is this dramatic, it's a good idea to set extra weight on the rear foot at address. This presets the loading action normally performed on the backswing and promotes a forward shift on the downswing, driving the body through the shot.

Topping can also result from a premature unhinging of the wrists, or scooping action, on the downswing, often caused by an overactive right hand. If this occurs and the clubhead passes the hands before impact, the swing arc is rising and contact will be high on the ball—slightly high means a thin shot, higher means a topped shot.

> ### *BEST TIP: Get to Your Front Foot*
>
> Topping often results from hanging back on your right side. Here's a good way to find out if your weight is getting back to your left foot by impact. Tee a ball a half inch off the ground and hit it with a 5-iron. But here's the kicker: Take a divot after impact without disturbing the tee. To hit a teed ball solidly and then take a divot, your weight has to be transferred to your front foot, with your upper body well into its forward rotation.
>
> —Craig Shankland, *GOLF Magazine*
> Top 100 Teacher

Shanking

Nothing strikes fear in the hearts of golfers like the shank, golf's mysterious malady. It occurs when the hosel of the club, instead of the clubface, contacts the ball and sends it darting off to the right. Many players won't even utter the word "shank" on the golf course out of fear that it might somehow bring on a bout of these alarming mishits.

But they're only as mysterious as you make them. The shank only rears its ugly head when the hosel of the clubhead moves closer to the ball at impact than it was at address. The problem could be that you're simply standing too close to the ball and your arms reroute the club during the swing into a less cramped

If your weight goes to your toes, you're asking for a shank.

To conquer the shanks, keep your weight toward your heels and your arms relaxed.

position. But most shanks happen for one of two reasons: Either the arms tense up and pull out away from the body on the downswing or the upper body leans toward the ball. Both can send the shot hard right.

Treating a case of the shanks has to start in the mind. After you hit one, let it go and approach the next shot with a positive and confident attitude— easy to say, tough to do. At address, make sure your hands are set a comfortable distance from your thighs, about the width of your hand, giving your arms room to swing back. As for the swing, which tends to become a short, tense swipe after a few shanks, take some deep, calming breaths and focus on keeping your weight toward your heels from setup to finish and making a smooth swing, with the arms staying soft through impact. Remember, every new swing is a chance to do something spectacular.

BEST TIP: Shank Cure

Place two balls side by side on the ground, about an inch apart. Address the ball that's farther from you, then swing and try to hit the near ball. If you can consistently hit the near ball, you're pulling the club closer to you during the swing—the opposite of a shank swing— and putting your move back on track.

—Martin Hall, *GOLF Magazine*
Master Teaching Professional

4

Practice

To many golfers, "practice" is a dirty word. They'd rather say "hitting balls" or "going to the range," which says a lot about how slack and unstructured their practice habits are. I'm not going to start preaching here, but if you see the practice tee as a place where you blow off some steam or have long-drive contests with your buddies, fine; just don't expect it to help your golf game. Hitting balls may be enjoyable, but you need to have a purpose to make it productive.

For starters, realize that you can change your golf swing. You can learn to hit the ball longer, straighter, higher—whatever you like. Sure, some faults are tougher to overcome than others, but if you know where you want to improve and implement a plan, how well you progress is up to you.

Practice hard and you may quickly see dramatic improvement; take it slowly and you'll have to wait. But you have to believe it will come along. Your efforts will be rewarded.

Practicing and Playing

You may find this hard to believe, but some golfers actually like to practice. They like the feeling of grooving their swing during long hours on the practice tee, finding the secret "in the dirt," as Ben Hogan used to say. Others would opt for a root canal over a bucket of balls. Instead, they spend their golf time on the course, engaged in battles with Old Man Par.

Most golfers fall into the latter group, claiming to have neither the time nor the motivation for the practice tee. In many cases, the real culprit is a lack of structure to their practice sessions. Twenty minutes of ball-beating, the last fifteen with the driver, and they start getting bored or tired, wondering why they're not playing golf. They're right to call these sessions meaningless, as practice without a purpose is simply time wasted.

First, understand that practicing and playing golf are totally different activities. In practice, you work on the mechanics of the swing, trying to achieve certain positions or moves. On the course, the game changes, the object is to forget about mechanics and focus on hitting targets. Sure, you're using the swing you've grooved on the practice tee, but most golfers play their best when they put aside thoughts of swing technique.

The good news is, you can learn things on the golf course—in fact, you need to. Since there is often no correlation between how well you perform on the range and how well you play, you need to keep track of where your game falters on the course. Are poor drives leading to double bogeys? Are you missing all your approaches to one side? Do you have trouble getting out of the rough? These are the types of questions you need to ask yourself, and the answers can only come from a careful analysis of your rounds.

If you watch the pros at Tour events, they often spend more time on the range after they play than before. They know that the intensity of playing "live" shots, having one swing to pull them off, exposes your weaknesses and shows how much you trust your swing. Heading to the range right after the round, when the highs and lows are still fresh in your mind, leads to a more focused, productive practice session.

You should also take advantage of practicing on the course whenever you can. The practice tee doesn't offer all the challenges of a round of golf, such as driving between tight treelines, playing from uneven lies, and hitting out of deep rough.

This is one reason to play an occasional round by yourself when the course isn't busy: You can play an extra ball or two from these situations to familiarize yourself with the strategy required.

BEST TIP: *Rehearsal Swings*

Think of practice swings on the course as "dress rehearsals" for the shot at hand. To accomplish this, you must have a clear image of the shot, with consideration for the lie of the ball, the overall terrain, and the distance and trajectory. Then pick a specific object on the ground, such as a broken tee or a dandelion, and try to strike it with your practice swing. This will focus your attention and lead to an accelerating, descending blow, just as you want in your actual swing.

—Eddie Merrins, *GOLF Magazine*
Top 100 Teacher

Home on the Range

The practice tee is the ideal spot for practicing or warming up before a round. Unfortunately, many golfers think these activities are one and the same. Truth is, practicing involves working on your technique, while warming up is simply a way of getting your golf muscles ready to play.

As for practicing, every session should begin with a plan. What has lead you to the practice tee? What do you hope to accomplish? Too many amateurs toil away, beating balls with blind fury, without thinking much about what they're doing. It's not enough to just put in the practice time; you have to take a critical look at where you need improvement, and then map out a plan to get there, including when to practice and what clubs, shots, or practice drills to work on.

Here are a few hints for getting started. Begin each practice session at the putting green. Stroke some short putts, then some lag putts, and hit a handful of chips and pitches before heading to the range. You might ask, "Why bother with the small stuff?" Because even the shortest putt is the golf swing in miniature—fewer moving parts but the same objective. It makes sense to start simple, where the targets are easier to hit and the swing is less complicated, and to build on the motion as you go.

Once you get to the practice tee, follow the same philosophy as above, starting with the short irons and gradually working your way up to the longer clubs. Whatever you're hitting, it's critical to pick a target for each shot, using range flags or target greens if possible, or at least a landmark on the horizon. Also, lay clubs on the ground as alignment guides,

Even short putts are the golf swing in miniature.

Use clubs on the ground to develop good alignment habits.

one at your toes and another just outside the ball, to make sure you're aimed where you think you are. Get into the habit of structuring your sessions.

Fine-Tuning

Most golfers practice to become more consistent when they play, to fine-tune what they have, not to make major swing changes. That being the case, the key is to simulate on-course situations as much as possible. To do this, imagine the confines of a fairway or the surface of a green and take aim on every swing. Use the treelines or boundary fences on the range as obstacles and play shots from different lies, even hitting out of a divot hole now and then. Also, change targets frequently, just as you do on the course.

When you have some time, do yourself a favor and find out how far you hit each club. Hit ten balls with each club in your bag, perhaps splitting it over two sessions, and figure out the average carry for each. Don't take the best shot with each—estimate the *average*. Too many golfers make club selections based on the maximum yardage they can stretch out of a given club. They think they can reproduce that distance every day. Avoid one of the biggest playing faults among amateurs by establishing a realistic distance for each club.

Practice Trajectory

Every round of golf presents situations where you need to hit a shot either over or under an intervening obstacle, such as a tree limb. Although it's tough to convince yourself to spend valuable range balls on trouble shots, you should spend a few minutes every so often trying to control trajectory. Practice high and low shots, as well as draws and fades—you'll need them all sooner than you're willing to admit.

Another valuable use of practice time is working on your tempo. Extended practice sessions, provided you aren't just blistering drive after drive, loosen your muscles and groove good rhythm. When the clubhead starts to feel heavy and you can sense the pull of centrifugal force during the swing, your muscles are warm and performing at their best. Try to internalize this feeling of relaxed power and recall it on the golf course.

You should also hit some shots going through your entire preshot routine, starting from behind the ball just as you should on the course. This can be tedious, so work out a system you can faithfully adhere to. Dr. Richard Coop, *GOLF Magazine*'s Mental Game Consultant, recommends performing the preshot routine before every fifth shot—that's about all most golfers have patience for.

Finally, don't try to be somebody you're not when you practice. If you get bored after thirty minutes, go back to the putting green for a while,

On the range, practice your preshot routine, too.

or take a short break. The trick is to make each shot count: If you're practicing with a friend, play a game of closest to the pin; if you're alone, put yourself on the last hole of the U.S. Open. When your mind wanders elsewhere, you're no longer practicing effectively. Come back another day.

> ### *BEST TIP: Groove Good Tempo*
>
> If your swing tends to get fast, especially on the range, hit balls with the image of a good finish position in your mind: arms and club high, chest facing the target, weight on the outside of the front foot. As you swing, hold on to this image and try to match it. You'll start thinking about swinging the club instead of hitting the ball, and as a result, you'll slow down and gain control.
>
> —Johnny Myers, *GOLF Magazine*
> Top 100 Teacher

Making Changes

Some trips to the practice tee are made out of necessity. Every golfer's swing slips off track now and then, requiring critical attention. The range is the perfect place—the only place—to work on swing mechanics. Playing golf with your mind cluttered with mechanical thoughts, such as swing plane or weight shift, is a recipe for frustration. The body works best when the mind stays out of its way. That means trusting your mechanics.

There are a couple of viable ways to improve your swing mechanics. First, you can seek the help of a PGA professional, whose experience and expertise can put you on the right path. It may cost you a few bucks, but in time you will almost certainly improve. Or, you can go it alone, using the lessons you read in books and magazines. This is a trickier proposition, as the golf swing can be deceptive—you aren't always doing what you think you're doing. That's why it's a good idea to periodically record your swing on video and review it as objectively as possible.

When working on a specific part of your swing, such as your takeaway or your position at the top, isolate your thinking to that area. This is one time when ball flight doesn't really matter; the key is grooving the proper sensation and getting it on video for later analysis. It's also advisable to make shorter, slower swings when changing your technique, as your body will more easily incorporate the changes, and to use clubs with which you're most comfortable—say, a 7-iron instead of a driver.

The problem with focusing on one particular area is that the golf swing is a single flowing motion. Sure, there are swing positions and checkpoints along the way, but motion is the glue that holds them all together. To make sure you never lose sight of this, always intersperse normal swings between any drills or modified swings you're working on. And if things ever get real ugly, make some swings, even half-swings, thinking only about producing smooth tempo back and through.

When making a swing change, focus your work in one area.

Warming Up

If you have the luxury of hitting balls before you play, by all means do it. But keep in mind that your objective is to ready your body for golf, not to practice. Tinkering with your swing before you play leads to mechanical thoughts on the course, and that spells trouble: confusion in your head, tension in your body, and big numbers on the scorecard.

The warm-up, like the practice session, should start on the putting green, where you can regain a feel for the basic golf stroke and for aiming at targets.

Playing Well? Take a Lesson

It makes perfect sense that the only time most golfers pay a visit to their local pro is when their game has left them. But consider taking a lesson when your swing feels right and you're hitting the ball the way you like. It's a good idea to have your pro see how your "A" game looks, even get it on video to check against that other swing that surfaces now and then. This is precisely what the Tour players do with their teachers.

From there, a few chips or pitches are useful, if time permits. Most golfers are eager to get to the practice tee, which is where you really need to discipline yourself. As tempting as it is to grab a full bucket of balls and start whacking them into outer space, stick to a simple plan, such as the following:

• Stretch your big rotational muscles. Standing up straight, hold a club across your back and practice turning to your right, then your left. Slowly assume your golf posture as you turn, tilting your upper body forward and flexing your knees.

• Rehearse the swinging motion. Take two clubs in a baseball grip and swing them back and through several times, increasing speed as you go. The extra weight will get the blood pumping to your hands, wrists, and arms.

• Start with half-wedge shots. Focus on smooth tempo and crisp contact, then hit some full shots with your wedge or another short iron.

> ### BEST TIP: How to Use Video
>
> Video is an indispensable tool in monitoring the golf swing. Have a friend film your swing from three angles: face-on (facing your chest), down-target (target in the background), and rear view (facing your back). To ensure consistency from session to session, shoot from the same exact perspective every time: From face-on and rear view, set the camera in line with the leading edge of the clubface; from down-target, align the camera halfway between the stance and the ball. Video sessions are always revealing—even with the world's best players.
>
> —Robert Baker, *GOLF Magazine*
> Master Teaching Professional

Pick a target for each shot and try to make all your actions relaxed and unhurried. Tension is reflected in every swing.

- Hit a handful of mid-irons. Again your focus should be establishing good rhythm and zeroing in on a target. If you've hit more than fifteen shots at this point, slow down—the worst thing you can do now is slip into rapid-fire mode.

- Play a few tee shots. Notice I didn't say "launch" or "pound" or "rip." Many amateurs kick their swing speed up a notch when they pull out the big stick. Remember why you're there: to warm up your muscles, not test their limits.

- Cool down with a wedge. By now you're ready to go, but you don't want to head off to the first tee with an aggressive mind-set. Go back to the wedge and pitch a few balls to a very demanding target, such as a range flag or even a single ball.

- Roll a few more. If you still have time to kill, stroke some short putts. Don't worry if you make or miss them, just enjoy the smooth motion that warm muscles produce. The critical point is not to waste your warm-up session by sitting idle until it's time to go. Now you're ready to play some golf.

The *GOLF Magazine*

Complete Guide to Golf

Book Five

Short Game

Peter Morrice

and the Editors of *GOLF Magazine*

Photography by Sam Greenwood

Introduction

What's the big deal about the short game? Green-side shots are not that hard to execute and even if you do totally bungle them, the consequences aren't exactly devastating. I mean, when's the last time you chipped a ball out of bounds or lost your Saturday Nassau on a poor bunker shot. Never, right?

Well, yes and no. You see, the short game—chipping, pitching, bunker shots, and the like—is stuck between the flashiness of the full swing and the finality of putting. After all, every hole starts with a tee shot and finishes with a putt. Errors around the green aren't as obvious because they're neither as dramatic as full-swing errors, where the ball can fly 40 or 50 yards off-line, nor as definitive as putting errors, which seem to make the difference between bogeys and pars, between the 80s and the 90s.

But the short game has hidden significance. For instance, when you chip from the fringe to eight feet then miss the putt for par, do you blame poor putting for a failed up-and-down? Probably. Would you dwell on a topped tee shot or a chunked chip after making a double bogey? Chances are, you'll remember that humiliating drive for the rest of the day. This is human nature: We want pretty shots and low scores. In the mix, golfers lose sight of the short game—the shots that allow them to recover from that poor drive or make that makable putt . . . well, *makable*.

Think of how many holes you play during a typical round without using your wedges, without chipping or pitching or blasting your way onto the green. Not many, I bet. And if you're using those wedges two or three times a hole, that's a good indication that your short game needs help. That's okay; most short games do. The real problem is that most golfers don't really analyze this part of their game, certainly not like they do their golf swing.

This book invites you to do just that—and then to do something about it. In the pages that follow you will find all the setup and swing keys for playing the standard chip, pitch, and bunker shots, as well as many other "specialty shots." You'll also find tips on greenside decision-making, strategy, the mental game, and how to best use your practice time. In addition, tips from Tour pros and many of *GOLF Magazine*'s Top 100 Teachers are included in a recurring feature called "Best Tip." Assembled from the archives of *GOLF Magazine,* these represent the finest short-game tips we've come across in our forty years of publishing golf instruction.

So, with some of the know-how presented in this book, and a little practice, you can dramatically improve your play around the greens. It really is up to you.

1

Chipping

Let's put some meaning to the "short" in short game. Here's the number-one rule in greenside play: Produce the "shortest" ball flight with the "shortest" possible swing that allows you to get the ball to the hole.

And what does that mean? It means keep the swing simple and get the ball rolling as soon as possible. If you can commit this concept to memory and recall it often, you'll save yourself countless strokes around the green. And that means lower scores, the quest for which no doubt has led you to this book.

Okay, so it's not quite that simple. Let me attach two conditions to our "short" philosophy. First, although you want the shortest ball flight, you should land the ball on the green whenever possible, where you'll get the most predictable bounce. Shoot to land the ball a yard or two onto the putting surface to allow some room for error on the short side.

The second condition involves the length of the swing. You want it to be as short as it can be, provided you maintain a smooth, natural rhythm from start to finish. In other words, don't make your backswing so short that you have to jerk the club on your downswing to get enough power. If you feel as if you have to help the club back down, your backswing is too short.

Let this rule, with its two conditions, guide your greenside play. If you do, you'll soon discover that most short shots can be run along the ground. Simply put, chipping is the backbone of the short game. It's the highest percentage play you can make, driven by a simple single-lever motion, with the left arm and the club essentially staying in a straight line from setup to finish. The swing is short and repeatable, and the ball flies low and rolls most of the way to the hole.

It's fitting that our analysis start with the standard chip shot. It may not be the most exciting shot in the game, but it is the easiest to learn and the safest to employ. In the words of the immortal Bobby Jones, "The chip is the great economist of golf."

What Is a Chip?

The first step in becoming a smarter, more effective player around the greens is understanding your options, understanding the difference between a chip, a pitch, a lob, and so on. Once you know the characteristics of each shot, you can confidently choose among them in a given situation, knowing that you have picked the right play. Such confidence breeds success.

The chip shot is generally thought to be any short shot that flies no more than a third of its total distance and rolls at least two thirds. Keep in mind these are the outside parameters that apply when chipping with a wedge; chips played with a short or middle iron can roll as much as five or six times farther than they carry in the air.

The chip shot comes with little risk. Its objective is to bump the ball out of the grass and onto the edge of the green. Except for a putt, it's the simplest motion in golf, and the simpler the motion, the less the chance of something going wrong. Add this to

The chip shot rolls at least two-thirds of its total distance.

the fact that a rolling ball is more predictable than a flying ball that can still take a bad hop when it lands, and you'll understand why the chip should be your first greenside choice.

The putting stroke is even safer, but putting from off the green requires an excellent lie and smooth ground the whole way. Otherwise, the chip is a better bet. Remember, your objective should be to minimize risk: Putt before you chip; chip before you pitch; pitch before you lob. Keep that in mind and you're on your way to getting the most out of your game around the greens.

When Not to Chip

For all its good qualities, there are times when a chip shot is the wrong choice. If you have to carry the ball more than a third of the way to the hole due to intervening obstacles, such as deep rough or sand, you should play a more lofted shot. The worst swing thought you can have around the green is that you have to help the ball into the air to land safely on the green. When this notion crosses your mind, stop and rethink your shot.

Likewise, when hitting to an elevated green, you may need more height than a standard chip provides to carry the ball onto the putting surface. Try-

---

BEST TIP: Grip-Down Drill

Good chipping demands firm wrists through impact and free body rotation back and through. To ingrain these fundamentals, practice your chipping motion with your hands choked down to the shaft and the butt of the grip touching your left side. Keeping the grip against your ribs, swing the clubhead back and through in the air, noting how your wrists remain stable and your body turns back and through with the swinging motion.

—Carl Welty, *GOLF Magazine* Top 100 Teacher

---

ing to bounce your ball into or up a slope is unpredictable. Plan your first bounce to be on the putting surface itself, where the ground usually is more level and the grass is uniform.

Sometimes a poor lie in deep rough also makes a chip shot inadvisable, since the ball needs to come out high enough to keep from getting snagged by the long grass. In fact, even when the ball itself is sitting up, the grass around it must be considered: A clump of thick grass behind the ball may require a steeper downswing than the standard chip provides, and long grass in front of the ball may require a higher launch angle off the clubface.

BEST TIP: Learn to rotate your body and keep your wrists firm by choking up on a club and swinging with the grip against your left side.

So, the chip shot is not the be-all and end-all of the short game, but it should be your favorite option around the green. Whenever putting is unwise—and it often is—set your sights on chipping. If you can't make a strong case *against* chipping, you have a strong case *for* it.

How to Plan a Chip

Chip-shot execution should begin as soon as your previous shot comes to rest. Say you've missed your approach shot to the right and your ball finds an uphill lie just off a slick downhill green. The best view of this shot is probably on your walk up to the green: You can see the nature of the terrain from start to finish, where the ball should land, the incline of the lie, and the decline of the green. These subtleties are tough to judge once you're at the ball. Take full advantage of your perspective on your walk to the green.

Once you reach the ball, develop a picture in your mind as to how you want the shot to look: the bounce, the roll, the final destination. Crouch down behind the ball and read the shot like you would a putt, first picking a spot on the green for the initial bounce. Remember, this landing spot should be at least a yard onto the green to provide room for error if you catch the shot a bit heavy or thin.

Next comes club selection. There are two schools of thought on how to pick a club for chipping. One theory says develop a comfort level with a single club, say a pitching wedge, and use it for all your chip shots, adjusting the length of the swing to dictate the distance of the shot. The other theory advocates a single swing for chipping that produces different shots with different clubs, anything from a sand wedge to a 5-iron. Both are reliable methods, although changing clubs rather than adjusting your swing to produce different results is a simpler approach.

We'll get into the mechanics of the setup and swing in a moment, but first consider two preshot factors that grow in importance as you get closer to the hole: precision and relaxation. Simply put, the shorter the shot, the greater your expectation of precision. For example, if you miss a green with a 3-iron, you may not be all that upset; but if you leave a little chip shot in the long grass, you want to bite the club in half. That's because you've fallen miserably short of your expectations.

As for relaxation, shorter shots require less big-muscle motion and therefore rely more on your sense of rhythm and timing. Tension is rhythm's

To bolster feel, make swings looking down the line.

biggest enemy, making it critical to ward off stress on short shots. To do this, commit to the shot and club you've chosen and focus on executing what you see in your mind's eye. Make a few rehearsal swings in a similar lie, looking down the line and sensing the effort required, then step up and hit the ball. Don't waste time second-guessing your decisions. Extra time means extra tension. Envision, commit, rehearse, and execute.

Chipping Setup

The basic motion of the chip shot is a downward hit, the clubface contacting the ball before the club has reached the bottom of its downswing arc. This de-

Free Chips

Next time you're walking down the fairway with your wedge in hand, stop for a minute and take a few practice chipping swings, trying to brush a leaf or loose grass off the turf. You'll be surprised how smooth and rhythmic your stroke is without the prospect of a difficult shot in front of you. Try to internalize this fluid action and recall it the next time you face an intimidating chip shot.

scending action is preferred because the most important factor in chipping is clean clubface-to-ball contact, and the most reliable method for doing this is making contact while the clubhead is still in its descent. Think of it as pinching the ball against the turf.

Clean contact in chipping is critical for two reasons: First, catching grass before the ball on a chipping swing kills the momentum of the clubhead, often cutting power significantly before it reaches the ball; and second, when grass gets trapped between the clubface and the ball, the nature of the contact and the spin imparted on the ball is unpredictable. Catching grass first may work out on full shots, where the clubhead often tears through the grass with little effect, but when playing from short range, you simply cannot take the chance of making poor contact.

Every aspect of the standard chipping setup is designed to promote a descending blow and a low, running shot that lands just on the green and rolls to the hole. Here are the specifics:

Play the ball back.   Position the ball opposite your right instep and push your hands toward the target, until they're even with your left thigh. This hands-ahead position sets up a steep backswing and a descending motion at impact, with the hands leading the clubhead until well after the ball is gone.

Set your weight left.   Place 60 to 70 percent of your body weight on your left foot at address. This further encourages a downward angle of approach but also discourages weight transfer during the swing by presetting the weight on the target side, where it has to end up. Weight transfer is an unnecessary complication in chipping.

For a standard chip, set the ball back and your weight left.

Take a narrow stance.   With your heels six to eight inches apart, you'll naturally resist weight movement during the swing. Keeping the feet close together also sets you more upright and therefore nearer the ball, which increases your control of the motion, as your hands and arms stay closer to the body.

Choke down for feel.   Slide your hands down the grip until your right hand is almost to the end of the handle. This effectively shortens the club, which reduces the power of the swing and bolsters control.

Set up square to slightly open.   A square stance makes sense, as it promotes a straight clubhead path through impact, but some golfers like to open up a bit to gain a better view of the line. This is a matter of preference: If you feel comfortable standing open, it can be beneficial, but if you find yourself hitting chips off-line, by all means use a square setup.

Square the clubface.   As you move the ball back in your stance, the tendency will be to flare the clubface open. And unless you make an in-swing compensation, you all but guarantee an open clubface at impact, which will send the ball right of your intended line. To guard against this, always make sure the leading edge, or bottom, of your clubface is perpendicular to your starting line, regardless of ball position. Then you can swing away knowing your clubface will be square when it meets the ball.

BEST TIP: Looking Ahead

In chipping, a slight lean toward the target at address promotes a steep downswing and clean contact with the ball. To create this leaning action, focus your eyes on the front half of the ball as you take your stance. This will ensure that your head is slightly in front of the ball and that the shaft is angled toward the target. From there, the backswing will be fairly upright, setting up a descending blow and crisp contact.

—Laird Small, *GOLF Magazine* Top 100 Teacher

Chipping Swing

You've no doubt heard the term "one-piece take-away" to describe the first move away from the ball in the full swing. Well, this concept of starting the arms, shoulders, and club in a unified, synchronized motion is a great mental image for the chipping swing as well—not only on the takeaway, but throughout the entire motion.

Picture the chipping setup just described or, better yet, take your address facing a full-length mirror. You'll notice your arms and shoulders form a large triangle—each arm being a side and the line of your shoulders representing the third side. The key to good chipping is keeping this triangle intact from the setup to the finish, meaning it should not change shape as you swing away from the ball or through to the target. This demands that the shoulders turn at the same rate that the arms swing.

The age-old concept that chipping is a hands-and-arms motion is dead wrong. The small muscles of the hands, wrists, and forearms are the least reliable actors in the golf swing, particularly under pressure, and therefore should be prohibited from leading any motion. Instead, think of the chipping swing as a mini-turn back and a mini-turn through—a one-piece motion all the way.

Here's the basic technique for chipping:

Start relaxed. Tension in the hands, arms, or body at address virtually guarantees a quick start, from which a chipping swing will rarely recover. To prevent tension and encourage a smooth first move, hover the clubhead at address, slowly wagging it back and forth as you track your eyes down the line. Watch Raymond Floyd, one of the game's best chippers, as he stands over chip shots; he looks as if he's drawing circles in the air with his clubhead.

Swing triangle back.   Keeping your weight left and your head stock-still, move the hands, arms, and shoulders away from the ball as a single unit. This is a pendulum-type motion similar to putting, where no part of the swing outraces any other and the body center stays firmly in place.

Let the body react.   Although you shouldn't consciously hinge your wrists during the chipping swing, they should be free to react naturally to the swinging of the club. This will happen automatically if you keep your grip soft. As for your lower body, it should also feel relaxed and responsive. The knees and hips should rotate back slightly in reaction to the swinging motion, without any thought on your part.

The arms and shoulders swing the club back together.

Reverse the motion. The downswing should be a mirror image of the backswing. If you've started from a good setup position, you need not think about making the downward blow required in chipping. Simply swing the arms-and-shoulders triangle to the target, letting the clubhead naturally accelerate through impact.

Let the clubhead accelerate through the strike.

Finish to the target. Assuming you have a decent lie, there should be nothing choppy in your chipping motion. Swing the clubhead through at least as far as you swung it back, never letting your wrists flip or your shoulders stop rotating. At the finish, the clubhead should be about shin-high and your upper body should be half-turned toward the target.

Follow through with the club and your body.

Common Faults

Chipping should be a piece of cake. The motion is only slightly more complicated than a long putt, yet many amateurs struggle to even make solid contact on chip shots, sending them half or twice their intended distance. If they were to do that in putting, they'd find something else to do on Saturday mornings.

Unfortunately, many golfers have learned to live with—even expect—poor chipping. They've dismissed it as an aspect of the game that requires a degree of touch or finesse they simply don't possess. Fact is, the motion is so simple, most problems stem more from a misunderstanding of the technique than from mechanical errors that occur during the swing.

We know the number-one requirement of effective chipping is clean contact with the ball. Why, then, do so many amateurs set up with the ball forward in their stance and their weight centered or even favoring their rear foot? These positions scream trouble. If the body is set behind the ball, a crisp, downward blow is difficult to produce, leaving the clubhead little chance of meeting the ball without first catching grass. The result is usually poor contact and therefore poor distance control.

BEST TIP: *Keep It Up*

Hitting chip shots fat from greenside rough is a common problem that often results when golfers sole the clubhead behind the ball at address. You see, grounding the clubhead in effect establishes the touchdown point of the swing: If you start with the clubhead resting behind the ball, you'll tend to swing it into the ground at that spot, producing contact behind the ball. To prevent this, hover the clubhead above the grass at address, setting up a downward swing into the ball and good contact.

—Jim Flick, *GOLF Magazine*
Master Teaching Professional

To make sure you're setting up correctly, focus on two things: playing the ball off your right instep and leaning the shaft toward the target, so the butt of the grip points at your left hip. With your hands well ahead of the ball at address, you're virtually guaranteed to make a descending blow, putting the clubface on the ball without any interference. Getting the setup right is more than half the battle in chipping: The swing is so short and simple, it has little chance to slip off-track.

BEST TIP: Hover the clubhead above the ground at address to promote crisp contact with the ball.

Setting the weight right usually leads to poor contact.

Aside from a faulty setup, many golfers have a poor understanding of how the chipping motion should feel. Perhaps the most harmful piece of advice on this subject is "chip like you putt." Players who try to do this tend to rock their shoulders stiffly up and down, instead of letting them rotate around the spine as they do for every other golf shot. This rocking action makes the upper body tip toward the target on the backswing and away on the downswing, which changes the bottom of the swing arc and leads to fat chips or contact on the upswing.

Other golfers don't let the shoulders move at all. In an attempt to keep the body perfectly still, they swing the club with only their hands and arms, letting the wrists hinge and the hands take control. Problem is, when the hands dictate the backswing, they also control the downswing and that means unpredictable bursts of speed and inconsistent contact.

> ### *Chipping Ratios*
>
> *GOLF Magazine* Top 100 Teachers Paul Runyan and Phil Rodgers developed a system of carry-to-roll ratios of chip shots hit with various clubs. For instance, the carry-to-roll relationship of a standard 9-iron chip is three parts roll for every one part flight. Here are the ratios for the common chipping clubs:
>
> | Club | Carry : Roll |
> |---|---|
> | 6-iron | 1 : 6 |
> | 7-iron | 1 : 5 |
> | 8-iron | 1 : 4 |
> | 9-iron | 1 : 3 |
> | Pitching wedge | 1 : 2 |

If you try to "chip like you putt," you'll make a stiff, mechanical swing.

To correct these faulty motions, think of the chipping swing as the golf swing in miniature. When the arms swing, the shoulders must turn, and nothing should be forced not to move. Forced actions mean tension, and tension kills feel. If you think you're a bad chipper, you're probably just getting in your own way. Remember, relax and keep it natural.

Chipping Variations

While there are conditions that make chipping inadvisable, such as limited green to work with or intervening obstacles, you're often better off adapting your chipping technique slightly than selecting a riskier play. Think of the chip as your default shot: If you can't eliminate it as a viable option, it's the right choice. Consider adding these variations of the chip shot to your short-game arsenal.

The Bump-and-Run

On standard greenside chip shots, landing the ball on the green is a top priority, but there are situations when bouncing the ball short is an acceptable play. The bump-and-run, which is essentially a long chip shot, is designed to land well short of the green and bounce several times before reaching the putting surface. It can cover anywhere from 20 to 100 yards, depending on the club used and the length of the swing (experiment with different clubs to get a feel for distance). But for this to be a wise play, you need to have a firm, unimpeded path to the hole.

The bump-and-run can be effective if you have a clear path.

The technique for the bump-and-run is similar to the chip shot, with two exceptions: The ball is played in the middle of the stance, not back; and the wrists are allowed to hinge a little more to lengthen the swing. But the motion looks a lot like a long chip: Arms and shoulders move back and through together, the lower body only reacting to the movement of the arms and upper body. Using anything from an 8-iron to a 4-iron, try to clip the ball off the turf with a level, sweeping motion, imparting minimal backspin so the ball bounds forward after landing.

The Super-Short Chip

At the other end of the spectrum from the bump-and-run is the super-short chip shot. This shot is useful in those pesky situations when your ball lies in long grass just off the green and the hole is cut very close to you. You need to bump the ball out—just a few feet—and stop it quickly.

In this situation, most amateurs grab their sand wedge and try to flip the ball over the long grass. In all honesty, that requires more touch and coordination than most golfers can muster. The usual result is either a fat or skulled shot. A better plan is to pop the ball out with a modified chipping motion, keep-

On super-short chip shots, cut across the ball to deaden the hit.

ing the swing simple and limiting the chance for disaster.

Using your sand or lob wedge, open your stance and play the ball off your right instep. Then open the clubface so it points slightly right of the target. From there, simply swing the clubhead back along your stance line, keeping your wrists firm, and try to slide the clubface under the ball. Forget about the follow-through; focus on making the clubface point to the sky after impact. Your objective is to cut across the ball, imparting a weak blow that pops the ball onto the green without enough energy to get away from you.

Chipping from Poor Lies

You simply cannot predict how the clubhead will react if it catches grass, not to mention ground, before it meets the ball. The chipping swing does not have enough energy to lose horsepower before impact and still produce a decent shot. In effect, you either hit it cleanly or you're hitting it again.

Let's look at a few lies that require special consideration. How about when your ball is sitting in a patch of thick, clumpy rough? To create the contact you need, make a more upright backswing to avoid

getting the clubhead caught in the grass and to promote a steep descent to the ball.

To accomplish this, play the ball farther back in
your stance at address—off your right toe or even

Out of thick grass, play the ball farther back in your
stance and set more weight left.

the outside of your right foot. Be sure to set your weight left and start with your hands well ahead of the ball. This setup promotes the steep up-and-down motion you need from this lie. Keep in mind also that playing the ball back delofts the clubface, making a pitching wedge play like a 7- or 8-iron. Club down accordingly.

You must make similar adjustments when playing from muddy or hardpan lies. In both cases, there is no room for error in the contact department—a premature touchdown means a chunked shot. On hardpan, the clubhead will sometimes ricochet off the ground and into the middle of the ball, producing a skulled shot. Either way, the results are disastrous.

To handle such lies, select an 8- or 9-iron, play the ball in line with the outside of the right foot, and set most of your weight on your left side—even more so than when playing from thick rough. Understand that the farther back the ball and the more weight you have on your left, the steeper the swing will be, without any hinging of the wrists. From extremely firm lies, try to pinch the back of the ball against the ground. The combination of a steep downward hit and firm ground to hit against will produce lots of backspin; expect the ball to bounce a few times and check up quickly.

Sometimes a ball rolls into a perched lie on top of the grass. Good contact may seem like a no-brainer from here, but you still need to allow for a different kind of impact. These lies create cushion under the ball, as the grass, not the ground, is supporting the ball's weight. If you hit down with a standard chipping motion, the clubface will either sink in the grass, causing weak contact on the top of the clubface, or the ball will dive down into the grass before popping out. In both instances, the ball will come out weakly, and you'll feel as if you've wasted a great opportunity.

BEST TIP: Aim for Hollows

Traditional instruction says to land your greenside shots on flat areas of the green whenever possible. However, if you can plan a shot that will land in the middle of a dip or hollow, go for it. If you land short, the downslope will kick the ball forward, making up for your lack of carry. Hit the ball a little too long and you'll catch the upslope on the far side of the dip, slowing its progress. Total distance for all three shots— landing in the middle, short, or long—will be about the same, providing the largest possible margin for error.

—Dave Pelz, *GOLF Magazine* Technical and Short Game Consultant

Take advantage of this teed-up lie by hitting the ball with a more level or sweeping motion, much like a long putting stroke. Play the ball in the middle of your stance and position your eyes directly over it. From there, make a simple arms-and-shoulders swing back and through, keeping the wrists firm. The ball will pop forward with little backspin, due to the level impact angle, and roll smoothly to the hole.

When the ball is sitting up, make a level, sweeping motion.

2

Pitching

Be honest now: When you think of someone who has a great short game—whether it's Tiger Woods or your regular weekend partner—you're thinking about how he lofts the ball high in the air and drops it dead to the hole, right? You don't care much about the running shot; heck, you can skull a sand wedge and make it run. But the guy who can get some air under the ball—there's a guy who has some short-game savvy.

Well, this kind of thinking is a reality of modern golf. The player with a showy short game, who plays it high when he could go low, who makes that long wristy swing when he could play a standard chip shot, is the player who will get the reputation as a whiz around the greens. There's some-

thing innately cool about missing a green and floating a shot from the edge of disaster to three feet—
and doing it five times a round. But mostly, people
love such players because they feel they could
never be one.

The general feeling among amateurs, it seems, is
that you basically have it or you don't when it
comes to hitting high-lofted, soft-landing shots.
You're either blessed with "good hands" and the
moxie to take on difficult situations, or you want to
run and hide every time a shot calls for a little finesse. Unfortunately, most golfers would put themselves in the latter group.

Given that fact, it's amazing that so many golfers
are quick to grab their sand or lob wedge and try to
loft the ball at every opportunity. This is a great
irony: Players who have no confidence in their
greenside touch routinely choose high-lofted shots
over low-risk running shots. It's as if they have no
memory of their track record around the greens.

In most instances, they choose the shot they'd
like to play, not the one they should play. They mis-
interpret the old adage "To be a great player you
have to think like a great player." That doesn't
mean attempting shots that are way over your head
(literally) but playing the best shot, given the situation and your skill level. There are plenty of Tour

pros making millions with chinks in their short-game armor. The secret is knowing where those weak spots are and playing away from them.

But pitching the ball in the air is neither as difficult nor as mysterious as many people make it out to be. Becoming a good pitcher starts with a basic understanding of the physics of a golf shot and the design characteristics of the clubs you're using. Are some golfers naturally better than you around the greens? Sure they are; that's life. But you can get better.

What Is a Pitch?

The basic objective of a pitch shot is to get the ball into the air quickly to carry obstacles that stand between you and the hole, obstacles such as bunkers, deep rough, or water. The other end of the shot, after the ball lands safely on the green, requires a soft bounce and a quick stop, as the ball has already flown a good way to the hole.

This second part of the equation takes care of itself. You see, a high-lofted shot lands at a steeper angle to the ground, causing it to bounce more upward than forward. When this happens, the energy of the shot is exerted downward upon landing and absorbed by the ground, producing a weak rebound and little forward momentum.

In terms of flight-to-roll ratios, the pitch takes over where the chip leaves off: The chip is *no more than* one third flight, while the pitch is *at least* one third flight. A standard pitch with a pitching wedge is generally thought to be about half flight and half roll.

The pitch has become more and more popular as courses have become better manicured and heavily irrigated, leading to better lies and added stopping power on the greens. Our forebears in the game had little use for the pitch shot, as the greens of those days were far too firm to accept even a high-lofted pitch. But today's golfers can fly shots well into a green and be reasonably confident they will come to rest without rolling over. And since any well-executed pitch carries trouble and sits down quickly, it appears to be low risk. This is simply not true: Loft means risk.

When most golfers see thick rough or sand between them and the green, they think one thing: "Gotta get over that stuff." Loft seems the obvious issue, but the lie of the ball is even more important, as it dictates how cleanly you can make contact. As you'll see, a standard pitch requires at least a decent lie and a longer, more complicated swing than the chip. The more things you have to factor in to a swing, the more things can go wrong; there is less

The pitch shot flies higher and rolls less than the chip.

room for error. This is the case with high-lofted shots, which makes them risky. Golfers lose sight of that, and they pay dearly for it.

BEST TIP: Aiming High

To hit higher pitch shots, open the clubface to increase its effective loft. However, since the ball flies in the direction the clubface points, you have to make a corresponding move or else lose these shots to the right. To properly add loft, rotate the clubface open, then take your grip and shift your stance to the left until the clubface points back to the target.

—Mike Adams, *GOLF Magazine*
Top 100 Teacher

When Not to Pitch

Think of pitching as a necessary evil. There are times around the green when the chip shot would fly too low or run too far to fit the situation. This is when the higher-risk pitch shot should be considered, but not before.

When should you pitch? Since a chip is maximum one third flight, and you want to land the ball on the green to ensure a predictable bounce, your green light for pitching comes whenever you can't chip the ball onto the green with your highest lofted chipping club. For instance, if you can't chip the ball onto the green with your sand wedge, it's time to consider the pitch.

Once you opt to pitch the ball, select the least lofted club you can to play the shot, always trying to maximize ground time. Keep in mind, as loft increases, your swing length must also increase to cover the same distance because the swing's energy is sending the ball both upward and outward. The greater upward force means a weaker outward force, and hence a shot that travels less distance.

Don't forget about roll. As you add loft, realize you are also taking away roll, due to the steeper angle of descent to the ground. See how the risk factor is escalating? Hitting the ball higher means you have to carry it closer to the hole, bringing your margin for error on the far side of the

Fly High, Stop Fast

If you're like most golfers, you're amazed when the pros drop a pitch shot next to the hole, bounce it twice, and draw it back like a yo-yo. You'd love to be able to make the ball stop like that. Trouble is, you probably don't play a soft enough ball to create that much backspin. Instead, when you have to stop the ball quickly, simply hit a higher shot that plops straight down with little forward momentum. It's a safer, more dependable way than adding backspin to make the ball stop in its tracks.

green into the picture: A slight mishit may spell big trouble over the back.

How to Plan a Pitch

In golf, great pitchers can eye up a situation, grab a wedge, and dial in the shot they need. This skill has nothing to do with natural ability: It comes from experience and practice. Nobody picks up golf with a knack for pitching the ball accurate distances; it results from planning and executing thousands of pitch shots until you learn to match the situation you see with the motion you've learned. To be sure, it's an art, not a science.

The shot process in pitching starts with a careful assessment of the situation at hand—the slope of the terrain, any obstacles to negotiate, and the quality of the lie. As with chipping, you should start to evaluate the shot on your trek to the green. As you approach, you'll face the first set of critical questions: Where should you land the ball? Any trouble at the far side? Where do you want to putt from? Such questions are often best answered from a panoramic perspective.

However, the lie of the ball stands above all others in the analysis of a pitch shot. Pitching features less of a descending blow than chipping, which means the grass behind the ball comes into play to a much greater degree. If you try to hit a standard pitch from a buried lie in the rough, you're likely to catch a clubface full of grass before the ball, resulting in a weak shot. Try to develop a sense for what to expect from various lies and how to handle them. Again, that comes with experience.

Okay, after considering the above factors, you've decided you're going to pitch the ball; now you need the right club. More specifically, you need the right wedge, as all your pitching should be done with a wedge. Why? Two reasons: First, you need the higher loft that the wedges provide; and second, the more lofted the club, the heavier the flange (bottom of the clubhead) and therefore the lower the center of gravity. Both of these design features help you slide the leading edge of the clubface under the ball at impact, producing a high, soft shot.

How do you know which wedge to use? Well, that's a personal decision. More loft may create a higher percentage play, if, for instance, it gives you more room for error in carrying intervening obstacles. But the trade-off is the longer swing that a more lofted club requires to cover the same distance. As I've said, a longer swing means greater risk of in-swing faults and poor results. You have to

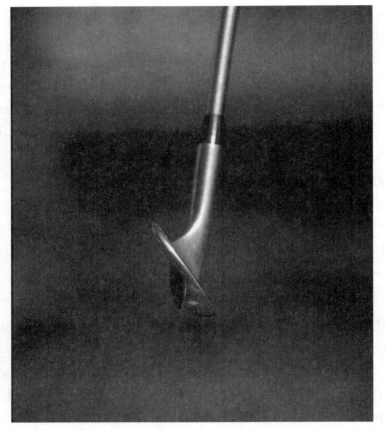

Wedges have heavy flanges to help get under the ball.

weigh your options, and make sure you're comfortable with the club you choose.

That said, you may want to use one club for all your pitch shots, as many golfers do in chipping. This creates a sense of familiarity that can be comforting when you have to face intimidating shots.

Pitching over obstacles creates tension in many players, and tension goes with touch like oil goes with water. Trust in your club selection is one good way to ease your fears and send yourself into the shot with a positive feeling.

BEST TIP: Watch Your Speed

Nothing makes a pitch swing more unpredictable than too much speed. When the hands and arms race out of sequence, they throw the swing off-track, leading to a variety of mishits. To learn speed control, practice hitting 30-yard shots with your pitching wedge using a full swing. It will feel as if you're swinging in slow motion, but don't cheat: Make sure you complete your backswing and follow-through. Gradually increase distance to 50, 70, and 100 yards. You'll gain an instant appreciation for how fast you're swinging the club.

—Craig Shankland, *GOLF Magazine*
Top 100 Teacher

Pitching Setup

Pitching can, at times, seem to be a hopeless endeavor. Consider the objectives: You want to loft the ball over obstacles and stop it quickly on the green, two things that you're probably not confident doing. As a result, you feel anxious over the ball, which leads to tense muscles, a tight grip, and quick tempo—three major obstacles in any pitch shot. What you need instead are soft hands and a little faith.

A tight grip obviously starts with the hands, but grip tension quickly spreads to the wrists, arms, and shoulders, inhibiting them from working naturally. The common by-product of this tension is unpredictable speed. If you take a stranglehold on the handle at address, you'll likely snatch the club away from the ball and make a quick swipe at it coming down.

In addition, tension reduces the range of motion in the wrists and shoulders, creating the need for the hands and arms to create hitting power (speed) on the downswing. This type of power production is unreliable, as it hinges on perfect timing of muscles in the hands and arms. It's simplest to avoid these speed issues altogether by taking a soft grip at address and keeping it soft throughout the swing, thereby de-emphasizing the hitting action of the hands and arms.

All this tension goes against our second setup essential: trust. Truth is, many amateurs doubt their ability to hit short shots high in the air. They don't trust the design of the club to help them get the ball up or their skill in putting it to use. As a result, they flip their hands quickly through the hitting area to try to create a lifting motion. That's a recipe for inconsistency.

To become a good pitcher, you have to go into every swing relaxed and confident about the outcome. Put yourself in the following setup positions every time and you'll have good reason to feel ready over the ball:

Center the ball. Position the ball midway between your heels and set your hands directly in line with the ball. With the hands just ahead of the clubface at address, the shaft leans slightly toward the target, setting up a descending angle of approach on the downswing for crisp contact.

Distribute your weight evenly. Since the pitch swing is a miniature full swing, with the same motions only performed on a reduced scale, it does feature a slight weight transfer to the back foot going back and the front foot coming down. To allow this natural weight shift in response to the

For a standard pitch, center the ball and distribute your weight evenly.

swinging motion, set your weight evenly at address, 50 percent left and 50 percent right.

Take a narrow stance. Place your heels ten to twelve inches apart. Although your weight should transfer, you don't want to complicate the swing by moving laterally off the ball and requiring a compensating movement on the downswing to get back. With your feet close together, you'll automatically limit lateral motion to keep your balance.

Use your normal grip. Don't grip down on the club, as you should when chipping. Gripping down lightens the club and reduces power, which, in pitching, means you'd need a longer, faster swing to compensate. Using the full length of the club also allows you to better feel the weight of the clubhead, letting it unhinge your wrists coming down and slide under the ball without any hitting action from your hands.

Set up square to slightly open. A square stance is the simplest, as body alignment tends to follow foot alignment and a square body promotes a straight swing path through impact. However, setting your alignment slightly open promotes another critical motion: body rotation toward the target on the downswing. This pivoting action is one of the keys to delivering the clubhead to the ball in a shallow, undercutting motion. Experiment with a square and a slightly open stance to find out which is better for you.

Aim the clubface square to slightly open.

In chipping, a square clubface is best because the swing is so short and slow that the ball simply rebounds off the clubface. But for longer, faster swings, the ball will start on a line somewhere between the direction of the swing path and the direction the clubface is pointing in at impact. If you play from a square stance, you'll tend to swing straight along the target line through impact, so square the clubface at address. If you open your stance at address, you'll tend to cut across the line from out to in through impact, so open the face to send the ball slightly to the right of the swing path. An open clubface also adds loft to the shot. There is no one best way—it comes down to what makes you comfortable and confident.

> ### *BEST TIP: Hoop Dreams*
>
> Most amateurs tend to leave the ball short when pitching to an elevated green and only the top of the flagstick is visible. To produce a longer shot, they need a sensory cue that makes them hit the ball harder. I have my students envision a basketball hoop, which stands ten feet tall, in place of the flag. If they try to swish their pitch shot through the hoop, they'll have a much better chance of getting the ball to the hole.
>
> —Dr. Richard Coop, *GOLF Magazine*
> Mental Game Consultant

Pitching Swing

As strange as it may sound, pitching requires power—quite a bit of power, in fact. You might not think so, considering the soft, floating shots it produces, but the pitching swing requires a forceful motion because the power is used to send the ball as much upward as forward. The force is more under the ball at impact than behind it.

Think of what happens when you hit a pitch shot thinly. The leading edge catches the middle of the ball and sends it screaming over the green. That's because the power of the swing launches the ball forward, not upward as expected. As a result, the ball flies three or four times farther than planned—all due to misdirected power.

The good news is, you don't have to worry about directing the power during the swing; you've set it up with your club selection and address positions. You see, by using the highest lofted clubs for pitching, you're hitting the ball with a clubface that's tilted away from the target. At impact, this produces oblique contact with the ball that pushes it upward as well as forward. The higher the loft, the more oblique the contact, with the energy of the swing farther under the ball, producing a higher shot.

The setup positions just discussed likewise force the swing's energy under the ball. By distributing your weight evenly and playing the ball in the middle of your stance, you promote a slight downward blow, as compared to the sharp descent used in chipping. This more level angle of attack puts the heavy sole of the clubhead under the ball at impact, producing a higher launch angle off the clubface and more lift.

Now you need to add power. To hit a pitch shot (which travels both forward and upward) the same distance as a chip shot (which travels essentially only forward), you need a much longer, faster swing. In chipping, the swing employs a single lever, from the left shoulder to the ball; in pitching, the swing uses two levers, the left arm and the club, with a hinge at the wrist. This hinge allows you to make a longer swing and to generate the added power you need.

As you may already be piecing together, the pitch swing is really the full swing in miniature. Not only does it feature a significant wrist hinge, but the need for more power also produces a fuller body turn and even a slight weight transfer back and through. These elements, which are crucial power producers in the full swing, can be found to smaller degrees in even the shortest pitch shots. So while you may not want to *think* power when pitching, you need to generate a fair amount of it to be an effective pitcher.

Here are the keys to executing a standard pitch shot, which, with a pitching wedge, should send the ball about 30 yards—15 yards in the air and another 15 on the ground.

Check your grip pressure.   In order for the wrists to hinge freely on the backswing, the hands have to keep a light grip on the club. Try slowly

The pitching swing features a full wrist hinge.

waggling the club back and forth at address to keep the hands soft and the wrists limber and ready to perform. Keeping the club in motion makes you more aware of your grip pressure and also serves to keep the hands and wrists active and therefore less susceptible to unwanted tension.

Start the arms and shoulders together.

As with the chip shot, the arms and shoulders start back together, causing the body to pivot away from the target. It's imperative to keep your head perfectly still; any vertical or lateral head movement on the backswing has to be "undone" before impact for solid contact to occur. Feel as if you're moving around a fixed axis, with your arms swinging and your body turning as a single unit.

Hinge the clubhead up.   Almost immediately as you swing back, start hinging the club up, pointing the toe of the clubhead to the sky. Even on a thirty-yard pitch shot, the wrists should hinge the club into nearly a 90-degree angle with the left arm. The longer swing created by this hinging action should be supported by added rotation in the shoulders and hips, even a slight weight transfer.

The shoulders turn as the arms swing the club back.

However, do not consciously shift your weight; the weight will move naturally as a result of the actions of the upper body. Your focus should be on making a smooth, unified move away from the ball.

Synchronize the downswing. To return the clubhead to the ball, simply swing everything through together, as if you were in a body cast and couldn't move any parts independently. The centrifugal force of the downswing will unhinge the wrists and pull the club into a straight line with the left arm at impact. Feel as if you're just letting the clubhead drop as you turn through with your entire body—knees, hips, chest, shoulders.

Let it go. You have to trust that you've established the necessary loft in your setup and the necessary power in your backswing; the downswing is a simple reversal of the backswing positions on the way to the finish. Too many amateurs see it as a last-ditch effort to manipulate the position or speed of the clubhead with their hands and arms. No golfer can save swings in this manner on a consistent basis.

Feel as if you're simply letting the club drop as you turn your body through.

Finish your pivot. If your body turns smoothly through impact, you've stayed relaxed and not tried to overcontrol the shot. To monitor hand and wrist tension, think about the club rehinging into a 90-degree angle with your right arm on the follow-through, a mirror image of your left arm and the club on the backswing. At the finish, your belt buckle and chest should face the target and almost all of your weight should be on your left heel. These positions indicate that you've used the big muscles of your body, not just the quickness of your hands and arms, to deliver the club to the ball.

BEST TIP: Release Your Fears

If your fear factor is high on pitch shots, I bet your lower body isn't working properly. Fear freezes the big muscles, locking the lower body in place, and activates the small muscles in the hands and arms. That is a risky prescription for a pitch shot.

To return leg action to its proper role, start your downswing by rolling your right ankle and knee toward the target. This move helps the big muscles stay loose and perform as they should and promotes high, soft shots that clear even the most fearsome obstacles.

—Paul Trittler, *GOLF Magazine* Top 100 Teacher

Relaxed hands and wrists will rehinge the club on the follow-through.

Common Faults

Most pitching faults occur when golfers try to help the ball into the air. With little faith in the club's built-in loft or the technique just described, they think they have to manufacture extra loft to carry the ball safely onto the green. As a result, they try to lift the ball by manipulating impact. Such manipulation has many forms, but consider the three most common.

Let's start with the setup. Golfers intent on producing a lifting motion often set up "behind the ball," meaning they set more weight on their rear foot, tilt their spine away from the target, and play the ball up toward their front foot. From there, they feel as if they can undercut the ball and thereby increase the height of the shot.

Other golfers set up okay, but then try to create these behind-the-ball positions during the swing. They shift to their rear foot on the backswing and stay there, swinging the clubhead up at the ball. The typical result in both cases is poor contact, since moving the ball up or moving the body back puts the bottom of the swing arc behind the ball. The club either bottoms out in the ground before it reaches the ball or catches it on the upswing. They're either chunking it or skulling it.

Another in-swing fault is "the scoop," or a premature unhinging of the right wrist in an attempt to lift the ball by flipping the hands. Although good players will sometimes use this unhinging motion to maximize loft, it's an ill-advised method for the middle to high handicapper, as it requires a keen feel for what the clubhead is doing. In effect, you're creating the bottom of the swing arc with your hands and wrists. If you don't catch the ball perfectly, the resulting shot will be either fat or thin.

Players who try to manufacture extra loft need to resign themselves to one simple truth: You can hit down on the ball and still hit a high shot. In fact, you should always make a slight downward strike on greenside shots to ensure flush contact; the wedges have plenty of

"This Is Not a Toy"

There's a serious problem spreading through the amateur ranks: lob-wedge dependence. More and more amateurs are grabbing their lob wedge for all sorts of greenside shots, instead of reserving it for when they really need extra height. Remember, the higher the shot, the longer the swing must be to cover any given distance; this sends the risk factor through the roof. Lob wedges should come with a warning label: "This is not a toy." For some, the novelty soon wears off, but too many have reinvented their short game around this modern-day weapon. Loft should inspire caution, not comfort.

"Scooping" through impact is a common pitching fault.

loft to launch the ball into the air. That's easy to say, but to become a believer you have to learn for yourself that "down means up," and then have the courage to trust it when you're standing over the ball.

Pitching Variations

Now that I've taken such pains to caution you against the perils of pitching, let's look at a few descendants of the pitch shot that demand even more prudence in planning and execution. They come in two forms: shots where the stance or lie of the ball is unusual and shots requiring greater height or distance than the standard pitch provides. Practice them before you put them in your bag; in time, they'll save you shots, if you use them wisely.

The Lob Shot

When you're asked to carry the ball over bunkers or deep rough and stop it quickly on the green, you need a shot that flies almost straight up in the air and dribbles to a stop after landing. This is com-

For a lob shot, hinge the club up abruptly.

monly referred to as the lob shot, and anyone who's tried it knows it takes some chutzpah.

First, take your most lofted wedge, preferably a lob wedge, although a sand wedge will do. However, do not use a sand wedge with a lot of "bounce," a design characteristic caused by the trailing edge of the sole being lower than the leading edge. This feature prevents the clubhead from digging on contact; it's great in the sand, but when used anywhere else can cause the clubhead to ricochet off the ground and into the ball.

To execute the lob shot, open your stance about 30 degrees and play the ball slightly ahead of center, with your weight evenly distributed. Whether you're using a sand or lob wedge, point the leading edge of the clubface at the target. From there, make a long, slow swing, hinging your wrists immediately on the backswing and rehinging them immediately after impact. You want to make a three-quarter swing at half-speed, sliding the clubface under the ball and continuing into the finish. As you might imagine, this is not the type of shot that can be used effectively with little practice. Work on it before you try it during an actual round.

> ### *BEST TIP: Right for Height*
>
> The lob shot takes some getting used to, as the swing is long but the shot is short. To generate a long enough swing and the necessary shallow approach into impact, try to feel an underarm throwing motion with the right arm. Take practice swings (then hit balls) with your left hand off the club and let your right arm create the wide arc and shallow approach necessary to slip the leading edge under the ball.
>
> —Dick Harmon, *GOLF Magazine*
> Top 100 Teacher

The Half-Wedge

Hitting a wedge half of its full distance is a tricky proposition for most. It catches the golfer between full-swing mode and short-game mode, with the result often being uncertainty and poor execution. The best way to deal with this shot is to steer clear of situations where you would need it: Half-wedges often stem from poor decisions, such as hitting a layup too far or punching out of trouble to an awkward distance. In short, don't put yourself in half-wedge territory.

But despite your best planning efforts, you'll still come across this shot now and then. When you do, your main objective should be to keep the arms and

---

BEST TIP: Steady as She Goes

On half-wedge shots, it's vital that the body's center of gravity remain stable. To ingrain stability, practice with a golf ball wedged under the outside of each foot. The balls prohibit the knees and hips from sliding laterally and force the muscles in the hips, back, and shoulders to turn and support the swinging motion.

—Kent Cayce, *GOLF Magazine* Top 100 Teacher

body linked throughout the entire motion. Many golfers try to take power off the swing by restricting body turn or decelerating the club on the downswing. These are unreliable ways of controlling distance; the former causes excess tension, the latter puts the hands in control.

To execute the half-wedge, start by taking a narrow stance, with your heels twelve to fifteen inches apart, and setting the ball in the middle. Then swing the club halfway back, the shaft reaching vertical, and keep your body centered. From there, swing the club and turn the body through together, keeping your left wrist firm through impact and letting the shaft reach vertical on the follow-through. With some practice, this shot will not be quite so intimidating.

Hilly Lies

Approach shots that miss the green often find uneven terrain, especially with all the greenside mounding and bunkering found on modern-day courses. That's why it's crucial to know how to adjust your standard pitching technique to accommodate uphill, downhill, and sidehill lies.

When pitching from hilly lies, swing with the slope, not into it.

When pitching uphill or downhill, it's easy to mishit the ball; you'll tend to hit fat shots going uphill and thin shots going downhill, because gravity pulls your body in the direction of the slope during the swing. To counter this, set more weight on your uphill foot at address and try to keep it there throughout the swing. Also, try to align your shoulders parallel to the angle of the ground and focus on swinging with the slope, not into it.

For sidehill lies, your main objective must be to make contact without the toe or heel of the clubhead catching the ground first. When the ball lies above your feet, the toe will tend to hit the ground first; when the ball lies below, the heel is likely to catch. To encourage solid contact, make sure you set the sole of your wedge flush to the ground at address. If the ball is above your feet, stand more upright and make a more around-the-body swing; if the ball is below your feet, bend your knees more and make a more up-and-down motion.

Deep Rough

There are times when you need the height of a pitch shot, but the lie is too thick to allow clean contact using the standard pitching technique. We all know that feeling of hopelessness when we catch a clump of heavy rough before the ball and the clubhead loses its will to go on.

The best option here is a modified pitch shot—something between a chip and a pitch. You need the steeper angle into the ball that a chip features to catch it cleanly, but you also need the higher loft and stopping power of a pitch shot. So, take what you need from each.

Using your sand or lob wedge, play the ball back toward your right instep and push your hands

To pitch from thick grass, move the ball back and make a steep swing.

ahead. With your weight favoring your left side, hinge the clubhead up quickly and then drop it back down to the ball. Don't worry about making a follow-through; your focus should be making good contact. The ball should pop out on a trajectory higher than a chip but lower than a pitch. That's how you handle the thick stuff.

3

Sand Play

Let's get something straight: Most amateurs are pathetic in the sand—and they know it. You may think you're a decent chipper; maybe you can even pitch the ball with a fair bit of confidence. But if you're like most golfers, you'd rather find your ball buried in six-inch rough than staring at you from a greenside bunker.

The simple truth is that most poor bunker play stems from a lack of understanding of what needs to happen at impact. You don't have to dig halfway to China to blast the ball out. In fact, the deeper you try to dig the better your chances of taking too much sand and—dare I say—leaving it in the bunker. The only thing worse than not getting out of the sand the first time is having the chance to do it over again.

So why do the pros look so darned comfortable in the sand? Because they know two advantages that sand shots have over other greenside shots: predictability and forgiveness. First, the pros know sand is a fairly predictable playing surface from one shot to the next, in terms of both firmness and depth. Assuming your ball is sitting on top of the sand, you know what lies underneath it. That's where you're guessing with other lies; even in seemingly good lies in the grass, you never know how firm it is underneath. You don't have that uncertainty when you're in the sand.

The second reason pros like sand is that it is forgiving; it leaves room for error. Since your clubface never comes in contact with the ball on bunker shots, solid contact—perhaps your biggest fear in other greenside shots—is simply not an issue. In fact, with the right swing, you can enter the sand an inch or so closer to or farther from the ball than you planned and still produce a decent shot. Where else can you say that around the green?

So before you conclude that you'll never be much of a bunker player, read through the instruction that follows. It's a lot simpler than you may think, and could easily become a strength in your game. Maybe you'll start wishing for bunker shots, like the pros sometimes do—or at least not feel as if you're doomed when your ball ends up on the beach.

How to Plan a Bunker Shot

Most golfers climb into bunkers with a fair amount of mental baggage. Each can tell you horror stories of disaster holes or career rounds ended in the sand. And every one of us can commiserate. But those are harmful thoughts as you step up to a bunker shot. You need a clear, confident approach and a simple plan of attack.

First, be thankful that the two major decisions you usually have to make next to the green—shot selection and club selection—are no-brainers in the sand. The basic bunker technique I'm about to discuss works for most greenside sand shots, and the sand wedge should be your weapon of choice in

> ### *No Choking*
> For most golfers, sand means tension. And the first place tension rears its ugly head is in the grip, where the fingers strangle the handle and send pressure up the arms and into the body. The usual result is a fast, jerky swing and inconsistent shots. To nip tension in the bud, "milk" the handle at address, exerting and releasing pressure with your fingers. Don't take the club back until your grip feels soft. Only then are you ready to go.

A simple plan and positive visualization are crucial in bunker play.

A club has "bounce" if the trailing edge of the sole is lower than the leading edge.

virtually every situation. (Due to its "bounce" feature, the sand wedge slides through the sand instead of digging.) So, there are two fewer things to
think about. And you thought this was hard?

Your first order of business, assuming you have a
decent lie, is deciding where you want to hit the
shot. This may sound obvious, but you don't always want to play directly to the hole. For instance,
if you're staring at the tallest part of the bunker lip

or you have deep trouble directly behind the hole, you may want to look for a safer route. That decision hinges on how much confidence you have in your sand game. But for most players, it's better to be thinking about getting on the green, not getting to the hole.

Once you know where you're going, pick a landing area. It may be difficult to zero in on a specific spot, but figure out the general area where you want the ball to touch down. This gives you something positive to focus on, rather than bad memories or the opportunity for disaster that the shot presents. Simply pick your shot, then your spot, and keep your thoughts focused and positive.

Although we're about to look at setup and swing mechanics, bunker play is largely about feel. Swinging through the sand produces a much different sensation than hitting the ball directly; you should pre-sense how you want your body and the club to feel as you prepare to hit the shot. Focus less on the technique of the swing and more on how the club should move through the impact area. As you become a better bunker player, you'll rely almost totally on your instincts in the sand.

One last point on preparation: Check your tension level. Negative thoughts and fear cause tension, which tightens the grip and quickens the swing. Take a few deep breaths and shake out your hands. And remember, try to draw on the good experiences you've had, not the heartbreakers.

Bunker Setup

First, realize that the prevailing technique used in bunker play has changed. Traditional instruction says the bunker swing is a steep, out-to-in swipe that slices across the line, digging under the ball and popping it out of the sand. Today, most instructors teach a shallower swing that slides the club-

---

BEST TIP: *Predictable Roll*

Tour pros rarely use the traditional out-to-in swing for bunker shots. We know it imparts a lot of left-to-right sidespin on the ball, which can be difficult to plan for on the landing. Instead, we prefer a more normal swing path, the clubhead cutting a swath in the sand that points to the target. Picture a rectangle in the sand with the ball in the middle and make a steep swing back and through, trying to slice the entire rectangle out of the sand. A straight swing will produce a straight roll.

—Curtis Strange, two-time
U.S. Open Champion

head just under the surface of the sand and clips the ball off the top. This new method has proven to be more effective and more forgiving.

As a result of this change in thinking, the traditional bunker setup has also undergone an overhaul. The old stance was dramatically open, with the feet sunk deep in the sand, to promote a backswing to the outside and a steep, explosive descent into the ball. The new setup is designed to let you move the clubhead in a normal swing arc, from the inside coming down and back to the inside on the follow-through. This path creates a shallower approach to the ball and a longer, thinner cut in the sand.

The following setup keys will put you in position to execute the modern bunker shot.

Open the clubface. This exposes the bounce on the bottom of the sole and adds loft to the clubface. However, you should open the face before you step into the bunker: With your left hand on the grip, rotate the club clockwise about 20 degrees with your right hand and then take your normal grip with both hands. If you merely turn the clubface open at address, without changing your hand positions, you haven't really opened the clubface at all.

Before you enter the sand, rotate the face open, then take your grip.

Play the ball forward.   Since you actually want to make fat contact, touching down in the sand first, position the ball about an inch in front of the center of your stance. Let your arms hang naturally; your hands should be slightly behind the ball at address, the shaft tilting neither toward nor away from the target. This promotes a fairly level swipe through the sand, with the ball in the middle of your sand divot.

Take a wider stance.   Even if you dig your feet in, your stance in a bunker is never rock-solid due to the shifting nature of the sand. To create a steady base, spread your feet apart so your insteps are at hip-width. You still won't be able to transfer much weight or move laterally off the ball, which will do wonders for your consistency. Your objective is to make a smooth, accelerating swing while staying in perfect balance.

Align slightly open.   Shift your stance, as well as your knees, hips, and shoulders, about 20 degrees open to the target. This open position presets a full rotation of the body through the shot, a move that many amateurs fail to make in the sand. Once your

For a standard shot, play the ball just ahead of center.

feet are positioned, twist them down into the sand about an inch, which lowers your entire body and therefore the bottom of the swing arc. Remember, you want the swing to bottom out in the sand under the ball, not at ball level.

Aim an inch behind the ball. You actually want to contact the sand about two or three inches behind the ball, but if you aim the leading edge about an inch behind it, the bounce factor of your sand wedge will cause the trailing edge to enter the sand first. But try not to get too stuck on this aiming point: If you make it the focus of the entire swing, you'll probably fail to swing the clubhead through the sand—a common amateur mistake.

BEST TIP: *Dial the Face*

Control the depth of your divot holes in the sand by increasing or decreasing the angle of the flange—the clubhead's protruding sole. The more you open the clubface—also known as "dialing the face"—the greater the angle of the flange, which prevents you from digging too deep in the sand. I like to play most of my bunker shots with the leading edge pointing toward 1:30 or 2 o'clock. This shallows out the divot and adds loft and spin to the shot.

—Phil Rodgers, *GOLF Magazine*
Top 100 Teacher

Bunker Swing

Many golfers feel as if they have to manufacture a totally different swing when they step into the sand. They try to make a steep, out-to-in motion that they use nowhere else on the golf course. This is a mistake.

Truth is, anyone who can make a simple pitch swing can hit a good bunker shot—and that means any golfer. The motion is essentially the same: Swing the club and turn the body in one motion, then move everything through together. The fact that you're hitting sand instead of a golf ball should not affect the swing; the only difference is that the bunker swing needs to be longer and faster to hit the ball the same distance as a normal pitch shot. Practice will tell you how far your standard bunker shot travels compared to your standard pitch.

Hank Johnson, one of *GOLF Magazine*'s Top 100 Teachers, discusses this relationship in his book *How to Win the Three Games of Golf:* "I usually count on a 3-to-1 ratio. A swing that would hit a standard pitch 30 yards would hit a bunker shot 10 yards. A stroke that would send a standard pitch 60 yards would result in a 20-yard bunker shot."

Relating your bunker swing to your pitching
swing should be helpful: It's a move away from the
old out-to-in method, and should help dispel the
mystique of sand play by linking it to something
with which you're more comfortable.

Here are the swing keys for a standard greenside
bunker shot:

Hover the clubhead. Be thankful for the
rule that prohibits you from grounding your
clubhead in the sand. By having to support the
weight of the club at address, you sustain a
constant grip pressure, which promotes a smooth,
unhurried takeaway. Given the tension that most
golfers feel in the sand, it's also a good idea to
waggle the clubhead back and forth or up and
down to quiet stress in the hands and arms.

Start the arms and shoulders together.
Make a one-piece takeaway, turning your
shoulders as your arms swing the club on a
slightly inside path. Let the wrists hinge the club
upward, an action that will happen naturally
provided your grip is light and your wrists are
supple. Think of the lower body as the base of the

swing: The hips and legs should support the actions of the arms and torso, responding to motion, not creating motion.

Make a three-quarter backswing.

Lengthening your backswing is the best way to promote more clubhead speed coming down so you can power through the sand. At the top, your wrists should be fully hinged, the club at a right angle to your left arm, and your hands should be at about shoulder height. Also, make a three-quarter body turn away from the ball, with your back almost to the target and your left shoulder nearly under your chin. These backswing positions set up a proper move into impact.

Turn and swing through impact. From

the top, turn your body and swing your arms down in one synchronized movement. Provided your arms don't rush out in front, the club will track back down to the ball on an inside path, producing a shallow entry into the sand and a long, thin divot. The old out-to-in technique produces bomb craters because the downswing is a steep motion controlled mainly by the arms. Today's method features more

Make a three-quarter backswing with a full wrist hinge.

Cut a shallow divot and keep the clubhead moving.

body rotation back and through, which shallows out the swing and helps the clubhead slip through the sand, rather than slam into it.

Continue to a three-quarter finish.   The shallower swing arc allows you to swing through

At the finish, the chest should be turned to the target.

the sand with less resistance and therefore achieve a fuller finish. Your clubhead should touch down two to three inches behind the ball and slide underneath it. As a result, the ball will fly out on a pillow of sand without ever making contact with the clubface. Impact should be a muffled "thump," like the sound of beating out an old rug. At the finish, your chest should face the target, indicating full body rotation on the downswing.

BEST TIP: *How to Vary Distance*

Many amateurs have trouble varying distance on bunker shots. Part of the problem is how they finish: They swing into a full follow-through regardless of the shot at hand. As a rule, the length of the follow-through should correspond to the length of the shot. A short shot needs a short follow-through, and a long shot needs a long follow-through. You wouldn't finish with the club up over your shoulder on a short pitch shot; so don't do it for a short bunker shot either. Match your finish to the shot you need.

—Martin Hall, *GOLF Magazine*
Master Teaching Professional

Common Faults

Most poor bunker shots result from one of two problems: fear or misunderstanding. The fear we can take care of with positive experiences, which come from understanding what you have to do to produce the desired results. It's as simple as that: Fix your technique, hit some effective shots, and the fear should shrink away.

That leaves us with grooving the right technique. To begin with, try to erase from your mind the image of a steep blast out of the sand, since that is the biggest technique fault among amateurs. If you try to make a steep swing, you'll instinctively freeze your body and swing the club up and down with only your hands and arms. The result is a fast, rigid lash—a move you see from virtually every poor bunker player.

Such a move can produce either fat or thin shots, often in alternating fashion. You see, a steep swing requires great precision, as the clubhead has to enter the sand very close to the ball to produce an acceptable shot. If a steep swing enters the sand a little too far behind the ball, the clubhead will lose too much momentum and yield a fat shot; if it enters too close, the result is the dreaded skulled shot.

Most golfers try to dig the ball out with a steep swing.

Simply put, a steep swing has to be a precise swing, and that's a lot to ask in an intimidating situation.

Instead, envision a shallow cut through the sand. To shallow out an overly steep swing, you need to add body rotation. Focus on the takeaway: Start the

Spinning from the Sand

To increase backspin on bunker shots, you have to swing the club faster through the bottom of the swing arc, sliding the clubface on a shallow angle through the sand. Think of it as knocking the legs out from under the ball. Visualize the clubhead passing under the ball and beating it out on the other side. To produce this fast cutting action, lay the clubface wide open at address and focus on fast body rotation back and through.

club back with the hands, arms, and shoulders moving as a single unit, the clubhead sweeping slightly to the inside and low to the ground. Provided you don't yank the club down from the top, the downswing will return on the same path and skim through the sand, pushing the ball up and out. A good swing thought to increase body rotation is "Turn your back to the target on the backswing, then turn your chest to the target on the through-swing." Don't get stuck thinking about impact; concentrate on the overall swing motion.

Bunker-Shot Variations

The Long Bunker Shot

When you're in the sand but need more than the standard 10- to 15-yard bunker shot, you need to transfer more energy to the ball at impact. To do this, many amateurs either swing harder or try to make contact closer to the ball. Problem is, hard swings mean wild swings, and closing the gap between the clubface and the ball at impact requires too much precision to be reliable.

There is a better option. First, put away your sand wedge, and opt for a pitching wedge or 9-iron—even an 8- or 7-iron for a longer shot. These clubs have more upright faces, which apply more forward propulsion and less upward propulsion as they enter the sand. Use the same technique described above, except square the stance and the clubface to produce more direct impact, and you'll hit a shot that comes out lower and hotter and rolls after landing.

The Buried Lie

Always a gruesome discovery, the buried bunker lie strikes fear in even the most experienced golfers. Knowing that the objective of a bunker shot is to swing the clubface under the ball, golfers typically try to pound down on buried lies, hoping that extra power will create deeper penetration into the sand. Sometimes this works, sometimes it doesn't.

For longer bunker shots, change clubs, not technique.

To get the ball up and out of a buried lie, you need the clubface to dig, not bounce. Play the ball farther back in your stance, just behind center, and push your hands slightly ahead—both promote more of a digging motion. Also, place a little more weight on your left foot and set the clubface square or even slightly closed. From there, just make your normal bunker swing; the setup changes will produce a steeper swing that helps the clubface cut through the sand and move under the ball. Expect a lower trajectory and minimal backspin.

BEST TIP: *Facing the Buried Lie*

To extricate a ball buried in a bunker, the clubhead must approach at a steep angle and dig deep into the sand. As a result, the hosel that connects the clubhead to the shaft plows into the sand just as the clubface does. In normal bunker shots, only the clubface compacts sand, and the ball flies out in the direction in which the clubface is aimed. With buried lies, the hosel also compacts sand, pushing it to the right. To compensate for this, aim the clubface farther to the left at address.

—David Feherty, television commentator and former Ryder Cup player

From a buried lie, play the ball back and lean left to promote a digging action.

From Wet Sand

You may think playing from wet sand should be much like playing from a buried lie, since both situations present the problem of getting under the ball. However, wet sand is very firm and difficult to penetrate. You need to adjust your approach.

When the sand is wet, use a wedge with as little bounce as possible, preferably a lob wedge, as you want to minimize the ricochet effect off the firm sand. Open both your clubface and your stance about 30 degrees, and play the ball off your left instep. Make your normal bunker swing, entering the sand about an inch farther behind the ball, which gives the clubface more time to dig into the firmer surface. Make sure you hold the clubface open through impact so that more of the clubhead can slide under the ball.

You may have to swing a little harder to keep the clubhead moving through the packed sand, but try to achieve at least a half-length finish, as this mind-set will ensure an accelerating motion through impact. Again, expect a lower ball flight and reduced backspin.

4

Specialty Shots

To borrow a phrase from Wall Street, an efficient short game is grounded in risk management. Smart golfers rarely play a risky shot when a safer one can produce similar results. This may seem like routine decision-making, but there are legions of golfers out there who overlook the risks involved in greenside shots, who pitch the ball when they could chip it or play the sky-high lob at every opportunity. These folks will never realize their potential as golfers.

This is not to suggest that every time a golfer strays from standard chipping, pitching, or bunker technique that he is taking unnecessary risk. Fact is, a risky shot in some circumstances is a smart play in others. For instance, the long swing required to hit a lob shot is risky, but in some cases

BEST TIP: *Ultrahigh Flop Shot*

When there is very little green to work with or a tall obstacle, such as a high bunker lip, between you and the hole, you need a high shot that stops immediately. Using a sand or lob wedge, place the ball off the middle of your front foot, open the clubface 30 to 40 degrees, and set your hands a couple of inches behind the ball. On the backswing, make a cupping action with the left wrist, arching the back of the left hand toward the forearm, to open the clubface even more. Imagine a pile of sand on the clubface at address; during the takeaway, rotate the clubface open so the sand dumps on the ground behind you. Make a full backswing, then swing the clubhead down along the target line. The result will be a very high, soft-landing shot.

—Lee Janzen, two-time U.S. Open Champion

it's safer than the standard pitch shot. Say a small green requires that you drop a pitch on the front fringe to avoid rolling over. In this case, the higher-flying lob gives you more room for error on the landing. It's a riskier swing but a safer shot.

Aside from the shot variations I've already discussed, there are times when you're really forced to

BEST TIP: To loft the ball high and stop it quickly, open the clubface at address and rotate it more open during the backswing.

think "outside the box" in greenside situations. From one shot to the next, your lie can go from firm to soft, the grass from thick to thin, and your path to the hole from unimpeded to seemingly impassable. Decide right now to accept that: You cannot control where your ball goes after you hit it, and you'll never play a good shot dwelling on what you perceive as a bad break. When your ball finds a tricky situation, think of it as a chance to be creative and have some fun.

Does this mean throw caution to the wind? Hardly. The shots we're about to look at are actually safer plays than the standard greenside shots we've been discussing—provided the situation calls for them. That's the key: You have to decide between a more familiar shot and a more inventive one designed for very specific situations. Are the circumstances strong enough to warrant a major departure in technique? Remember, your confidence in the shot will show in your execution.

So, keep that decision process in mind as you read through the specialty shots that follow. First, make sure the circumstances at hand demand the shot you want to play, then check your comfort level. If one of the standard greenside shots is a viable option, use it; if you think a specialty shot is the way to go, commit to it and enjoy being creative.

The Bellied Wedge

The Situation:

Your ball has run through the fringe and nestled up against the edge of the rough. Although the ball actually lies on closely mown grass, where you'd typically putt or chip, the long grass behind the ball will grab the clubhead if you use a normal putting or chipping motion. You need a swing that will slide the clubhead through the grass without it getting stuck.

The Shot:

All you need to play from this precarious situation are a sand wedge and a little common sense. First, realize that the thick, heavy sole of a sand wedge slides through long grass fairly easily, provided it doesn't sink too deep. Since you only have to nudge the ball forward and get it rolling, the best way to handle this lie is to play an intentional thin shot, contacting the middle of the ball with the leading edge of the clubface.

To do this, set up as you normally would for a putt—ball centered, hands slightly ahead of the

With the ball up against the collar, try "The Bellied Wedge."

clubhead, eyes over the ball—except grip down about an inch on the handle. If you stay in your normal putting posture, choking down should raise the clubhead up about an inch off the ground. Then, simply line up the leading edge with the ball's equator and make a straight-back, straight-through sweep, like a putting stroke, keeping your head and lower body perfectly still. The ball will skip forward and roll smoothly.

The Wood Chip

The Situation:

Again, you've narrowly missed the green, but this time you find yourself in thick grass just off the fringe. A standard chip shot could do the job, but it would be difficult to catch the ball cleanly in the heavy grass without dropping the clubhead almost directly on top of the ball, which can make the shot very unpredictable.

The Shot:

Similar to the bottom of a sand wedge, the rounded head of a fairway wood glides through long grass more easily than an iron head. In fact, the molded bottoms of most fairway woods help the clubhead slide instead of dig, parting grass as it goes and promoting a clean hit. This sliding action comes in handy on greenside shots, provided you

A fairway wood can be an effective chipping club.

don't need to carry the ball, as these clubs feature minimal loft.

The first step in executing a fairway-wood chip is choking down to the bottom of the grip to wield better control over the long shaft. Then take your normal pitching setup—ball centered, hands slightly ahead of the ball, weight evenly distributed—and make a simple pendulum motion with the arms and shoulders, letting the club-head slide through the grass. You may trap some grass between the clubface and the ball, but the grass will not grab the wood head like it does an iron. Get used to this shot on the practice green before trying it on the course.

> ### Get a Good Leave
>
> As golf architect Robert Trent Jones Jr. notes in his book *Golf By Design,* "like pool, golf is primarily a game of position ... The key is to get a good 'leave,' or an ideal position for the next shot." On greenside plays, this means leaving yourself with a makable putt, or at least an easy two-putt. If the greens are fast or severely sloped, you'd sometimes rather be ten feet below the hole than five feet above it. Point is, your target doesn't always have to be the hole; be aware of areas you want to avoid.

The Bunker Putt

The Situation:

Chasing a hole cut close to a side bunker, you get too cute with your approach shot and find the sand. Now you face a ticklish little shot with just a few paces of green between you and the hole. Your standard bunker shot will get you out of the sand but will release to the far side of the green. In this situation, consider putting the ball, instead of trying to finesse a bunker shot.

The Shot:

For the bunker putt to be a smart play, several conditions first need to be satisfied. To begin with, the sand must be firm and smooth, and your ball must be sitting up cleanly in a flat area. Next, the bunker lip must be flat enough so the ball doesn't jump straight up as it rolls over it. Finally, the grass between the bunker and the putting surface must be dry and fairly short to allow the ball to bounce through it.

If these conditions are met, this simple shot can be very effective. The key to executing it correctly is contacting the ball at the exact bottom of the swing arc to produce a forward skipping action through the sand. If you make a downward strike, you'll drive the ball into the sand; if you make contact on the upswing, you'll hit the ball weakly and leave it short.

Take your normal putting stance and play the ball precisely between your heels. Do not dig your feet into the sand—you want a level stroke into the back of the ball without contacting the sand. As for

Putting from the sand requires a very still body.

the stroke itself, think of it as a long lag putt. You may have to let your wrists hinge slightly going back to create a long enough backswing, but try to keep your head and lower body very quiet. Then, swing the putterhead through the ball aggressively, never letting it touch the sand.

The Banker

The Situation:

Your approach to an elevated green sails wide and your ball trickles down to the base of the green's bank. You can see only the top of the flagstick, which is unsettling in itself, and you feel like you need to loft the ball up in the air and land it perfectly on the near fringe. But given the flat lie and the precise landing required, the high pitch is a low-percentage play.

The Shot:

Hitting the ball into the bank and bouncing it onto the green may be your best option, provided the grass on the bank is not so thick as to smother the ball on contact. If you feel confident that the ball will bounce up the hill, take a middle to short iron, whatever will put the first bounce about two thirds of the way up the hill, and make a short punch swing. Play the ball back in your stance and set your weight left to promote clean contact.

When you play this shot, you may be fighting your instincts in two areas. First, you probably have

Hitting into the slope can be smarter than going over it.

to hit the ball about twice as hard as you think, as the first bounce into the slope is like hitting a wall; it takes a tremendous amount of energy off the shot. Second, you're so accustomed to using a wedge for greenside shots, you'll probably pick a club with too much loft and risk clearing the hill instead of bouncing into it. Keep these tendencies in mind and practice this shot into hills of varying grades to develop a feel for when and how to use it.

BEST TIP: The Chop Shot

When your ball finds shin-high rough around the green, you need a shot that will power through the grass and dig it out; that's "the chop shot." Play the ball off your back foot and lean toward the target, keeping your weight there throughout the swing. Swing the club back abruptly, cocking the wrists fully, and deliver a descending blow, cutting the grass behind the ball on the approach. Try to take a divot in front of the ball and strive to keep the club moving through the grass at least two feet past impact.

—Dave Pelz, *GOLF Magazine* Technical and Short Game Consultant

The Grassy Blast

The Situation:

At first glance, this shot doesn't look so bad: your ball lies in moderate rough only 15 or 20 feet off the fringe, with plenty of green to work with. A standard pitch should do the trick, right? Not so quick. On more careful examination, you see the grass, although not long, is very dense, surrounding the ball like a bird's nest (called a "nesty lie"). Your normal pitch swing will trap too much grass between the clubface and the ball, making contact and distance unpredictable. In this case, you have to give in to the lie; you simply cannot manufacture clean contact.

The Shot:

The best way to handle a nesty lie is to blast out of it as if you were hitting a bunker shot. Your weapon of choice should be one of the wedges: a sand wedge with bounce if the ball is sitting up; a lob or pitching wedge if the clubface needs to dig to accommodate a deeper lie.

From a nesty lie, play the ball forward and hit it like a bunker shot.

At address, play the ball two inches ahead of center, open the clubface, and aim about an inch behind the ball. Then make a half-swing, letting the wrists hinge the club back to vertical and through to vertical, trying to slide the clubface under the ball. Like in a bunker, the clubface never actually hits the ball, and therefore you need a more forceful swing than you might expect.

The ball will come out high and soft, with minimal backspin, due to the cushioned impact provided by the thick grass. Be forewarned: It takes some guts to hit this shot as hard as you have to, especially if the grass is growing away from the target, which will further kill the clubhead's momentum on contact. However, once you get comfortable with it, this shot can be a major stroke-saver.

The Hook Chip

The Situation:

You've come up just short of the green and the hole is cut way in the back. With only a few yards of fairway and all that green to cover, you could easily play a standard chip with a mid-iron, bouncing the ball onto the front edge and letting it roll the rest of the way. However, the longer irons can be unwieldy for chipping and choking down for control throws off the balance of the club and can lead to sloppy execution.

The Shot:

A better bet is to play the hook chip. Essentially, this is a standard chip shot, except with right-to-left sidespin, which promotes added roll. Using your 7- or 8-iron, play the ball off your right instep and push your hands ahead. Close the clubface slightly at address and swing the clubhead in to out

"The Hook Chip" runs hard for back hole locations.

through impact, just as you would to play a hook with your full swing.

This mini-hook will come off with more running power because the closed clubface creates the effect of a less-lofted club through impact without the awkwardness of the longer shaft. This shot is particularly useful when chipping to a top tier, since the ball needs extra forward momentum to climb uphill. In effect, you're hitting a shot that would normally require a longer swing or a longer club just by imparting hook spin on the ball.

BEST TIP: The Low Roller

When your ball is sitting up in grass just off the green, the low roller is an effective option that presents minimal risk. First, select the lowest lofted club you can use and still land the shot on the putting surface. Set up very close to the ball, with the club up on its toe and the ball off your right instep. Bend both elbows slightly to promote a level, sweeping swing. From there, make a simple putting-type motion with the arms and shoulders. The ball will skip forward with virtually no back-spin and roll to the hole.

—Jerry Mowlds, *GOLF Magazine* Top 100 Teacher

The Trap Shot

The Situation:

Your ball has come to rest on a severe upslope to the green. The lie itself is good, but you can't possibly set up the way you're supposed to for uphill lies, primarily by aligning your shoulders parallel to the slope. If you try, you'll risk toppling down the hill during the swing. Instead, you need to find a way to hit the ball while leaning into the slope so you can keep your balance.

The Shot:

No matter how determined you are, if you start to lose your balance during the swing, your body will instinctively try to save itself from falling; as a result, shot execution takes a back seat. That said, the key to handling this situation is to find firm footing and maintain it throughout the swing.

Start by selecting one of your wedges and taking a wide stance, leaning your weight into the hill like a mountain climber balancing between steps. Play the ball off your front instep and choke down to the shaft to make up for being closer to the ball. From

On severe upslopes, try to trap the ball against the ground.

there, make an abbreviated backswing and simply try to trap the back of the ball against the hill. The upslope will provide all the loft you need; concentrate on making clean contact with the back of the ball and keeping your balance.

The Half-Grass, Half-Sand Shot

The Situation:

Around the edges of bunkers, you often find sandy areas with grass growing through them—you're not really in the bunker, but you're not in the grass either. You will find it almost impossible to judge what the ground is like underneath the ball, thereby making it extremely difficult to select the appropriate shot. If you play a pitch shot and the lie turns out to be soft, you'll have to pick it perfectly, or else risk chunking it. If you try a bunker blast and the ground is firm, you'll launch your ball over the green.

The Shot:

Don't be a hero. It's not often you find one of these lies, which means you're never really comfortable standing over one. This is not the time to have visions of floating the ball to the pin and stopping it on a dime. Instead, your objective here should be to get the ball somewhere on the dance floor. Unless you have a good feel for the firmness of the lie—remember, if you're not in the bunker, you can

Play the ball back and chip it from half-grass, half-sand lies.

take practice divots—play a standard chip to the nearest spot on the green.

The uncertainty of the lie makes it imperative to hit the ball first. To ensure that you do, play the ball off your back instep and settle more weight over your front foot. Using as little loft as possible, make a simple arms-and-shoulders swing, clipping the ball off its perch and landing it on the closest edge of the putting surface. Resist the temptation of playing a riskier shot, trying to guess how the ball will come out; a little discipline and a safe play will at least keep you in the hole.

BEST TIP: Ball in Shallow Water

Hitting a ball out of water is not as unpredictable as you might think; in fact, it's a lot like hitting a greenside bunker shot. As in bunker play, the key is the setup, positioning both the ball (in your stance) and face alignment so the club will cut into the water about as deep as the bottom of the ball. Then you make an aggressive swing and continue into a full finish. Here are the adjustments to make depending on how deep the ball lies:

1. Ball mostly above the surface: clubface wide open, ball off left heel.

2. Ball one half to two thirds below surface: clubface partially open, ball between left heel and stance center.

3. Ball almost or completely below the surface: clubface square to slightly closed, ball in center to slightly behind.

—Dave Pelz, *GOLF Magazine* Technical and Short Game Consultant

5

Practice

Golfers typically practice for one of two reasons: They want to hit the ball more consistently, or they want to shoot lower scores. To meet the first goal, they go to the driving range and hit balls until they can't feel their hands. For the second, they go to the practice putting green, because putting is the most obvious culprit in high scores.

As a result of such practice habits, most golfers have grossly underdeveloped skills when it comes to greenside play. For instance, say you're a poor bunker player but you never hit a sand shot outside of an actual round. If you play twenty rounds a year and hit into five bunkers a round, you only hit 100 bunker shots during the course of an entire golf season. How can you expect to get any better, especially when every shot is a hit-and-hope experience?

Point is, you simply have to practice; there is no other way to develop your talents and gain confidence around the greens. But short-game practice can be much more interesting than working on your putting or your full swing. Think about it: You can play all sorts of different shots with different swings, using your imagination and playing games and competitions against yourself or a friend. The variety is as limitless as the short game itself. Enjoy the process and watch your scores start to drop.

BEST TIP: *Height Makes Right*

In the short game, trajectory is the key to controlling the total distance and the flight-to-roll ratio of the shot. I create trajectory mostly by changing clubs and altering my setup. Once I take my setup, I focus on where I want the ball to land, not the hole. When practicing shots of different trajectories, place towels on the green as your landing spots and develop a feel for picking a club and a shot that will get you to those spots.

—Annika Sorenstam, two-time
U.S. Women's Open Champion

The Short of It

If you're not sure about the importance of the short game, don't take my word for it: Keep track of your strokes. Every time you play a shot within 100 yards of the green, mark it on the scorecard and then rate your execution of the shot on a scale of 1 to 5. I bet you'll find two things: You play a lot more shots than you think you do from 100 yards in and your execution is not as sharp as it should be.

Keeping track of your rounds, you'll also find that you're better in some areas than others. You may be a fairly confident chipper, but become a nervous wreck when you have to pitch over sand or water. You may discover that you always take the air route over the

Keep track of your short-game shots and rate them 1 to 5.

***BEST TIP:** Club Drills*

Sometimes the best feedback you can get while practicing comes from a club—not the one you're swinging, but a club on the ground. Here are two simple drills to groove your chipping technique. First, place a club along the outside of your right foot and perpendicular to the target line. With the ball off your right instep, practice chipping balls with the clubhead missing the club on the ground (see photo at right5). Second, create a track for your clubhead with two clubs about four inches apart and aimed at the target. Practice chipping between the shafts to ensure an on-track swing path.

—Martin Hall, *GOLF Magazine*
Master Teaching Professional

ground route, or that you have an aversion toward your sand wedge. These are all useful things to know as you look at ways to improve your short game.

Once you know where your weaknesses are, you know where to focus your practice efforts. The old adage "play to your strengths" is wise advice, but around the green you can't always control where your ball ends up. You have to learn how to play all of the basic short-game shots, and that starts with making sure your technique is sound.

Review the basic instruction contained in this book and devise your own improvement plan. Re-

member, practicing just for the sake of practicing is useless. As Dave Pelz puts it in *Dave Pelz's Short Game Bible*, "Practice doesn't make perfect; practice makes permanent. If you practice poorly, you will become consistently poor . . . perfect practice makes for good progress and improvement."

To begin with, practice your worst shots first; they're probably causing the biggest disasters on your scorecard. Devote some time to these dreaded shots in every practice session, before you go onto the ones you play with confidence. And for those who say they have no place to practice, think again. You may have to use your imagination, but there's always a way to practice most of the shots in your short game.

Take your own backyard. Okay, so you don't have a practice bunker back there, like some Tour players do, but you can still find plenty to practice. Try pitching over picnic benches or chipping to tree trunks. No doubt you could find some pretty ugly lies in your yard—thick, clumpy lies, maybe even some hardpan. Indoors, try chipping to table legs or clipping specks of dirt off the carpet. These activities are not only fun diversions; they're at your disposal every day. If you look at it this way, the short game is easier to practice than either the full swing or putting. Any other excuses?

Make It Real

While practicing at home can be useful, try to simulate on-course conditions as often as possible when you practice. If your course has a short-game practice area, stake out a spot there and put some time in chipping and pitching the ball various distances from various lies.

At the very least, hit shots from grass cut the same length as the rough you find around your greens. And practice hitting balls from less-than-perfect lies. Without conscious thought, most golfers instinctively roll their practice balls into fluffed-up lies and then feel cheated when they don't get them on the course. One way to create realistic lies is to throw the balls up in the air and play them from wherever they come to rest. In addition, make sure you practice with the same kind of ball you play with. If you prefer a soft-covered ball but practice your short game with range balls, you'll develop two sets of sensations. That's no way to keep it simple.

Another thing that amateurs often fail to do when they practice is attach value to the shots. It's easy to think of every shot as a "freebie" when you practice; after all, just rake over another ball and you can try it again. But instead, try to discipline yourself into thinking that every shot counts. Make up contests for yourself, such as refusing to go home until you chip eight out of ten balls into an imaginary five-foot circle around the hole. Give the shots meaning. Remember, there are no do-overs on the course.

Finally, divide your practice time to mirror your game. For instance, if you shoot around 100, you probably play about 60 shots per round within 100 yards of the green. So spend 60 percent of your practice time on short shots—maybe 30 percent on putting and the other 30 on chipping, pitching, and sand play. To stick to this, spend fifteen minutes on the putting green before you hit the range, then intersperse short wedge shots between every five full swings you make, and end your session in the short-game area. Without a plan like this, your practice sessions will tend to be ball-beating exhibitions. Adher-

Focus your practice by imagining a five-foot circle around the hole.

ing to a plan may take some discipline, but you'll develop a more well-rounded, more satisfying game.

Make It Fun

To many golfers, practicing the short game is about as exciting as watching grass grow. If you're of this mentality, you need to overcome that feeling of drudgery by recognizing the importance of short-game practice and then making it more engaging. As Bobby Jones put it in his famous instructional *Bobby Jones on Golf,* "Practice must be interesting, even absorbing, if it is to be of any use. Monotony palls, and nothing can be more monotonous than playing over and over the same shot from the same place."

To elevate your interest level, strive to create a sense of challenge or competition when you practice by playing a friend or pitting one ball against another. A few simple games for your practice green come to mind: playing a nine-hole match trying to get up and down from various spots around the green; chipping three balls and then putting out your worst effort; pitching one ball and chipping another to the same hole. If you really want to make things interesting, have you and your opponent create each other's lies and designate the club to be used.

Local Knowledge

Does your home course often call for a certain kind of shot? For instance, the greens may be elevated and propped up by steep banks, making the bank shot a useful weapon. If so, practice hitting into steep upslopes whenever you get the opportunity. Or, you may find the need for a specially designed club, such as a lob wedge or a sand wedge with a lot of bounce, to handle situations you commonly encounter. Point is, keep track of the types of greenside shots your course presents and make sure you have the skills and the equipment required to execute them.

That'll test your imagination and your ability to think quickly and manufacture shots.

If you still find short-game practice uninteresting, limit the time of your sessions to ten minutes each. Alternate your practice from putting to full-swing work to the short game, keeping the stimuli fresh by jumping from one to the other before your mind can start to wander. Remember, practice loses

Practice getting up and down: Chip the ball, then try to sink the putt.

its effectiveness when you fall into a routine of just going through the motions. Stay focused.

The Rewards of Hard Work

Progress in your short game comes in two forms: actual and perceived. It cannot be disputed that every golfer can improve his short game with a fair amount of focused practice. If you keep statistics on your rounds, you'll start to see a higher up-and-down percentage, closer putts for par, and generally better scores.

> ### BEST TIP: Rhythm Method
>
> Good rhythm is crucial to pitching and chipping. But it's difficult to keep in rhythm if the lengths of the backswing and follow-through don't match. A short backswing causes overacceleration at impact and an overly long follow-through; a long backswing leads to deceleration at impact. Practice making the backward and forward motions equal in length. Once you get a feel for these "mirror-image" motions, your short-game swings will have smooth rhythm, producing solid contact and better distance control.
> —Keith Lyford, *GOLF Magazine* Top 100 Teacher

You'll also notice a capability for making quicker, smarter decisions regarding which shot to play in a given situation and which club to play it with. This is a by-product of increased practice: You'll be the proud owner of a better feel for how to manage your short game. That's real progress.

Perhaps even more important is your perceived progress. If you can stand up to greenside shots with the confidence to execute them with a free mind uncluttered by negative or anxious thoughts, your entire game will improve. It's true, a confident short game takes the pressure off the rest of your game. Imagine how much more relaxed you'll feel on approach shots, and tee shots for that matter, knowing you can miss a green and still have a good chance at par. Good feelings can be just as infectious as bad ones.

So get out there and start practicing, because an ability to read and handle greenside situations is the most effective protection against wasted strokes. Practice is the only thing that will get you thinking better, executing better, and therefore scoring lower. Now that sounds like something every golfer should do. Simply put, it is.

As your short game improves, your confidence around the green will soar.

The *GOLF Magazine*

Complete Guide to Golf

Book Six

Putting

Peter Morrice

and the Editors of *GOLF Magazine*

Photography by Sam Greenwood

Introduction

Admit it: You hate putting. Before you object, there's plenty of evidence to support this contention. Consider: If you shoot ninety for eighteen holes with 36 putts (an average of two per green), 40 percent of your strokes are made with the putter. Compare that to maybe 20 strokes with the wedge, 14 with the driver, and another 20 or so with all the remaining clubs in the bag. But you don't spend 40 percent of your practice time putting. Nobody does, because *everybody* hates putting.

If people really liked to putt, there'd be multitiered practice putting facilities popping up all over the country. Holes would be reserved by the hour, and people would rush from work to roll a few before dinner. And the average American handicap would be way down. Fact is, putting has the biggest effect on how well you score, yet folks would much rather spend time whacking balls off rubber mats with the driver, a club that's used less than half as much.

Then again, maybe you don't hate putting; maybe you just don't understand it. It can be something to enjoy, obsess about even, if you approach it not just as a shorter version of all the other shots you hit in golf, but a completely different game in itself. It's contained and precise; a thinking man's game, like billiards or chess. It doesn't require near the amount of coordination it takes to crush a 270-yard drive, yet it would be hard to find a physically more awkward feeling than missing a three-foot putt. It's mysterious and paradoxical: The great Ben Hogan, perhaps the finest and most consistent ball-striker ever, once said, "I'd enjoy the game a lot more if I didn't have to putt." Hogan won nine major titles, including back-to-back U.S. Opens in 1950 and 1951, but nobody ever accused him of being particularly strong on the greens. Perhaps he didn't understand putting either.

But don't let that fool you into thinking that good putting is some sort of mystical blessing bestowed by the golf gods. Success with the putter comes from a simple formula: a combination of proper technique and a confidence that comes from knowing what you're doing as you stand over each putt. And anybody can make that happen. The technique is not particularly complicated or physically demanding, and you don't have to be a rocket scientist to read greens and understand smart putting strategy. So, there's no reason why a high handicapper can't be a good putter and a middle-handicapper a great putter well before either masters the game from tee to green.

If that doesn't inspire you, go back to that hypothetical 90 you shot with the 36 putts. Say you eliminate a few three putts and sink a couple of 10-footers that you ordinarily miss. Now you've taken 30 putts, and that bloated 90 is suddenly a lean and mean 84, a much more exciting number to see at the bottom of the scorecard. The next round you play, there's less pressure on your game from tee to green because *you know* you're putting well. You relax, swing a little freer, and *presto*—hit four more greens in regulation than you did the round before. Add your 30 putts, and you're actually threatening to break 80! A 10-stroke improvement, and that's without hitting one driver off a rubber mat.

Of course, 10 strokes is optimistic. It's completely plausible for a high handicapper, but maybe there's only six or seven strokes to be had for a 15-handi-capper. And maybe a single-digit player can only hope to cut three or four—but those are still precious strokes. Nevertheless, one thing is certain: Whatever your level of play, the fastest way to take it to the next level is by improving your play on the greens. You may have hated putting before, but you'll love it when your scores start to drop.

If this reads like a sermon on the value of putting, fine—the purpose of this book is not only to teach, but to inspire as well. You'll have the opportunity to familiarize (or refamiliarize) yourself with the fundamentals, brush up on strategy, and learn some new ways to make those sessions on the practice green actually bearable. You'll also find some of the most helpful putting tips ever published in *GOLF Magazine*, in a feature called "Best Tip." Not that any of it will ever make putting as exciting as nailing a perfect drive or sticking an approach shot close to the pin, but it should show you that real improvement is well within your reach. And that's the exciting part.

1

The Setup

Any discussion of putting technique has to begin with two acknowledgments. The first one is that at the end of the day, there is no "right" way to putt. Because putting is such a make-or-break part of the game, whatever happens to get the ball in the hole in the least number of strokes is perfect. If you digest all the information in this book and then realize that you're deadly from inside 10 feet standing on one foot, stick with it. That technique is right for you. On the Tour, making putts is the difference between big money and just scraping by. So it's not surprising to see a wide variety of putting styles among the pros, from tall posture to crouched posture, from narrow to wide stances, from short, poppy strokes to long, slow sweeps. Players do what works.

Second acknowledgment: Even though there are no hard-and-fast rules of putting technique, there are a handful of fundamentals that work for most golfers. Those fundamentals will be the primary focus of the technical section of this book. More specifically, most golfers will find the greatest success by making a putting stroke that is controlled almost entirely by moving the arms and shoulders as a unit, while the hands simply follow along. *For most golfers*, it's easier to keep the putterface pointed at the target if the hands and wrists aren't doing anything except stabilizing the club.

For sure, there have been great putters who used wristy strokes—and "alternative techniques" will also be addressed in the book—but most of the fundamentals of grip, stance, and alignment are designed to promote an arms-and-shoulders stroke, because that's the simplest way to do it. And simple means easy to do well, and easy to repeat. So, before you jump to the conclusion that your stroke is decidedly idiosyncratic, get to know and understand these basic fundamentals. See how they work for you. If you're a better player, use them to check yourself. A prolonged stretch of inconsistency might indicate that you've wandered too far away from them. But no matter your level of play, let simplicity be the foundation of your putting stroke. Once that's established, you can go about discovering the nuances that will make your stroke distinctly yours.

The Pendulum Motion

Imagine a tower with a pendulum hanging from a fixed point at the top, like a grandfather clock. The pendulum swings back and forth while the clock tower remains still. It's a time-worn yet perfect analogy for an arms-and-shoulders putting stroke. Your body is the tower, and your shoulders, arms, hands, and putter form the pendulum. The fixed point is right between your shoulders—the very top of your sternum. The body remains still while the shoulders, arms, hands, and club swing back and through. If you think in those terms, it's easy to see why grip and stance are such important parts of putting. If your hands and wrists move independently, the pendulum breaks down. If your stance is unstable, the pendulum won't swing from a fixed point.

You can see and feel the pendulum motion by standing in front of a full-length mirror without a golf club. Bend forward from the hips and clap your palms together so your hands, arms, and shoulders form a large triangle (remember this triangle image, as we'll come back to it often). Keeping the palms together, swing the arms back and through by rocking the shoulders. Notice how the triangle is maintained throughout the motion; the relationship between the hands, arms, and shoulders never changes. This is the

To feel the pendulum, swing your hands and arms back as a triangle.

essence of the arms-and-shoulders stroke; it changes slightly when there's an actual club in your hands, but your grip and stance should be designed to make the difference as small as possible.

As you swing through, maintain the shape of the triangle.

Grip

When the palms face each other directly below your sternum, as they do when you create the triangle, they are perpendicular to the target line. In other words, the back of the left hand and the palm of the right hand face the hole, which makes it easier to swing the arms back and through on a straight line. That's the goal with the putting grip; there are many different variations, but you'll find it easiest to make a straight arms-and-shoulders stroke if the palms face each other.

Fortunately, most putter grips are designed to help you do this. Find the flat ridge running down the middle of the grip; if you hold the club with both thumbs resting on top of that ridge, your palms will be effectively facing each other. (The palms don't *really* face each other, not as they do in the triangle exercise, because the right hand is below the left on the grip.) Generally, the hands are closer together on the putter than they are in a regular full-swing grip. That way, they operate much more as a single unit, keeping the connection between the arms and putter as seamless as possible so the pendulum can swing without any unnecessary complications.

In the traditional Vardon, or overlapping, grip used in the full swing, the club sits in the fingers of

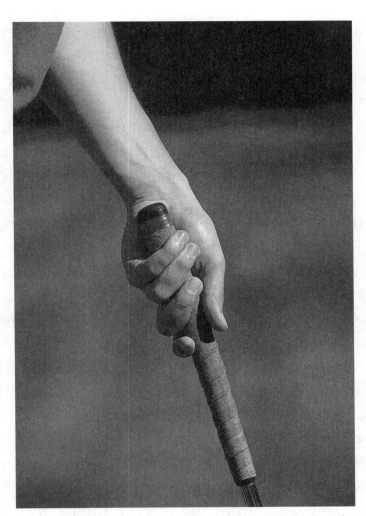

The grip should run down the middle of the left palm.

the left hand, allowing the wrist the necessary mobility to hinge during the swing. With a putter, however, the grip is nestled into the palm of the hand, locked right into the channel created by the thumb pad and the heel. Holding the handle in the palm not only points the back of the hand to the target, but has the effect of immobilizing the left wrist as well, so the swinging of the putter can be a natural extension of the arms-and-shoulders movement. (Incidentally, this is why some players prefer a thicker grip on their putters—it makes it easier to grip in the palm, thereby reducing the risk of unwanted contribution from the hands and wrists.) The left thumb sits on top of the grip, on the flat ridge, and, although the fingers should never apply more than moderate pressure to the handle, the bulk of the squeezing in the left hand is done by the last two fingers.

Place the right hand on the grip so the right thumb pad covers the left thumb and the right thumb rests on the flat ridge. Wrap all four fingers of the right hand around the handle so the palm directly faces the target. In the reverse-overlap grip— the accepted "standard" for putting—the left forefinger, and sometimes the middle finger, too, rests on top of the fingers of the right hand. It's this overlapping of fingers that makes it possible for the hands to be as close together as possible. First try overlapping the left forefinger only. Does the grip feel as if it's seated securely in your left palm between the heel and thumb pad? If it doesn't, you

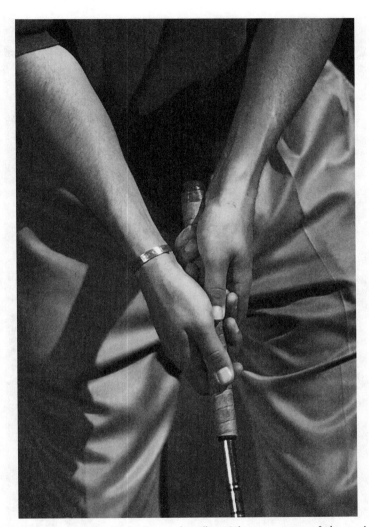

Both thumbs should sit on the flat ridge on top of the grip.

can try extending the left forefinger so it points down the shaft, across the first knuckles of the fingers of the right hand. Let the middle finger of the left hand overlap the pinkie or ring finger of the

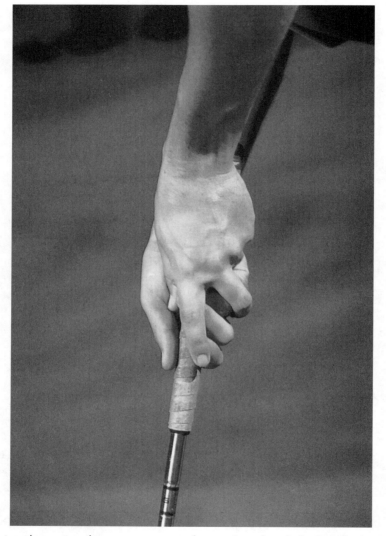

In the popular reverse-overlap grip, the left forefinger "overlaps" the right hand.

right. You may find it easier to set the grip in the palm of the left hand this way. Certainly with two fingers overlapping, the hands are closer together. If you feel like you can control the putter with this grip, it's a great way to keep the hands operating as a single unit.

Already you can see that there are viable options when it comes to gripping the putter. If you decide to experiment, remember the goals of a conventional grip: to keep the hands close together, the palms facing each other, and wrist action to a minimum. With a good grip, you have in place the critical first piece of the putting puzzle.

Stance and Posture

Like the hands, the position of the body has a major effect on your ability to make a straight, smooth pendu-

First and Foremost

The reverse-overlap grip was invented by Walter J. Travis, a putting pioneer who won three of the first four U.S. Amateur Championships of the 20th century. A late bloomer who didn't take up the game until his mid-30s, Travis was a notoriously short hitter who compensated by infuriating his opponents with stellar putting. Nobody complained about his grip (he later taught it to the great Bobby Jones), but his putter—one of the first center-shafted models, known as "The Schenectady"—was banned in Britain after he won the 1904 British Amateur.

lum stroke. Go back to the triangle exercise: If you stand perfectly straight and tall, there won't be any room for your arms to swing back and through; your body will be in the way. Similarly, if your stance points 45 degrees to the left, your arms will want to swing that way, instead of to the target. Positioning the body to putt is not a complicated process, but it is something to be meticulous about. Good body position breeds a good stroke; poor position breeds compensations and mistakes.

In a standard putting stroke, only the pendulum moves—the shoulders, arms, and hands. The rest of the body—legs, hips, torso, head—remains still from the moment the stroke starts until after contact is made. You should always be relaxed, but at the same time, your stance serves to lock your body into place.

Start without a club. Stand with your feet 15 to 20 inches apart and square to the target line (imagine a line drawn across the tops of your toes; if that line is parallel to the line running from the ball to the target, your stance is square). Stability is the prime objective here, so distribute your weight evenly between each foot and allow the knees to flex slightly. Locking the knees may feel stable, but it actually creates tension in the body, which will eventually creep into your stroke. Bend forward slightly from the hips; notice how this allows the arms to hang from the shoulders, away from the torso. If you feel your weight moving onto your toes, you're bending too far.

This posture puts the body in position to make a straight-back, straight-through pendulum stroke. It's a square setup—if you drew imaginary lines across the feet, knees, hips, and shoulders, all would be parallel to the target line. Also, notice

With proper posture, the hands hang below the shoulders.

from a down-the-line view how the hands hang under the shoulders. That way, they can easily swing straight back and through on a line parallel to the target line.

Now try it with a putter and a ball. Everything stays the same: feet square, knees slightly flexed, torso bent forward from the hips, hands directly under shoulders . . . plus one more thing. Draw an-

A square stance promotes an on-line stroke.

other imaginary line—this time from your eyes to the ball. That line should be vertical, or very close to vertical, indicating that your eyes are over the ball. This is a must if you're going to see the line of the putt clearly. Otherwise, you're looking at the line from an odd angle, which will distort your perception. Generally, if your eyes are well inside the ball, what appears to be a straight line at the hole will actually point to the right of the hole; if the eyes are outside the ball, what appears to be a straight line will actually point to the left. Only if your eyes are over the ball can you be sure that what you see is what you actually get.

BEST TIP: Stay Balanced

Here are two quick ways to make sure that your body is balanced at the setup, with the arms hanging naturally from the shoulders: 1. If you lift the putter off the ground slightly, it should remain in place, not drift one way or another; 2. Have a friend try to push you off balance. If you're set up properly, it shouldn't have much effect. If you stumble, you weren't very stable in your setup.

—Gregor Jamieson, *GOLF Magazine*
Top 100 Teacher

BEST TIP: Check Your Eyeline

You can be sure that your eyes are over the ball by dropping a second ball from the bridge of your nose; it should hit the ball you're addressing. But it's just as important that your eyeline be parallel to the target line. To check this, take your stance, then hold your putter horizontally at waist level so it is directly under your eyes. If your eyes are over the ball, the shaft should appear to cover the ball; and you know your eyeline is parallel to the target line when you swivel your head and see that the shaft points directly at the hole.

—Eddie Merrins, *GOLF Magazine*
Top 100 Teacher

Square vs. Open

It's simplest to putt with your feet—and the rest of your body—perfectly parallel to the target line, but it's not uncommon to see good players adopting an open stance, in which an imaginary line drawn across the feet angles to the left of the target. Two of the best putters in history, Jack Nicklaus and Ben Crenshaw, have frequently used an open stance, claiming that it makes it easier to see the line of the putt. While that may be true, understand that if your feet are angled to the left of the target, your shoulders probably will be, as well. This alignment will then encourage your arms to swing in the same direction—to the left. Given that, the only way to

Arnie's Unusual Stance

How important is it for your body to be stable? If you go by the great Arnold Palmer, at his best one of the top pressure putters ever, a still body is crucial, no matter what the cost. Palmer was an athletic, charismatic player when his aggressive style of play captured the world's imagination in the 1950s and '60s, but he looked rather unconventional doing it. His full swing was a fast, swiping motion, and his putting stance looked as if he was a long way from a bathroom—and knew it. Knees knocked, feet pigeon-toed, thighs pinched together, he bent way over from the hips to get close to the ball. It wasn't pretty, but it served to lock his body into place so the only thing moving during the stroke would be his shoulders, arms, and hands. And the results he achieved speak for themselves.

swing the putterhead straight down the target line is to reroute it with the hands and arms during the stroke, which is probably more complication than you want to add to your putting motion.

Nicklaus and Crenshaw pulled it off because both had razor-sharp touch in their prime, but for the average golfer, it's much more practical to adopt a square stance. With a square setup, the arms can just follow the lead of the shoulders, without any extra manipulation required.

To Crouch or Not to Crouch

How much should you crouch over when you putt? Again, look at Nicklaus and Crenshaw: Jack always crouched as much as anybody on Tour, while Ben stood tall. Both, obviously, can be fantastic ways to putt. But keep this in mind: Crouching gets you closer to the ball, which can offer a better sense of control, but it also creates angles in the elbows and wrists. For some, those angles can destabilize the triangle formed by the shoulders, arms, and hands, so the shoulders are no longer in complete control of the stroke.

Standing tall, on the other hand, allows the arms to hang straight, or nearly straight, from the shoul-

Crouching over can bolster feel but complicate the stroke.

ders. Being farther from the ball doesn't provide the same sense of control, but you may find it easier to make a smooth pendulum stroke if the arms and wrists are essentially straight and the integrity of the triangle is maintained. Experiment to find what feels best for you.

Standing tall can simplify the stroke but may reduce feel.

The Importance of Ball Position

All theories aside, the putting stroke is not a perfect pendulum motion. In order for that to happen, the putter would have to be built like a croquet mallet, so the arms and shaft could form a vertical line down from the shoulders to the ball. And the shoulders would have to make a perfectly vertical rocking motion, like a hanger on a coat rack.

In reality, the putter is more like a hockey stick, with the shaft angled toward the player. Also, the shoulders don't rock on a perfectly vertical line; they rotate around the spine, as they do in the full swing. As a result, the motion that the putterhead makes during the stroke is *pendulum-like*, but also slightly rounded. That is, not only does the putterhead lift off the ground as it swings back, it also moves slightly to the inside of the target line. As it swings through, it returns down to the target line, then swings up and through to the inside again. It's not very pronounced, and in most cases, it's not even noticeable, but that rounded path is precisely why ball position is critical.

Consider how this path affects the angle of the putterface. When the putterhead goes back slightly inside the line, the putterface naturally rotates open relative to the target. It returns to square at the bottom of the swing arc, stays square for a couple of inches, then rotates closed to the target as the putterhead swings through. So, all else being equal, unless you make contact when the putterhead is within a couple of inches of the bottom of the swing arc, the ball will not roll on the line you've intended. And that's not all. In order for the ball to roll as smoothly as possible, contact must be made when the putterhead is moving parallel to the ground or just slightly on the upswing. If contact is made too early or too late, the ball may skid excessively or hop before rolling, both of which can affect distance control. In other words, you can make a perfect stroke and still miss—and miss badly—if you haven't positioned the ball in your stance correctly.

The good news is that the legs and torso don't move during the stroke, so the low point of the swing arc will generally be in the same place relative to your body every time. To find that spot, go back to the pendulum; the low point of a pendulum's arc is opposite the fixed point where the top of the pendulum connects to the tower. Now think in terms of the triangle exercise: The fixed point is a spot between your shoulders, at the top of the sternum. When the hands are directly under that spot, they are at the bottom of the swing arc. That should be your reference point when positioning your body to the ball.

The putterface should make contact at the low point or just slightly ahead of it (remember, you've got a two-inch window before the putterface begins to rotate off-line). So, position the ball just ahead of the middle of your sternum, about an inch. Assuming your weight is evenly distributed between both feet, that's far enough forward to ensure you don't hit the ball with a descending blow, which can

For optimum contact, play the ball one inch ahead of your sternum.

pinch the ball against the turf and influence the roll. It's also far enough back in your stance that the putterface will still be square to the target, assuming your stroke hasn't broken down.

You might wonder why the sternum is used as the initial point of reference for ball position, and not the feet. That would be simpler, wouldn't it, considering that they're so much closer to the ball? Yes, but the feet aren't always reliable. Consider this: If you position the ball just ahead of center relative to your feet, it will also be just ahead of the center of your sternum—if your weight is evenly distributed between both feet. But if you favor the front leg in your stance (Greg Norman and Nick Faldo do it), your torso shifts forward with your weight, so that same ball position—just ahead of center in your stance—will actually be *behind* the center of your sternum. You'll make contact before the putterhead reaches the bottom of its arc and trap the ball against the green. On the other hand, if you use your sternum as the reference point, you can be sure the ball position is correct every time.

A Word on Aim

All these specifics about the setup are actually only half of what you need to hit the ball the way you want. Aim is the other factor. Good aim is about setting the putterface square to the target; a good setup aligns the body relative to the putterface. Since aim is closely associated with the routine of actually executing a putt on the course, it will be discussed in the next chapter, "The Stroke."

2

The Stroke

Why does putting have to be so complicated? It's just a short little stroke made with a short little club. It's easy—certainly easier than hitting a full shot with, say, a 3-iron. Right?

Well, kind of. It's easier to make solid contact on a putt than it is on a long-iron shot, but in other ways, a putt is much more demanding. First of all, there's far less margin for error. If you hit a 3-iron from 190 yards to a green that's 20 yards wide, you can have varying degrees of success. Hitting the ball next to the pin is great, but just getting it on the green is pretty good, too. For that matter, missing the green but leaving yourself an easy chip shot isn't so bad, either—you still have a good chance at par. You can miss your target by 10 yards—that's 30 feet—and still feel good about yourself.

With putting, the target is only 4¼ inches wide, and there's only one way to be successful: by making the ball go in the hole. Missing is failure, whether it's by an inch or a foot, unless you're a long way from the hole and just trying to get down in two. But from inside 15 feet, there are only misses—which are no fun—and bad misses, when you leave yourself in position where you might miss again.

And what about distance control? You know approximately how far that 3-iron is going to go if you hit it well. So you only use it when you're the appropriate distance from the green; if you're closer, you take less club and make virtually the same swing. Distance control, for the most part, is out of your hands: The loft of the club and length of the shaft largely determine how far the ball will go. But on the green, the putter is the only club you use, regardless of distance. You determine how far the ball will roll based on how much effort you put into the stroke; it's all on you. So it may not be a physically challenging move, but the putting stroke demands a better sense for direction and distance than any other shot in golf.

A more familiar way to describe direction and distance on the green is by using the words "line" and "speed." To make an effective stroke for any given putt, you need to know what the line of the putt is (the path the ball will take to the hole) and have a sense for the speed (how hard to hit the ball so that it reaches the hole). These factors are fairly simple on a short, straight putt, but if the green is sloped between the ball and the hole, they're dependent on each other: You can't know the right line of a putt unless you have a feel for the speed; and the proper speed varies based on what line you want the ball to take. In that case, understanding line and speed is a process in itself, something that will be explored at length in Chapter Three. First, you have to be able to hit the ball straight. And that begins with proper alignment.

Aim and Alignment

Think in terms of a straight, 10-foot putt. As with full shots, it's easiest to aim the putterface to the hole first, then align your body perpendicular to the putterface. To begin the process, the putterface should be square—at a right angle to the line of the putt. Most putters have a little horizontal line etched into the top of the head designed to help you make sure the face is square. Once the face is square, align your body accordingly, starting with your feet. In a square setup, the lines of your feet,

Square the putterface first, then set your stance
perpendicular to the face.

knees, hips, and shoulders are parallel to the line of
the putt, or perpendicular to the putterface. So,
with square aim and alignment and a straight-back,
straight-through stroke that returns the putterface
to the same square position at impact, the ball will
roll perfectly straight.

Aligning yourself for putts that break (curve to the right or left because of undulations in the green) is only slightly different. Instead of aiming the putterface at the hole, square it to the line on which the ball should start. That is, if the putt breaks six inches from right to left, aim the putterface six inches right of the hole, then align your body square to the putterface. From there, make the same straight-back, straight-through stroke you would for a straight putt. It's really that simple.

Spot Putting

Aiming the putterface is easy when the hole is three feet away, but what if it's 20 feet? It's much tougher to be precise and, therefore, feel confident that you're aiming the putter and yourself in the right direction. Wouldn't it be a shame to make a perfect stroke and miss the putt because your putterface and body were aligned just a fraction off-line?

Try spot putting instead. Crouch behind the ball and picture in your mind the line it will take to the hole. Then, choose a spot—an old ball mark or discolored patch of grass—about three feet in front of the ball and on that imaginary line. Instead of aim-

For accurate aim, line up to a spot a few feet in front of the ball.

ing the putterface at the hole, aim it to the spot you've chosen, three feet away. It's much easier to be sure of yourself with such a close target. Then, align your body perpendicular to the putterface and make your stroke. If you've read the putt correctly, the ball will roll over the spot and continue on into the hole.

The Three Elements of a Perfect Putt

To hit a perfect, on-line putt, three things have to happen at impact: The path of the putterhead has to be straight along the target line; the putterface has to be square to the target; and contact has to be made on the sweet spot of the putterface. To tell the truth, you can hit the ball on-line without perfect path, face angle, or contact, but it's a much easier game without trying to offset mistakes.

Two things occur if you strike a putt when your path is not straight along the target line. Assuming the face is still square to the target, sidespin is imparted to the ball, just like in the full swing. If the path goes from in to out, the ball will spin slightly from right to left as it rolls, encouraging the ball to go left and slowing it down. When the path is out to in, the ball spins from left to right, and tends to drift weakly to the right.

The other effect a faulty path has on a putt is starting direction. If the path goes to the left, the ball will typically start left. If the path is right, the ball will usually start right—even if the face remains square to the target line. That said, a faulty path probably gets too much credit for most missed putts. Since it's easy to see when your path is off, many players naturally assume that it's the main reason why the ball went off-line. But according to Dave Pelz, *GOLF Magazine*'s Technical and Short Game Consultant, there's a more likely culprit: face angle. A former scientist at NASA, Pelz has conducted exhaustive research on the physics of putting, and one of the many things he has discovered is that only 20 percent of a golfer's error in path is actually transmitted to the golf ball. Translated, that means if the putterhead is moving out to in, five degrees to the left of the target line, the ball will roll only one degree left of the target line, assuming the face is square to the target. That's about two inches on a 20-foot putt. So, a faulty path, while easy to see, has less effect on the ball's direction than you might imagine.

An error in face angle, on the other hand, is difficult to see—especially in somebody else's stroke—but Pelz's research shows that 90 percent of a golfer's error in face angle is transmitted to the golf ball. That means if the face is 10 degrees closed at impact, the ball will go 9 degrees left of the target line—and miss the hole by almost two feet on a 20-foot putt. So, when your putts miss the hole significantly to the right or left, your path may be off, but your face angle almost definitely is.

> ## BEST TIP: Hit the Tee
>
> Want to check your face angle at impact? Stick a tee in the end of a grip and lay the club on the green. Pretend the shaft is your target line. Set up to the tee and make your normal stroke: If the face is square, you'll tap the tee solidly; if it's open or closed, you'll knock the club off-line.
>
> —Martin Hall, *GOLF Magazine* Master Teaching Professional

How about the third factor: solid contact? How important is that? First, you should understand what happens when you make contact off the sweet spot. If, for example, you make contact toward the toe of the putter, the heel kicks forward, the face twists open, and less energy is imparted to the ball.

BEST TIP: Band-Aid Cure

Wrap two Band-Aids around the face of the putter so the pads form a half-inch frame of the sweet spot. If you make contact in the middle of the face, the putt will come off as usual. But if you make contact off center, the ball will hit one of the pads and roll about half as far. As solid contact becomes easier, move the Band-Aids closer together.

—Darrell Kestner, *GOLF Magazine*
Top 100 Teacher

Chances are, the putt will finish farther right and shorter than you were expecting. Exactly how much depends on how the putter you're using is constructed, but Pelz found that, on average, an eight-foot putt hit a quarter inch toward the toe will miss the hole 95 percent of the time. Clearly, the farther you get from the hole, the worse the odds get. The putting stroke may be a small motion, but don't take solid contact for granted; it's too important to ignore.

Common Faults

Straight stroke, square face, solid contact—simple, right? Think about it for a second: It's not like you're trying to make a full shoulder turn and drive the legs and clear the hips and finish in balance. It's a simple, pendulum-like motion controlled by the arms and shoulders. Weather and course conditions play a part, but mostly, if you're missing putts it's because you're making mistakes—adding flaws to a simple activity. The physical challenge of putting is less about achieving kinesthetic brilliance than it is avoiding mistakes. Next, we'll cover some of the most common errors and point to solutions.

Make a Stroke with Two Clubs

For a consistent stroke, you must have a feeling of unification between the shoulders, arms, hands, and club. Want to make it easy? Try it the hard way first: With a putter in one hand and a sand wedge in the other, make strokes with both, keeping the clubs parallel and about three inches apart throughout. If you can move both shoulders, arms, hands, and clubs in unison, doing it with one club will be a piece of cake.

Fault

Jerking the putter back away from the ball.

Effect

If the backstroke is rushed or jerky, you can bet something's going to move out of sequence, most likely the hands. That usually means the putterhead will swing off-line, or the putterface will rotate open or closed. As a result, whatever mistakes were made in the backstroke have to be undone in the through-stroke to hit a straight putt. Since the extraneous movement that occurred has to be repeated in reverse, the chances of hitting the ball where you've aimed are slim.

Cure

It can be hard to start the stroke smoothly when the body and club are dead still. The muscles can

A slight forward press often prevents a jerky start.

get "twitchy" and throw the backstroke out of whack. If this is a problem for you, try using a trigger to initiate the stroke. Before starting the putterhead back, tap it gently on the turf or press your hands just slightly toward the hole. Those are just two examples; the point is that setting the body in motion before the stroke makes it much easier to take the putterhead away from the ball smoothly. If you're smooth, you're much more likely to keep the putterface square and on-line. Experiment to find a trigger that works for you.

BEST TIP: Don't Drop the Ball

To keep the putterhead on-line and the putterface square in the backstroke, there can't be any unnecessary movement in the wrists. Try this drill to check your wrists: Assume your normal setup and grip, then have a friend wedge a golf ball between your right wrist and the grip. Stroke the putt. If the ball falls out, your wrists have hinged on the backstroke. Only if the wrists remain still will the ball stay lodged in place.

—Bill Davis, *GOLF Magazine* Top 100 Teacher

Fault

Making an excessively short (or long) backstroke and then having to accelerate (or decelerate) on the forward stroke.

Swing the putter back smoothly with the arms and shoulders.

Effect

The natural putting stroke is like a pendulum—the backstroke should match the through-stroke. Any effort to change that natural motion—like slowing the putterhead down to compensate for an overly long backstroke, or making an very short backstroke then jerking the putterhead through— makes it very difficult to keep the putterface square and to maintain a feel for speed.

Cure

The big misconception when it comes to putting tempo is that you have to *try* to accelerate the put-

Let the natural swinging motion power the through-stroke.

terhead into the ball. You simply don't. Remember, the putterhead comes to a complete stop, however brief, at the top of the backstroke, then starts moving again, which means it's accelerating. Even if you apply no effort at all and just let gravity pull the putterhead through, it will accelerate into the ball. So don't try to control the acceleration of the putter on the through-stroke. Think of the arms, hands, and putter as one unit, and let gravity drive the motion, like a pendulum. If you've made a solid backstroke, the putterhead will naturally swing through on the right line with a square putterface. You'll have a better feel for speed, too: Like a slingshot, the farther back you swing the putter, the faster the ball will roll. In time, you'll develop a feel for how the length of the stroke determines distance.

Fault

Peeking to watch the ball roll.

Effect

Unless your head swivels perfectly, it's almost impossible to move it without somehow moving your body as well, and even the slightest body movement before contact, especially on short putts, can make the difference between a miss and a make. Remember the pendulum: If the tower moves, the pendulum won't swing on the same path. In other words, you'll throw the putterhead off-line.

Cure

Focus not only on watching the ball during the stroke, but also watching the spot the ball occupied after impact is made. Keeping your eyes down ensures that the head—and the body—remains still. On putts over 10 feet, you'll still have enough time

On short putts, keep your eyes down and listen for the ball to drop.

to look up and see the ball roll to the hole. On short putts, keep your head down and listen for the sound of the ball going into the cup.

Fault

Letting the left wrist break down as the putter approaches impact.

Effect

Ideally, the back of the left hand should match the angle of the putterface. If the left wrist hinges before impact, the putterface flips out of position, usually sending the ball left of the target. Left-wrist breakdown usually happens when a putter gets nervous and makes a tentative stroke—almost always on short putts when, for whatever reason, there is a lack of aggression. That's what makes it so frustrating; it usually involves a very makable putt.

Cure

There are two basic ways to attack left-wrist breakdown. One is to resolve to be aggressive, especially on short putts. Hit them firmly, so the ball hits the back of the cup and falls in. Take a look to make sure your backstroke isn't longer than it should be on those short putts. With a shorter backstroke, you can make an aggressive forward stroke without the risk of hitting the ball past the hole.

To cure left-wrist breakdown, keep your backstroke short and make an aggressive through-stroke.

However, resolving to be aggressive on short putts is no cure-all, because what your mind tells your body to do and what your body actually does can often be two different things. And it's not just limited to the average golfer; Tour pros battle left-wrist breakdown all the time. They practice and make resolutions, and see sports psychologists. They change putters. They change caddies. And when none of that works—when their left wrist still makes the occasional ill-timed flip—they change the way they hold the club. At least some do. Fred Couples, Tom Kite, and Karrie Webb, to name a few, all have experimented with or switched to a cross-handed grip, which is much more effective in controlling left-wrist breakdown and its evil cousin, the yips, than a standard reverse-overlap grip.

Fault

"The yips," or convulsive movements of the hand and wrist muscles on short putts.

Effect

The yips often begin with chronic left-wrist breakdown and evolve into a problem rooted more in the mind than the body, ultimately affecting the entire stroke. At their worst, the yips make it almost impossible to draw the putterhead away from the ball without making a flipping motion. They're insidious because they strike seemingly at random and can just as easily disappear, although some of the world's greatest players (Sam Snead and Johnny Miller, among others) spent huge chunks of their careers battling them.

Cure

Two popular remedies for curing the yips are gripping the putter cross-handed and switching to a long putter. The term "cross-handed" implies something quite complicated, but it simply means reversing the hands so the left is below the right on the grip instead of above it. It's also referred to as "left-hand-low," which is not as catchy but might be more appropriate. Whatever you call it, it's a powerful weapon against left-wrist breakdown. Whereas in a standard grip, the lower position of the right hand encourages the left wrist to hinge, the cross-handed grip promotes the opposite—the right hand and arm stabilize the left wrist.

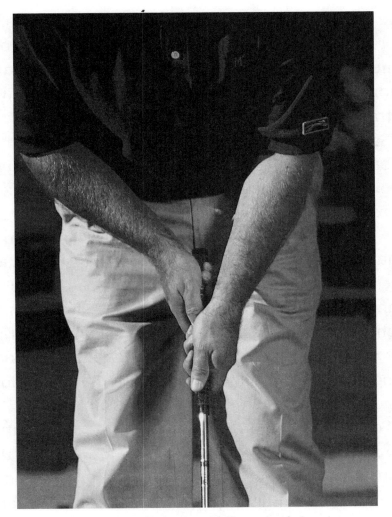

The cross-handed grip stabilizes the left wrist.

There's another big difference between cross-handed and traditional: With a standard grip, the right shoulder is significantly lower than the left at address, because the right hand is below the left on the grip. Reversing the hands realigns the shoulders, which actually makes the stroke more of a true pendulum motion. So, in some ways, it makes more sense to grip the club cross-handed than with a traditional grip.

Start by wrapping all four fingers of the left hand around the club near the bottom of the grip, so there's room for the right hand to go above it. As with a standard grip, the back of the left hand faces the target and the left thumb rests on top of the grip. Place the right hand on the club with the palm facing the target and the thumb slipped under the thumb pad of the left hand. You can hold the club with all the fingers of the right hand, or, if it's more comfortable, lay the right forefinger over the knuckles of the left hand. Overlapping in this manner will bring the hands slightly closer together but comfort is the primary issue.

Your other option, of course, is the long putter. Choosing this recourse, however, also means that you can throw out most of the instruction you've read so far. The long putter, nothing more than a regular putterhead attached to a shaft that is about 50 inches long (standard length for a men's putter is 35 inches), was developed in the early 1990s by Charlie Owens, a Senior PGA Tour player who was looking to fight the effects that age was having on his putting stroke—and to beat the yips.

The long putter has been a savior for many players with "the yips."

Being the first, Owens also had to develop a method for using the long putter. The technique is unusual: Holding the end of the putter with your left hand, you anchor it against the top of your breastbone, or under your chin. In terms of a pendulum, this anchor is the fixed point from which the pendulum swings. The right hand holds on to the club halfway down the shaft. Using light grip

Langer's Solution

Besides winning the Masters, Bernhard Langer is also well known for having a nasty case of the yips. He experimented with just about everything under the sun to beat them, with varying levels of success. One of his most successful experiments was an alternative method of gripping the putter that eliminated any chance of left-wrist breakdown. First, he held the putter below the grip with his left hand, on the shaft of the club. Then, with his right hand, he held the grip against the inside of his left forearm. The result was that the shaft of the putter served as a splint for his left wrist. He had to crouch severely to reach the ball, but there was no chance that his left wrist would hinge.

pressure, you pull the club away from the ball with the right hand, then guide it through by extending the right arm down the target line. The club is so long that it almost swings itself—very little assistance from the right hand is required. As a result, good tempo is easier to achieve and yips are very rare. Plus, the technique produces such a pure pendulum motion that getting a good roll on the ball is virtually guaranteed.

The downside to the long putter is that the length and weight of the club can be hard to control. If you make a mistake in the backstroke with a short putter, there's a chance you might be able to compensate for it on the forward stroke, rerouting the putterhead to where it should be. With the long putter, manipulating the head during

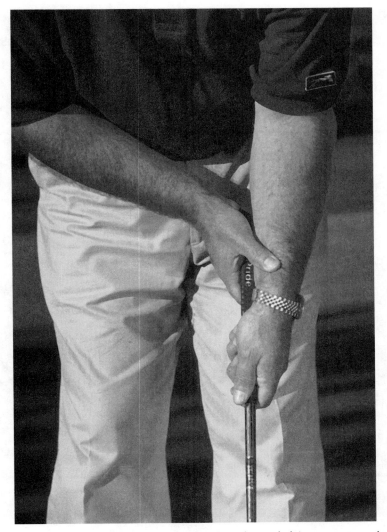

Famous yipper Bernhard Langer developed this strange grip.

the stroke is tough to do. If you make a mistake in the backstroke—like moving the putterhead outside the line—you're basically stuck with it for the rest of the stroke.

BEST TIP: *Look at the Hole*

Most golfers I've seen suffer from the yips have a problem with peeking—looking up at the hole just before contact—which throws the putterhead off-line. Unfortunately, telling them not to peek is like telling them not to think of pink elephants. Instead, I tell yippers to look at the hole throughout the stroke, even when they play. Not only does it eliminate peeking, but taking your eyes off the ball helps you relax and stroke it smoothly.

—John Gerring, *GOLF Magazine*
Top 100 Teacher

3

Strategy

Good technique gives you the potential to be a good putter, but to reach that potential you have to put it all together on the golf course. It's the difference between making a good stroke and actually *putting well*, which requires a set of perceptive eyes, intelligent strategy, and a fair dose of mental toughness. Applying what you know is the fun part; it's actually playing the chess match after learning how to move each piece. And on the course is where you have the most to learn, no matter your level of play.

The rules for putting, one might say, are much more universal than the rules for putting technique, so you must abide by them. For example, if the green is sloped from right to left, the putt is go-

Good putting requires perceptive eyes, smart strategy, and guts.

ing to break to the left, whether you use a reverse-overlap or a cross-handed grip; if you're putting against the grain on Bermudagrass greens, the ball will roll slower than usual. Regardless of your technique, you've got no chance of making putts if you don't recognize such on-course factors.

But there is more. You need a putter that suits you, something you can feel comfortable with as you stand over the ball. You need to know how to practice, so you can maintain your stroke and ensure that your putter remains your friend, not your enemy. That's what the remainder of this book is all about: getting out of the theoretical, and getting into the practical.

The Mental Side?

The old saying is that golf is "90 percent mental," but it's one of the more misunderstood truths in the game. Most folks associate the mental side with confidence, and confidence with emotional strength. That's part of it, but what people don't pay much attention to is how that confidence is developed. It's looked upon as a sort of magical quality that arbitrarily attaches itself to a lucky someone. You hear stories of Tour players seeing sports psychologists in an effort to regain their confidence, which may give the impression to the average golfer that these gurus have a unique insight into what must be a complicated process. Okay, for the pros, maybe confidence is a bit complex. They're the best players in the world, and they're playing for millions of dollars, not to mention their livelihood. But for the rest of us, the primary source of confidence is simple: It comes from having a specific plan, standing over a putt with no questions in your mind. You know how much the putt will break and how fast the green is, and you know your stroke is solid. The questions—or worries— aren't there because you've taken care of business. You've read the putt correctly, you've gauged the speed of the green, and you've spent enough time practicing to feel good about your mechanics. You're confident, but there's nothing magical about it. It comes from being smart and prepared.

The preparation part is simple: practice, practice, practice (see Chapter Four). But how do you get the smarts? There's a wealth of strategic knowledge to be had, from recognizing undulations to understanding the effect of different grass conditions. It's not the kind of knowledge that can simply be absorbed through reading; much of it comes from experience. Consider this chapter, then, as your guide.

Reading Greens

Put simply, most greens are sloped in some way, which affects how the ball will roll. Reading a green means identifying what slopes exist between your ball and the hole, then determining how the line

Most putts can be effectively read from directly behind the ball.

and speed will be affected by them. Despite the pains you see the pros taking on television, reading a green is not that complicated. Standing a few feet directly behind your ball, crouch down and survey the terrain between your ball and the cup. From there you should be able to see what slopes exist. If the green is sloped to the left, the putt will curve, or break, to the left, so you must aim to the right of the hole to compensate. If the green is sloped to the right, the ball will break to the right, so aim left. How far outside the hole do you aim? It depends on how angled the slope is, for one, and how hard you plan to hit the ball. You might be able to read the slopes in a green the first time you play, but knowing how much a putt will break comes with experience. The more you play, the better your green-reading skills will become.

You don't have to rely solely on crouching behind the ball to read the slope in a green, although if that angle seems to give you a conclusive view, there's little need to gather more information. But greens are usually sloped in several ways, so many putts will have more than one break in them. If crouching behind the ball still leaves you with questions in your mind, check the line from behind the hole. Sometimes getting a reverse angle can reveal things you didn't see from behind the ball.

And, as long as you're walking the length of the putt anyway, looking at the line from the side can reveal hidden upslopes or downslopes that will affect the roll of the ball. If you're still not sure, remember that your eyes can fool you, but your feet can't. You can feel when you're not walking on a flat surface, so pay attention as you walk along the line of your putt. However, don't get carried away with reading greens. Most of the time, the first impression you get when you crouch behind the ball is correct; if you continually second-guess yourself and check all the angles, your pace of play will be unbearably slow.

Every Putt Is Straight

Don't ever compensate for a slope in the green by altering your stroke. Even if there are six feet of break, play it straight. That is, pick a secondary target—in this case, a spot six feet outside the hole—and go about your business as if that spot were the hole, and you're about to hit a straight putt. Aim the putterface at the secondary target, align your body to the putterface, and make a straight-back, straight-through stroke along the target line that extends from the ball to the secondary target. Your alignment, not your stroke, allows for the break. If you've read the putt correctly, the slope will take care of bringing the ball down to the hole.

Play breaking putts just like straight ones, only adjust your aim.

The Linchpin: Speed

Every time you read a slope in a green, how much break you play—how far outside the hole you aim—depends on how fast you intend to hit the ball. This is especially true for short putts. A simple example: You're faced with a seven-foot putt, slightly downhill and sloped from right to left. If you hit the putt softly, so it would fall into the hole on its last rotation, you'd aim maybe four inches to the right so the slope could bring it back. But with the ball rolling that slowly, it's more likely to be thrown off-line by whatever imperfections exist on the green. So do you have to play that much break? Not at all. You could aim at the right edge of the cup instead of four inches outside it and still make the putt—but you'd have to hit the ball much harder. This presents some potential problems: If the ball doesn't hit the cup in exactly the right spot, it won't go in; and if it misses the cup altogether, it'll roll way past, maybe leaving you an even longer putt coming back.

So what's the happy medium? According to Pelz, it's 17 inches. He has found that a putt has the best chance to go in if it's hit hard enough to roll 17 inches past the hole. No more, no less. That's fast enough to resist most of a green's imperfections, yet slow enough that it will fall into the cup even if it isn't dead-center.

The challenge, then, is twofold: Being able to "read" speed in a green, and then, being able to dial in the right stroke. There are a few factors that influence how fast the ball will roll. First is the height of the grass on the green; the closer it is shaved, the faster the ball will roll. However, it's nearly impos-

Hitting short putts firmly takes away break, but if you miss . . .

sible to tell just by looking. Your best bet is to hit a few putts on the practice green before you play; it should reflect the speed of all the greens on the course.

The second is the incline or decline of the green. Obviously, a putt going downhill will be faster than one headed uphill. Most of the time these slopes are pretty apparent as you stand on the green. However, if the golf course itself is built on fairly uneven terrain, some slopes aren't so obvious. That's why it's smart to start reading the greens before you get to them. As you walk or ride up the fairway, pay attention to the overall slope of the green and the surrounding area. Is the entire green pitched in a certain direction? If so, you can bet the ball will tend to roll that way.

An Uphill Battle

Your ball's heading straight for the hole, about to drop in, but then curls away at the last moment and misses. Blame the golf gods if you want, but Pelz blames "the lumpy doughnut." During the course of a day, the average green is crushed by thousands of footprints that depress the grass everywhere except within a few inches of the hole, where nobody steps. So the hole and a small circle around it are slightly raised, meaning the ball has to go up a tiny ramp the last six inches or so to the hole, exactly when it's moving the slowest. The upshot: You can make a perfect read and a seemingly perfect stroke, and still miss the putt. That's one reason you need a little speed on the putt as it approaches the hole.

BEST TIP: *The Lower Half*

The best perspective for reading a long putt is halfway along the line on the low side. Assessing the putt from the halfway point gives a good feel for the overall distance, and the low side reveals any rise or fall. Keep in mind, distance is the key on long putts. Reading putts from behind the ball is more important from short range, where the break should be your primary concern.

—Jim Flick, *GOLF Magazine*
Master Teaching Professional

Another factor that influences a putt's speed is grain. Grain refers to the direction the grass grows on the green: A ball rolling with the grain will be faster than a ball rolling against it. Look for drainage patterns on the greens to determine the direction of the grain. If there's a water hazard around the green, the grain will usually run toward it. If the green is cut into a hill or mountain, the grain will tend to run down the slope, even if the undulations in the green appear different. On flat greens, the grain usually grows toward the setting sun. If you're looking at the green and the grain is running away from you, the grass will appear shiny; if the grain is coming toward you, it has a duller look. In some circumstances, grain can affect the break of the putt but for the most part, its impact is on the speed.

Once you've taken into account all the factors that can affect the speed of a putt, you're faced with the second part of the equation: How to make the proper adjustments in your stroke. How big a stroke do you have to make? How hard do you have to hit the ball so it has enough speed to reach, even roll past, the hole? Unfortunately, the answer to this one is not so black and white. It's a question of feel—an instinctive communication from your eyes, which take in all the visual information just discussed, to your brain,

The Amateur Side

If you're unfamiliar with the expression "never up, never in," it means that a putt that finishes short of the hole never had a chance to go in. Simple enough. But there's a similar philosophy to breaking putts: If the ball goes past the hole on the low side, it likewise never had a chance to drop. This, unfortunately, is a typical amateur mistake; you have to play away from the hole on a breaking putt and hit the ball a little harder, which can be hard to make yourself do. That's why the low side of the cup on a breaking putt is known as "the amateur side." But consider that a ball rolling on the high, or "pro," side of the cup—even if you've played too much break—always has a chance to hit something or lose speed and fall in. But once the ball is rolling below the hole, nothing can make it go back up the slope.

which processes the information, and finally, to your body, which makes a stroke based on what the brain tells it. Perfecting those lines of communication comes with practice and repetition: After you've done it enough, your body knows how to make a putt roll three feet or 30 without reinventing the wheel.

On long putts, make your stroke longer, not quicker.

One thing is for certain: You'll find it easier to gauge speed if your tempo is consistent from stroke to stroke. Tempo is the relationship between the pace of your backstroke and the pace of your through-stroke. If you swing the putterhead back very slowly then jerk it through, your tempo is uneven. If you take it back quickly and decelerate

Try to make your backstroke and through-stroke at the same pace.

going through, you're in no better shape. Strive for a smooth, even tempo, where the putterhead moves away from the ball slowly, then swings through at what feels to be the same pace, like a free-swinging pendulum.

Then maintain that tempo on all putts. If the putt is long, don't quicken the stroke, just lengthen it. On shorter putts, make a shorter stroke with the same tempo. You'll have a better feel for different speeds if your tempo is consistent. If the tempo changes from one stroke to the next, it's just another variable to complicate the equation.

Strategizing: Short Putts

In a nutshell, putts of about eight feet and less are why so many golfers hate putting. They look easy, they *should be* easy, but somehow they're frightening propositions. Maybe it's because they are easier to miss than they are to make. And not just for weekend golfers: Pelz's research shows that, on average, even the best putters on the PGA Tour make less than 60 percent of the six-footers they face. Remember, that's on average: When they shoot low scores, you can bet they're doing better than 60 percent. With this in mind, you shouldn't expect to be flawless from close range, but you should also recognize that improving your short putting is probably the first thing to do if you're looking to cut strokes.

Essentially, good short putting is about making a sound stroke despite your nerves. Alignment is important on any putt, of course, but it's the key on short putts, as you expect to roll them perfectly on-line. From inside six feet, you'll rarely have to aim more than a ball's width outside the cup. If you miss, it's usually because of a mechanical glitch that caused you to open or close the putterface, move your head or body, or make contact off the sweet spot. You can guard against these breakdowns by practicing and perfecting your mechanics on the practice green. That's taking care of the physical side of things. To take care of the mental side, a preputt routine is a big help.

A preputt routine is exactly that: a specific ritual you go through before every putt. For example, crouch behind the ball, read the break of the putt, and pick an intermediate target along the line. Walk to the side of the ball and make a practice stroke or two, sensing the effort required. Set the putterhead behind the ball, aligning it to your intermediate target. Take your grip, then align your body so it's parallel to the target line. Swivel your head to look at the hole, swivel your head back to the ball, then make your stroke. That's a preputt routine. Doing it

First, square the putterface to your intended line.

before every putt breeds familiarity and consistency and helps establish a rhythm. Plus, it's great on short putts because it gives you a chance to focus on something else besides your nerves and all the things that could go wrong. Develop your own preputt routine (the one above is just a good example) and discipline

With the face square, take your grip and align your body.

yourself to complete it before every putt, long or short. If you can repeat a good routine, you have a better chance of repeating a good stroke, too.

You also have to take a different approach to a short putt's line and speed. For instance, you're facing a left-to-right four-footer that reads like you should aim the ball outside the left edge. "Don't give the hole away" is an expression you'll hear from experienced golfers, which means don't aim outside the parameters of the hole if it isn't necessary. On this particular four-footer, you could aim at the left side of the hole instead of outside the edge; you'd just have to hit the ball a little harder.

For better players, this is not a bad idea. Since the ball is so close to the hole, more precise targeting is possible, and it's often easier to make a smooth, confident stroke when the target is inside, instead of outside, the hole. For most golfers, however, taking on a more aggressive strategy for short putts can wreak havoc with the stroke, throwing off tempo. It all depends on how confident you feel over the short ones.

BEST TIP: Head Still

To train yourself to keep your head and body still during the stroke, make practice strokes with the top of your head against a wall. With the head forced to remain still, the body will do the same, and you'll get a feeling for controlling the stroke with only the arms and shoulders. Try to reproduce this feeling on the golf course.

—Darrell Kestner, *GOLF Magazine*
Top 100 Teacher

Strategizing: Long Putts

Putts of 30 feet and longer aren't nearly as nerve-wracking as short putts since you don't have any real expectations of making them. Unfortunately, this attitude most often leads to a lack of concentration, which is a big mistake; it takes as much precision to hit a 30-footer within a few feet of the hole as it does to drain a five-footer. Another thing to remember is that if you're consistently facing knee-knockers for your second putts, you're often going to find yourself three-putting—the cardinal sin. The average golfer could cut three to five strokes a round just by eliminating three-putts. In other words, the ability to hit long putts close to the hole is a great scoring tool.

The key to long putts, also known as lag putts, is distance and therefore speed. Line is less of an issue because your target is wider, as your goal is to leave the ball within a couple feet of the hole. Nevertheless, on lag putts, most amateurs focus too intently on the line and so tend to make many more mistakes in distance. To gauge the proper speed, make several practice strokes to help your body adjust to the distance. Then, go through your normal preputt routine of reading the line and aligning the putterface then your body. During the stroke, stick to your same smooth, even tempo. You'll be surprised how good your feel is for distance if your tempo is consistent.

BEST TIP: Use a Mini-Swing on Long Putts

Controlling the speed of the ball on long putts is much easier when you make a long, smooth backstroke—like the mini-swing of a chip shot. If the putt is extra long—more than 50 feet—don't fight the feeling that you have to hit the ball hard. Allow for a little play in the wrists; you'll be able to generate more swing speed while still staying relaxed. If the longer stroke causes your body to move slightly, let it. The less tension you have, the better your tempo, and the better your touch.

—Brad Faxon, 6-time
Winner on the PGA Tour

No matter how good you are at lag putting, you can't always count on being left with a tap-in. So you have to consider the best place—and the worst place—for your next putt. Take the time to analyze the slopes around the hole. If at all possible, you want to be left with a straight, flat putt. If not, straight and uphill is the next best option. In general, uphill putts are easier than downhillers, so take that into account. Also, be aware of what type of break is more comfortable for you. Most right-handed golfers find right-to-left putts easier than left-to-righters. Favor the side of the hole that leaves you in your comfort zone. And if you roll the ball well past the hole, don't turn away in disgust. Watch the ball carefully; it's giving you a free read of your next putt.

Watch your ball roll past for a free read of your next putt.

Tiered Greens

Multilevel, or tiered, greens—those with two or more "shelves" connected by steep slopes—present a unique challenge on long putts. If your ball is on one level and the hole is on another, you basically have three reads to make: the break of the green on the level you're on; how the connecting slope will affect the roll; and the break on the level of the hole. With multiple angles to consider, it's easy to get confused about how the hills are going to affect the putt. But keep in mind that whether the putt is going down to a lower level or up to a higher level, the effect of the slope will always be to pull the ball down the hill. The ball likes going downhill, and will sometimes even reverse direction to do so. It sounds obvious, but when you're analyzing the slopes on tiered greens, it's a helpful thing to remember.

The good news is that most tiered greens are built the same way. Usually, from front to back, the lower level feeds into a slope that rises to an upper level, which is generally pretty flat. This hill profile means that if you're putting down from the upper level, usually all you have to do is hit the ball hard enough so it reaches the downslope. There are always exceptions, but more often than not, the slope will give the ball plenty of momentum to reach hole locations on the lower level.

Going up the slope to a higher level is usually a tougher putt. The ball has to roll significantly faster than normal to get up the hill, and it can be hard to convince your body to make such a long stroke. But if you don't hit the ball hard enough to reach the upper level, it might roll right back and leave you with a second putt longer than your first. At the same time, you can't just whack the ball; the upper level on tiered greens tends to be a bit quicker, as it's flatter. Too much speed and your ball will roll off the back and then you really have a tough play.

If you're having trouble gauging the proper speed, try tricking yourself into hitting it harder. Ignore the shelf, then imagine that the hole is about 10 feet farther back than it actually is. Gauge the length of your stroke as if you're hitting a straight uphill putt to the imaginary hole farther away. That should give the ball just enough momentum to roll up the hill without rolling over the green.

Different Speeds

Depending on how many different courses you play, you're likely to encounter a variety of greens,

When putting to a top tier, aim for an imaginary Hole 10 feet farther away.

some faster and some slower. To be a consistent scorer, then, you have to know how to handle greens of different speeds. The biggest key is not to get taken by surprise. Always take the time to hit a few putts on the practice green before the round, and ask your playing partners or the club pro if the speed of the practice green reflects the speed of the greens on the course. Usually, it will. Make any necessary adjustments on the practice green: a shorter stroke if the green is fast and a longer stroke if it's slow, never changing that smooth-back, smooth-through tempo. You'll adapt to the speed of the greens much more quickly if you don't have to adjust to a change in tempo.

A couple of things to keep in mind. Assuming that the greens are fast because they're well manicured and cut very short (rather than just baked-out hardpan), the ball will tend to break a little bit more. You'll notice this as you warm up. On the course, let the speed of the greens work for you. On most short putts—especially downhillers—all you usually have to do is get the ball rolling for it to reach the hole. That takes some of the guesswork out of speed control, allowing you to focus less on making the perfect stroke and more on finding the right line. Fast greens are usually pretty true, so if you get the ball rolling on line, it should behave as you expect it to.

Slow greens work exactly the opposite way: Whatever speed the ball gets, it's getting from

On fast greens, just get downhill putts started.

you—the green isn't going to help at all. On the other hand, slow greens also tend to break less. They can be very easy to score on once you get used to the speed because so many of the putts are straight (even if they look slightly sloped). Keep the green-reading simple and maintain a smooth stroke, focusing on consistent tempo.

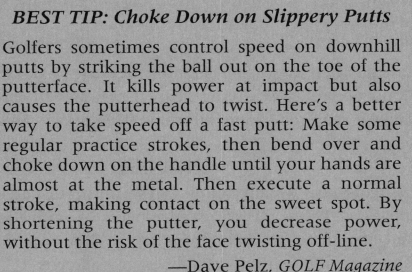

BEST TIP: *Choke Down on Slippery Putts*

Golfers sometimes control speed on downhill putts by striking the ball out on the toe of the putterface. It kills power at impact but also causes the putterhead to twist. Here's a better way to take speed off a fast putt: Make some regular practice strokes, then bend over and choke down on the handle until your hands are almost at the metal. Then execute a normal stroke, making contact on the sweet spot. By shortening the putter, you decrease power, without the risk of the face twisting off-line.

—Dave Pelz, *GOLF Magazine*
Technical and Short Game Consultant

Types of Grasses

Golf course agronomy is pretty complicated stuff, with all sorts of different grasses at the course designer's disposal, each with different characteristics based on climate and resistance to certain weeds. Luckily, not all of them have significantly different playing qualities; what a nightmare that would be for the golfer. As it is, there are essentially three different types of grasses you need to be aware of: bentgrass, Bermudagrass, and ryegrass.

Bentgrass has traditionally been reserved for courses in four-season climates, because it doesn't stand up well to extreme heat. If maintained carefully (it requires a lot of attention), bentgrass can be very lush; the grain grows very tightly and can be cut very short, so most of the fastest greens you'll see are bentgrass. It's usually found in the northern part of the country, but recent advancements in cultivation and maintenance techniques have allowed more courses in the South to install bentgrass greens.

Bermudagrass requires less maintenance and handles extreme heat much better than bent, so it's prevalent in desert or tropical climates. However, since it doesn't grow as tightly and can't be cut as short, it's hard to make Bermudagrass greens as fast as bentgrass greens. Because the individual blades are longer, grain is much more of a factor when putting on Bermuda greens. Not only will grain affect the speed of your putts, it can also contribute to the break. Putts going with the grain often break more; those going against the grain break less. It usually takes a round or two to get used to these differences if you normally play on bentgrass.

Ryegrass greens are far less common than bent or Bermuda. Rye is generally not the primary grass on a course, but is often used during the winter months in a process called "overseeding." In the desert of Palm Springs, for example, winter mornings often leave a thin layer of frost on the greens. The Bermudagrass that holds up so well to the blistering summer heat doesn't like the cold at all, so many of the courses in the area overseed with ryegrass in the fall. Its playing characteristics lie somewhere in the middle. It can be cut shorter than Bermuda, but the grain isn't very consistent, so the surface generally isn't as true as bentgrass greens.

Weather Considerations

In Scotland, wind and rain are almost a daily event on the golf course. In the U.S., inclement weather is less frequent—and golfers are less willing to endure it—but sometimes you have no choice. There are a few things to keep in mind.

When it comes to your putting, light rain is mostly just annoying; it shouldn't interfere with the short, simple motion of your stroke. Your main concern should be to keep the ball and the face of your putter as dry as possible, to ensure normal contact. However, rain makes the greens wet, and that can require some adjustments on your part. If the greens are slightly damp, they'll just be a little

From Off the Green

The putter doesn't have to be restricted to use on the green. From the fringe, or even from a greenside bunker, the putter can be a valuable weapon. But the conditions have to be right. Unless you're right on the edge of the fringe, make sure the grass isn't too much longer than the green and the ground is level. If the conditions are going to significantly slow down your ball or possibly kick it off-line, it's better to chip.

Putting from a greenside bunker is only a viable option if the lip of the bunker is very low, allowing the ball to roll out without jumping into the air. There shouldn't be any more than a few feet of rough between the bunker and the green, and make sure the sand is firm. Remember, don't touch the putterhead to the sand at address—that's a Rules violation.

Putting from the fringe is fine, as long as you can judge the roll.

When the wind is up, widen your stance for stability.

slower. But if water is accumulating, your ball will have a tendency to skid off the face of the putter, hydroplaning on top of a thin layer of water, like a car on a wet road. This could send the ball off-line slightly, especially if contact is made off the sweet spot. Once the ball stops skidding and makes contact with the grass, it will slow down considerably. With the water providing resistance, the ball will also break less than usual. Nevertheless, since most of your putts will be playing slower and straighter, wet greens give you an opportunity to make more aggressive strokes. Keep that benefit in mind.

Wind, on the other hand, can have a very definite effect on your stroke: It can blow you off balance. If you're feeling unstable, widen your stance slightly, so your feet are shoulder-width apart or even wider; this will help anchor you to the ground. Even then, making your normal stroke on a windy day requires a little extra concentration. In your preputt routine, focus on making a smooth practice stroke with an even tempo. And take your time; don't let the wind rush you into hitting the putt before you're ready or with a quicker pace.

In extreme circumstances, wind can affect the break of a putt. Your ball will never be blown wildly off-line unless the playing conditions are, well, unplayable. But when the breeze is blowing at 20 mph or better, wind's influence on a putt is similar to the effect of grain. Downwind putts will be faster; upwind will be slower. If the wind blows with the break, play the ball a little farther outside the hole; if the wind blows against the break, play it closer. If you find yourself with a downhill, down-wind, downgrain putt: Hit it lightly. Then hope.

One final point: Wind also acts as a drying agent. If you're playing on a damp course, and the wind picks up, expect the greens to dry out. And dry, windblown greens tend to be fast.

4

Practice

For those of you who are fed up with the constant reminders in golf books and magazines that you can't
improve without practice, here's the bad news: Not
only do you have to practice regularly to improve, but
your putting will quickly deteriorate without it. How
much you know about making a good stroke is unim-
portant. You have to constantly reinforce the muscle
memory that produces the precise pendulum motion
of the putting stroke. And even if your mechanics are
excellent, without practice you'll have a hard time
gauging speed, and your stroke will have a tendency
to break down in pressure situations. If your mechanics aren't perfect, practice is the one chance you have
to make corrections; an actual round of golf is not the
time to tinker with your stroke.

So you have to practice. (Yawn.) But here's the good news: Hitting a putt may not be as exciting as hitting a drive, but practicing putting can be much more fun than pounding tee shots. Drills, games, competitions—there's a host of things you can do to improve on the green aside from standing in one place and hitting putt after putt after putt. It's easy for the mind to wander while you're beating balls on the driving range; on the other hand, if you plan your putting practice sessions wisely, there's no reason to ever get bored on the practice green.

Setting Goals

"Practice with a purpose" is another time-worn cliché. Nevertheless, if putting practice has a reputation for being tedious, it's because most people do it aimlessly, just going from hole to hole and quickly losing interest. It's a much more engaging activity if you're actually trying to accomplish something, so set a goal for yourself before each session. Think about your tendencies and choose a daily objective; for example, working on lag putting by hitting a certain number of 30-footers within a six-foot circle around the hole. With a goal, you can track your progress along the way, which keeps things more interesting.

Set goals when you practice, such as trying to make 10 four-footers in a row.

Once you have a goal, don't put pressure on yourself to practice until your back goes out. Is there anyone who wouldn't go a little crazy from spending two hours straight just working on, say, stroke mechanics? Even with multiple goals, two hours is overdoing it. If you need work on short putts and big breakers, for instance, try to break the practice up over a couple of days. Stick to one goal per session and keep the sessions short—half an hour is plenty of time if you work steadily. Ultimately, you'll retain more information if you stay fresh throughout the session.

BEST TIP: Diagnose Your Stroke

The putts just aren't dropping for you lately, but you don't know why. To find the answer, buy 15 feet of yellow string and two 10-inch gutter spikes (about the cost of a Sunday paper). Attach the string to the spikes and find a flat portion of the practice green. Stick one spike about 17 inches behind the middle of the hole, then stretch the cord taut and spike the other in the green. The string should be about four inches above the ground. Hit putts, using the string as a guide to be sure the putterhead is moving straight back and through. If it is and the ball is starting right or left of the string, the putterface is opening or closing at impact. You can check your speed, too: If the ball misses, it should finish even with the far spike, 17 inches past the hole.

—Kent Cayce, *GOLF Magazine*
Top 100 Teacher

Working on Mechanics

If you're consistently missing makable putts, you might want to brush up on your mechanics. Bad habits can creep into your stroke like weeds, causing problems without you knowing it.

Maybe there's some hidden flaw in your stroke that only the trained eye of a golf professional can uncover. But before you jump to that conclusion, spend a practice session checking and working on your alignment, putterhead path, and face angle. It may be that refamiliarizing yourself with the fundamentals is all you need to get back on track.

Practicing mechanics is easier than working on anything else, because you don't need a hole, or even a ball. There are dozens of simple things you can do, from practicing a straight stroke against the line of the fringe to checking your alignment at home in a mirror. But the most complete way to monitor your mechanics is to use a practice station.

It's similar to laying down clubs on the range: Find a flat portion of the practice green and drop a ball eight to 10 feet from a hole. If you can, snap a chalk line from the ball to the hole; this is the target line. Put the putterhead behind the ball so the face is square to the target line, then mark this position with two tees, one a quarter inch outside the toe of the putterhead, the other a quarter inch outside the heel. Then create two rows of tees on either side of the target line (including the two marking the putterface) to guide the putterhead on a straight-back, straight-through path. The track may have to be slightly rounded to accommodate the shape of your stroke.

Putting with a Range Ball

Do you wonder whether you're making pure contact with the ball? You can find out simply by hitting straight 10-foot putts with a range ball. Align the stripe on the ball so it points down the target line, then make your normal stroke. If the stripe looks like a solid line as the ball rolls to the cup, you've made perfect contact and haven't imparted any sidespin. But if the stripe wobbles, it's an indication of sidespin, and you either cut across the ball or your putterface wasn't square at impact.

Practice with a range ball and make sure the stripe doesn't wobble.

Create a track with tees to check your path and face angle.

Start by making practice strokes without a ball to get a feel for a square putterface and proper path. Then put a ball down and hit a dozen or so putts to the hole. Make whatever adjustments are necessary to roll the ball down the target line and make it drop. If the putterhead doesn't hit the tees during the stroke, your path is essentially straight. If the ball still isn't going in, it's because the putterface isn't square at impact. Stick with the practice station until you make six or seven putts in a row. Then end the session by hitting a handful of putts with no alignment aids, trying to retain the feeling you had while working at the practice station.

Short Putts

What's the point of practicing putts of less than five feet? You may miss them on the course occasionally, but they don't even hold your attention on the practice green. So why bother? It's a good point, actually—there isn't much to be gained from spending a lot of time on something that isn't challenging. But ask yourself: Why are short putts challenging on the course? Because there's pressure—after all, you could always miss and cost yourself a precious stroke. That pressure gets to your nerves, and if your nerves get the better of you, they disrupt your mechanics.

In practicing short putts, your goal should be to strengthen your nerves. This means that you have to create pressure situations for yourself. For example, you could vow not to leave the putting green until you've made 15 three-footers in a row. Use only one ball. Every time you miss, start the count over. You can bet by the time you get to 10 in a row, your nerves will start to kick in. Want to crank the pressure up even more? Make a wager with a friend: First one to sink 15 wins. The extra competition raises the stakes, and the higher the stakes, the higher the pressure.

Long Putts

Practicing from long range means practicing distance control; direction is secondary. So your first priority should be to stroke every putt with a smooth, even tempo. Don't worry about making your mechanics flawless, focus on speed instead. To make sure you develop an overall feel for speed and not just a feel for one particular putt, move around the green as you practice. Spend as much time hitting putts up and down hills as you do in flat areas. To keep you challenged, going from hole to hole can be helpful, but add a little twist to make sure it stays interesting. Dave Pelz invented a game called "Safety Drawback" that is perfect for working on speed control.

The goal is to hit every putt, regardless of distance, either in the hole or so it finishes within a "Safe Zone" around the cup. Seventeen inches past the hole indicates perfect speed, but give yourself a little more room with the Safe Zone. Imagine a circle around the cup with a 34-inch radius. Now, since a putt that finishes short of the hole never has a chance to go in, slice off the half of the circle that is in front of the hole. You're left with a semicircle that begins at the hole an extends 34 inches to the sides and behind it. That's the Safe Zone.

To play the game, start by hitting a lag putt of 20 feet or more. If it finishes within the Safe Zone, you may tap it in. (To measure 34 inches, use the shaft of your putter—most are 35 inches long). If the ball finishes short of the hole or otherwise outside the Safe Zone, you must pull the ball back away from the hole another putter length. So, if you rolled the ball four feet past, you have to pull it away from the hole about three more feet and try to make a seven-foot putt. The same rules apply for the second putt: Leave it outside the Safe Zone, and you have to pull it back again. This game forces you to focus on the proper speed, or you could spend all day at one hole.

Play a game called "Safety Drawback" to test your distance control.

There are variations, as well. If you're working on really long putts—more than 40 feet—you can enlarge the Safe Zone to a full circle, so any putt that finishes within 34 inches of the hole, in any direction, is acceptable. Again, a little competition applies the heat and makes the game more interesting.

> ### BEST TIP: Putt With Your Eyes Closed
>
> During practice, I sometimes putt with my eyes closed, then guess where the ball will finish. Only after the ball stops rolling do I open my eyes to see if I'm right. This drill teaches you to have a better feel for the stroke and what the putterface is doing as it makes contact.
>
> —Greg Norman, 2-time
> British Open Champion

Breaking Putts

As with long putts, it's important to vary your practice with breaking putts. You don't want to just groove your stroke to one particular left-to-right 10-footer. You want to become skilled at the process of handling breaking putts, which means reading the line, gauging the speed, choosing a secondary target, and making a straight-back, straight-through stroke. That doesn't mean you have to crouch behind the ball and line up every putt on the practice green (although going through your preputt routine every few strokes is a good idea), but try to keep the putts as fresh as possible. Don't spend too much time on any one putt, and vary your distances between five and 20 feet. If left-to-right putts traditionally give you the most problems, focus on them during the session, but don't ignore right-to-lefters completely. Balancing the two protects the integrity of your mechanics, so you don't get used to making a stroke grooved on only one type of break.

Grooving Tempo

Because good tempo is so closely associated with speed control, practicing long putts is a great way to work on your tempo. Plus, it's easier to get a feel for the putterhead moving back and through at the same pace if you're making a longer stroke. To start, don't pay much attention to distance or direction, just hit a handful of putts from 20 feet or more, working with a light grip pressure and the sense that the putter is moving smoothly and evenly back and

BEST TIP: Four Corners

Stick four tees around a hole in the shape of a diamond, with each tee four to five feet from the cup. Use an area with some slope, so that putts from opposite sides of the hole feature opposite breaks.

Stroke three putts from one tee, then rotate to the next station and putt three from there, and so on. The objective is to make 12 putts in a row, three from each tee. If you miss, start over from where you are. If making 12 consecutive putts seems too tough for you, try sinking two at each station.

This drill makes for great practice because you eventually have to make pressure putts from all four stations, each of which features a different break and speed. Don't quit before you meet your objective.

—Karrie Webb, Winner of 17 LPGA Tour Events

through. As you stroke the ball, try saying the words to yourself slowly: "back . . . and . . . through."

Still having a hard time finding the rhythm? Try practicing with headphones on, listening to some steady, soothing music that you like. Or use a metronome if you have one. The beat of the music or the steady "tick-tock" of the metronome will encourage you to keep things on an even keel, without any sudden increases or decreases in speed.

BEST TIP: *The Putting Ladder*

Here's a great drill to help you regain a feel for distance and stop three-putting. Standing on one side of the practice green, pick a spot just short of the fringe on the other side. Putt a ball as close as you can to that spot without rolling it into the fringe. Putt a second ball as close as possible to the first one without going past it. See how many balls you can roll between the fringe and a point eight feet back, each putt shorter than the one before (see photo at right). You're in mid-season form if you can stop six balls within the eight-foot "ladder."

—Mike Bender, *GOLF Magazine*
Top 100 Teacher

Getting off the Three-Putt Train

Nothing adds more unnecessary strokes to your score than three-putting. If it happens to you more than twice a round, it's definitely something you should address in your practice sessions. Most likely, you're having trouble getting your long putts close to the hole. You're probably leaving yourself

with second putts of five feet or longer, and missing a few of those in a row can really do damage to your confidence. That feeling carries over to the next short putt you have, and suddenly, even if you hit the ball close, two-putting is no guarantee.

So, distance control and confidence are the main areas you should focus on to curb your three-putting. Try working on them together. Spend ten minutes working on three-footers, doing the 15-in-a-row drill to boost your confidence. Then play 18 holes of the Safety Drawback game just discussed, choosing first putts of at least 20 feet each time. That way, you hit a short putt after every long putt, just the way you do on the course. Keep score; par is 36. If you score under 38, you're doing very well.

The Value of Friends

Putting practice is always easier and more enjoyable if you have somebody to do it with. Not only does a partner provide competition for whatever putting drills and contests you devise, but also a second set of eyes. This is especially helpful with alignment; it's fairly easy to be sure the putterface is square at address, but a partner has a much better view of the alignment of your feet, knees, hips, and shoulders relative to the target line. He or she also may spot some flaws in your setup and stroke.

However, don't put too much stock in what your friend says about your mechanics unless he or she is a PGA professional. The first thing that average golfers see when they watch other golfers' strokes is

Have a friend check your setup, especially your alignment.

Play 11

Here's a simple yet challenging game to play with a friend: Go from hole to hole on the practice green, choosing putts of various distances and breaks. On each hole, the player whose first putt finishes closest to the hole gets one point. If a player three-putts, his opponent receives a point. Sinking the first putt earns three points. The first player to reach 11 points wins. Want to go a step further? Play with two balls each, and go to 21. Because points are awarded for lag putting and three-putts, there's pressure on all parts of your putting game.

the path of the putterhead, because it's the most visible part of the stroke. They'll tell you that you missed a putt left because you pulled it, but they can't see if you closed the putterface at impact or made contact on the heel, both of which can also make the ball go left. So they won't tell you all you need to know, and maybe not even the main cause of your misses. Nevertheless, a quick critique can be helpful; just know who it's coming from.

Warming Up Before a Round

Here's a riddle: When are you on the practice green, hitting putts, but not practicing? During the preround warm-up, which may look like practice but is actually something quite different. Practice is a time to work out the kinks in your stroke, to focus on your weaknesses, and sometimes, to take a step back before taking two steps forward. But 20 minutes before you tee off is no time to be thinking anything but positive thoughts. The purpose of the warm-up is not to fix anything; it's to make sure you have a feel for your stroke—and the greens— so that when you get out on the course, nothing takes you by surprise.

Typically, you have already stretched and hit some balls before arriving at the putting green, so your body is already loose. Start by hitting three or

---

BEST TIP: *Abbreviated Warm-Up*

The sad truth is that most golfers don't give themselves enough time to warm up properly before a round. If you've only got five minutes to putt before you're called to the first tee, here's what to do. Spend two minutes getting a feel for speed by putting back and forth across the length of the practice green. Each time, try to stop the ball just short of the fringe. Use the remaining time to hit dead-straight three-footers and short breaking putts. Limit yourself to only one ball on the short putts; this intensifies your focus and eases you into an on-course mind-set.

—Mike McGetrick, *GOLF Magazine*
Top 100 Teacher

To bolster confidence, finish your warm-up with a few short ones.

four long putts—30 feet or more—to get a feel for the speed of the greens. Don't worry about making the putts or even getting them close; you're hitting them merely for information. Once you have a sense for how the green is rolling, move in to about 20 feet. Again, don't worry about making anything.

Hit another 3 or 4 putts, and consider them successful if your tempo feels good.

Then hit a couple of 10-foot putts that break, just to see if grain is going to be a big factor. Move in and roll a few from seven feet or so, then finish up with five or six putts from three feet. These short putts let you finish your warm-up with the sound of the ball dropping in the hole ringing in your ears. The key to the warm-up is to cover most of the situations you might see on the course, but with different goals. Keeping pressure to a minimum will keep you loose and confident going into your round.

Practicing at Home

What golfer hasn't hit a few putts into a glass on the living room carpet? It's a time-honored tradition. It is not a good way to work on reading greens or distance control—carpets have a way of actually throwing off your feel for speed—but there are plenty of valuable things you can do at home when weather or a lack of time keeps you away from the course.

The most obvious work you can do is on your setup. In fact, you should make regular check-ins with a full-length mirror. Here's a reminder of what to look for: Facing the mirror, check to see that your feet are 15 to 20 inches apart, the ball is positioned opposite a point just left of your chest's center, and the angle of the putter shaft is vertical, not angled forward or back. Also, make sure that your weight is evenly distributed between both feet. From the down-the-line view, make sure your hands are directly underneath your shoulders and your eyes are over the ball. If you draw imaginary lines across your feet, knees, hips, and shoulders, they should all be parallel to each other.

Home is also a good place to work on stroke mechanics. Find some parallel lines on a rug or tiled floor and you have a perfect guide for a square putterface and a straight-back, straight-through path. Also, try taking your address with your putterface against a doorjamb and making strokes so the face hits the doorjamb at the place in your stance where the ball would be. Making contact with such a big, flat surface provides great sensory feedback and helps train you to get the putterface square at impact.

Want to really challenge yourself? Try the drill Johnny Miller used to hone his control of the putterhead: Lay a dime on a smooth floor and address it as you would a ball. Then make a stroke and try to hit the edge of the dime without banging the putterhead down. Only if you make a perfect stroke will the dime slide across the floor.

5

Equipment

Ask most Tour pros what the best putter on the market is, and you'd have a hard time getting a straight answer. Endorsement deals aside, if they're putting well, they'll say whatever putter they're using is the best. If they're in a slump, their putter is the worst, a piece of trash. In fact, they've probably already switched to something else. Since hundreds of thousands of dollars rest on a handful of putts on Sunday, it's understandable if they're impatient when their current flatstick isn't cooperating. If their mallet-shaped head isn't sinking putts, maybe they'll go to a blade, or a heel-toe model. Whatever works.

The point is not that you should have a stableful of putters to choose from, but that the only real rule of what makes a putter good is *if it sinks putts.*

That being said, there are some guidelines for picking the best putter for you: It should feel comfortable in your hands; you should like the feel of it as it swings back and through and the sensation you get when it hits the ball; and you should like the way it looks. Looking down at something that pleases your eye engenders confidence, and you can never have too much of that.

Like any other purchase, however, it's smart to know all your options before you make a choice. The following few pages detail the various specifications and styles to consider.

Specs and Options

Shaft Length

The length of the shaft is important because putters are designed to be held at the end of the grip. If the putter is too long and you have to choke up, it changes the balance and feel of the head. So, unless you prefer to crouch over the ball, choose a shaft length that allows you stand fairly erect and extend your arms straight down from your shoulders. Most putters are available in a variety of lengths, but the accepted standard is 35 inches. Experiment to find the length that's best for you.

Lie Angle

This is the angle formed between the shaft and the ground when the putterhead is soled flat. There are a couple of reasons why this is important. First, most putters feature a few degrees of loft, so if the putterhead is not flat on the ground, the face will actually point left or right of your intended target. Therefore, the lie of whatever putter you use should fit your natural stance. Second, it's important to set up with your eyes over the ball for a clear view of the line; if the lie of the putter is too flat (imagine putting with a driver), it will be impossible to sole the putter properly and still position your eyes over the ball.

Many popular putters on the market come in a choice of lies: upright, standard, and flat. Be sure the putter you choose has the appropriate lie, and if it doesn't, see if other lies are available in the same model. A trained PGA pro will help fit you for the proper lie, and most putters can be special ordered with a custom lie if necessary.

Head Style

A look through the history of putters will reveal some pretty bizarre-looking clubs—the putterhead shaped like a hot dog always comes to mind—but for all intents and purposes, there are three basic head shapes to choose from: Heel-toe weighted, mallet, and blade. Heel-toe weighted means the majority of the weight in the head is distributed at the ends—the heel and the toe—with almost no weight behind the sweet spot. The advantage to this style is that if you make contact toward the heel or toe, the head has less of a tendency to twist, and more energy is transmitted to the ball than if the head had an even distribution of weight. Heel-toe weighted putters are generally the most forgiving of mishits, and are therefore the most popular style on the market. The trade-off, however, is that there is less feedback transmitted to the hands on off-center hits, so you won't always know when you've missed the sweet spot. Without a clear reminder that you've goofed, you have to be careful about breeding bad habits.

Mallet putterheads are shaped like a semicircle, with variations among different brands and models. They're generally bigger than the average heel-toe weighted model, which, for some golfers, makes them easier to align and swing on a straight path. Some mallets have the majority of their head weight distributed around the perimeter, which has the same forgiving effect of heel-toe weighting. In that case, the only thing that makes one better than the other is how it putts, feels, and looks to you.

This mallet putter is heel-toe weighted for forgiveness on mishits.

Once popular, the blade putter is now used mostly by golf purists.

> ### Find the Sweet Spot
>
> Most putters have a little line etched into the top of the putterhead to aid in alignment. These lines are almost always exactly halfway between the heel and toe of the putterhead, which, in some cases, is not where you will find the sweet spot! So, here's how you do find the actual sweet spot: Hold the putter by the shaft, between your thumb and forefinger, and let it hang in front of you. Using the end of a tee, tap along the face gently until the putterhead doesn't twist one way or the other. When the tapping makes the head swing straight back and through—like a pendulum—you've found the real sweet spot.

Blade putters were popular in the 1970s and earlier, but they're mostly found in the bags of golf purists these days. Most blades consist of a small, skinny head with the weight evenly distributed from heel to toe. As a result, they're less forgiving: Putts hit toward the ends twist the head and come off the face with reduced energy. The advantage of the blade is that the putterhead's lines are generally clean and uncluttered, which some golfers find easier to align. And there's no mystery: If a putt feels solid and goes straight, you know you've made a good stroke and hit the sweet spot.

Offset Hosel vs. Standard Hosel

Most putters nowadays are offset, which means the neck of the putterhead is bent forward, so the shaft

To find the sweet spot, tap the face with a tee until you find the point where the head doesn't twist.

is slightly closer to the target than the face. There is no real mechanical advantage to the offset hosel, but many golfers feel that it gives a better view of the putterface, making it easier to aim. At the same time, it can be argued that standard hosels, with the shaft and putterface in a straight line, make alignment less complicated. In the end, it's a matter of personal taste.

Head Material

You'll find putterheads made from all sorts of different materials: steel, brass, copper, aluminum, even graphite and wood. No material putts better

The offset hosel sets the shaft forward and can aid in face alignment.

than any other, although some—like brass—have a slightly softer feel at impact. Steel is the most common material: it's inexpensive and can be cast into any shape with relative ease.

Face Material

Until recently, the face was always made of the same material as the putterhead. Now many manufacturers are putting plastic or rubber inserts in the faces of steel or beryllium copper putterheads to reduce the shock of impact. The resulting softer feel is only better if that's what you prefer. If you play hard-feeling, two-piece golf balls, these inserts may bring a welcome mellowness to contact, which can feel better in the hands.

Insert putters are designed to soften the feel of hard balls.

Weight

The general rule of thumb has always been that lighter putters are more effective on fast greens, while heavier putters are more suitable for slower greens. Obviously, it depends on the individual, but as you experiment with different weights, you'll find that heavy putters are great for making long, smooth strokes but more difficult to control on shorter ones. If you're going to own one putter, it makes sense to choose one that feels like it's somewhere in the middle. That way it can be effective no matter what the speed of the greens.

Grip Size

This is largely about personal preference, and most putters don't come with grip-size options. But there is something you should know: The thicker the grip, the easier it is to immobilize the hands and wrists. Thinner grips have a tendency to sit in the fingers and encourage mobility in the hands and wrists. If you feel like this is happening or you simply have large hands, talk to your local pro about switching to a thicker grip or building up the one you use. But be aware that a thicker grip adds weight to the end of the putter, which changes the balance of the club.

Classics and Oddities

Suppose you don't want to be a sheep. You take a look around and decide you don't like any of the putters that are popular in the current market. Suppose you want to be a lone wolf. In that case, you can go in one of two directions: classic or weird.

Most classic putters were first produced in the 1960s or earlier. They earn the "classic" designation because of a certain timelessness: As technology evolves, they remain popular because of a simplicity of design and superior feel. One such putter is the Titleist Bulls Eye, a brass, center-shafted blade that was introduced in the 1930s. It can still be found in pro shops today, and although it isn't as popular as it used to be, a survey of PGA Tour pros would probably reveal that more own a Bulls Eye than don't.

Another classic design is the flange putter, which is like a blade, except there's a small flange on the back of the head. Most of the classic putters of the 1950s, such as the MacGregor IMG and the Wilson 8802, were flanged designs. Today, these putters are bought and sold by collectors for hundreds of

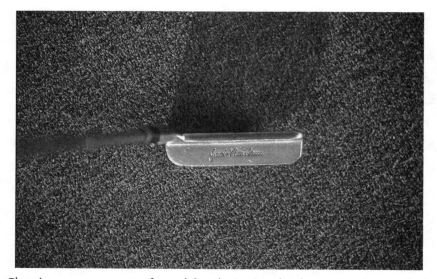

Classic putters are preferred for their simple design and pure feel.

dollars, and there are several models currently on the market that are based on their designs. Flanged putters are usually heel-shafted and, like a blade, require near-perfect contact to produce good results. But one thing you can count on with a classic putter: It looks awfully good sitting in your bag.

Not so with weird putters. There are countless small companies and small-time inventors trying to make a splash in a very crowded putter market. The pressure to create something that will revolutionize putting has inspired some pretty strange-looking offerings, usually with the claim that they will change your game forever. Any such promises should be taken with a healthy grain of salt, but feel free to experiment with "alternative" designs if you wish. You'll find them mostly in mail-order catalogs and discount golf shops, and you never know, you might find your perfect putter.

Occasionally, a weird putter will find its way into the hands of a Tour pro, and even more occasionally, that pro will win a televised tournament using it. That immediately legitimizes the company that made it—at least temporarily. For example, in the 1983 Los Angeles Open, then 52-year-old Gene Littler charged to the third-round lead, one-putting nine greens with something called the Basakwerd putter, which featured a hosel that connected with the toe of the putterhead. During the next two days, the club's manufacturer, a little-known company called Orizaba, sold 7,000 Basakwerds.

In 1986, Jack Nicklaus shot a stunning final-round 65 to win The Masters using the Response ZT putter from MacGregor, a heel-toe model with a giant head, more than twice as big as the average putter on the market. MacGregor took 70,000 orders for the ZT the week following the tournament, but just as quickly, interest in the club died, as many golfers found feel to be lacking in the giant head. The lesson of these stories is actually a good one to keep in mind when you're in the market for any putter, regular or not-so-regular: Don't make a purchase based on how a particular putter works for someone else. Always try it for yourself before you buy.

Who Needs a Putter?

When all is said and done, it's not the putter that makes putts, it's the golfer. And if the golfer is feeling particularly confident, it doesn't matter what kind of putter he's using—or whether he's even using a putter at all.

Consider the story of Ben Crenshaw at the 1987 Ryder Cup matches at Muirfield Village. In a singles match against Europe's Eamonn Darcy, Crenshaw had quickly fallen three down after only six holes when he broke his putter in anger. The Rules of Golf don't allow you to replace a club broken in anger in the middle of a round, so Crenshaw was forced to play the remaining 12 holes without a putter. Widely considered to have one of the best putting strokes ever, Crenshaw started using his 1-iron on the green—and fought back to go one up with two holes remaining. Unfortunately, his brilliant comeback fell short when he lost the last two holes because of some wild shots. It just goes to show you that putting is important, but it's not the only key to scoring. Maybe there is some value in whacking a few drives off rubber mats after all.

NOTES

NOTES

NOTES

NOTES

NOTES

NOTES